blue
rider
press

Citizens of the Green Room

Also by Mark Leibovich

*This Town: Two Parties and a Funeral—Plus Plenty
of Valet Parking!—in America's Gilded Capital*

*The New Imperialists: How Five Restless Kids
Grew Up to Virtually Rule Your World*

Citizens of the Green Room

*Profiles in Courage
and Self-Delusion*

MARK LEIBOVICH

BLUE RIDER PRESS

A MEMBER OF PENGUIN GROUP (USA)

NEW YORK

blue
rider
press

Published by the Penguin Group
Penguin Group (USA) LLC
375 Hudson Street
New York, New York 10014

USA · Canada · UK · Ireland · Australia
New Zealand · India · South Africa · China

penguin.com
A Penguin Random House Company

ISBN 978-0-399-17192-5

Printed in the United States of America
1   3   5   7   9   10   8   6   4   2

BOOK DESIGN BY AMANDA DEWEY

To my family

Contents

"I'M RUNNING FOR OFFICE, FOR PETE'S SAKE"

"WE WILL EAT ALL COLORS OF M&M'S"

Public Actors: Hillary Drank Two Glasses of Red Wine

Early in my ramble as a political reporter, I would come back to the office after a trip to, say, a presidential debate, or a convention, or a campaign event with candidate so-and-so. Steve Reiss, my sagacious editor at the *Washington Post*'s Style section, would always begin his debriefing with the same question: "What was it like?" It struck me as a strange construction. He would not say, "How was your trip?" or "What'd you get?" or—in the case of an encounter with a profile subject—"What was he/she like?" He always said, "What was *it* like," and after a while I took the "it" to incorporate the whole unnatural experience that these subjects endure on their daily high wires. In halting responses, I would share with Steve little stories and impressions and off-color details about my expeditions: how, say, John Edwards walked like a duck, or that Dick Cheney had no idea who John Travolta was, or that Nancy Pelosi had never heard of curly fries.

Steve later observed that very little of what I shared with him in his office would ever wind up in my stories. Quite often there was good reason: ground rules (they were off the record), or good taste (former POW John McCain telling me a joke about prison rape), or the fact that Mike Huckabee's scatological humor was ill-suited to a profile pegged to his new diet and nutrition book. But a lot of the good material also evaded print for bad reasons. It didn't fit, in part because I was too attentive to the banal conventions of so much political reporting; I was too conscientious about including talking points, pro forma quotes from "experts" and the requisite "others disagree" paragraphs (on the one hand, on the other hand, etc.). Steve urged me to listen to the stories I was telling my friends, was telling him, and was myself chuckling at, and then to liberate them into print as often as I could.

In the course of these conversations, I came to recognize that Steve was highlighting for me a basic dichotomy between what a reporter sees and what a reporter knows. The better the reporter becomes at integrating these, the more illuminating his material becomes. Whether he meant it or not, Steve was getting me to train my eyes and ears on the things that were revelatory rather than, say, dutiful (or merely quotable). I started listening differently to the people I was talking to, both in real time and on tape. Did Chris Matthews really just say that thing about Koreans? Did Haley Barbour just pat his wife on the ass as she walked by him? Did Teresa Heinz Kerry just snap at her husband again? I came to notice how nervous, glib, or confident they sounded; and I also learned how to interact with these people in a way that best elicited more authentic expressions. Over time, and this took years, I developed better senses to go to battle with. I also learned that a key to writing about people in public life is recognizing another core dichotomy: the one between what a subject wants to project to the world (and devotes a great deal of time, energy, and manpower to) and who they truly are.

Clearly for the writer, the idea is to convey as much of the latter as possible and as little of the spin and bullshit of the former. For the public actor, the relentless challenge they endure in trying to manage that gap—what to reveal and what to withhold, what to emphasize and what to obscure—is a wholly consuming experience. In many ways, it defines their realities. Steve would always ask me another question, too. "What's different about them?" By "them" he meant the public actors. They were often people of great renown and acclaim. They were recognized around town, usually Washington, DC, in those double-take instances that a public actor becomes an actual person before you. (*Hey, isn't that . . . ? It looks like Newt Gingrich. Or an overgrown kid playing Newt for Halloween? Yes, it is the real Newt—an actual sighting, just a few seconds ago, here at the Starbucks near the United Airlines counter at Reagan National Airport. And he is standing with someone who has the same silver-haired helmet on her head as his wife Callista does. So it must be Newt!*)

Public actors carry themselves with a jumpy expectation that they are being studied at all times. Often they are. They have a special sense that others are squinting in their directions. Their voices assume a deeper tone as if they are always speaking into a microphone. (*"It's good to see you again, Wolf."*) They walk faster. Their assistant will follow up with you later. They know the names of the makeup ladies and the valet guys and where the Snickers bars are kept in the green rooms.

"The rich are different from you and me," F. Scott Fitzgerald wrote memorably in *The Great Gatsby*. And so are the citizens of the green room. After a while, they acquire a shiny *otherness*—a stately gaze, a sweeping pace of movement, and sometimes comet trails of entourages. They navigate life in a perpetual "on" state, as naturally as a trout inhabits a stream. And they sweep into green rooms, the safe habitat where upcoming TV guests, debate participants, and various lofty haircuts get touched up, miked, and fed before their spotlight turns. Political green rooms in particular embody the unreality these paragons endure. Unlike, say, a diva's green room on Broadway or Van Halen's on tour (sans brown M&M's), political green rooms don't guarantee privacy. In joint appearances or debate settings, combatants are often joined, awkwardly, in rich anthropological scenarios: like Howard Dean, John Edwards, and John Kerry jockeying in line outside a public backstage men's room before a Democratic presidential debate. They are suspicious rivals (Dean eyeing Kerry for allegedly cutting him in line), but they also, clearly, all belong.

Not everyone in a green room is a legal citizen of the place. It takes repeated exposure and a quiet sense developed over time. That is the vague path to citizenship in the green room, which becomes a proxy for being an accredited citizen of public life. You are seen *around*. Tip O'Neill—a Golden Green-Room God back in his day—used to diminish certain past-primers by saying, "You know, you never see him *around* anymore." What could be more dismissive? Are they even still alive?

Full citizenship in the green room has both advantages and killer burdens. "There is relentless scrutiny that now stalks not only people in politics but people in all kinds of public arenas," Hillary Clinton said in an April 2014 speech in Portland, Oregon. "And it gives you a sense of being kind of dehumanized." I was struck by her word choices, some of them jarring: "stalked" and, especially, "dehumanized."

I think of those studies about the effect of life in prison; inmates who are brutalized or placed in solitary confinement. "Dehumanized" gets thrown around in those contexts, too. What is it like to be a human object in a dehumanizing machine? To be a prisoner in makeup?

B ack when she was running for president in 2008, or maybe it was late 2007—it was winter in New Hampshire—Clinton was having a "relaxed" drink in a hotel lobby in Manchester with a bunch of reporters. Hillary drank two glasses of red wine. She was playing relaxed, laughed a lot. For the heck of it, during one lag, I asked the then senator what state she would choose to live in if not New York. (I ask this question of politicians sometimes.) Hillary frowned. "I like all the states," she said, smirking to convey that she knew that I knew that a presidential candidate could not possibly answer that question. She wanted to hold the most powerful job in the world. But the reality is that that job holds complete power over the person who is holding it, or wants to. The requirements of it stalk an ambitious public actor, forcing them to withhold even their most inane preferences—like a favorite state. It would seem the essence of dehumanizing. I recalled when Bill Clinton was in the White House and he could not even pick a family vacation spot without first getting Dick Morris to poll on the matter (Wyoming won out, deemed better in his reelection year than Martha's Vineyard).

Given her aspirations, Clinton was certainly correct not to produce a state. To wit, a few years earlier, in 2004, I was writing about John McCain and we went to see the Arizona Diamondbacks play the San Diego Padres at what was then called Bank One Ballpark in Phoenix. Late in the game, after several hours of random chatter between us, I asked McCain where he would least like to live. "I would hate to live in Milwaukee," he said, and seemed to think nothing of it. I included this quip late in my story. And wouldn't you know it, four years later McCain would find himself running for president in the swing state of Wisconsin and trying to explain away this long-forgotten throwaway (the Obama campaign was nice enough to ensure it be fully resurrected).

To be a public actor is to be entrapped by persona. To be casual in this game is to be reckless (the Clintons know this better than most). You live in a physical place—New York and DC and airplanes—but you are public property once you become a citizen of the green room.

A few months before our relaxed drink in New Hampshire, I had obtained a cache of letters that the college-aged Hillary Rodham had written to a high school friend while she was attending Wellesley College in the late '60s. What was remarkable about the letters was how pre-persona they were, how they contrasted so eerily with the straitjacketed candidate who liked to describe herself as "the most famous person you don't really know." The letters offered forty-year-old proof that there's someone in there after all. They were by turns angst-ridden and prosaic, glib and brooding, anguished and ebullient.

"Since Xmas vacation, I've gone through three and a half metamorphoses and am beginning to feel as though there is a smorgasbord of personalities spread before me," Hillary Rodham wrote to her friend John Peavoy, who was then attending Princeton. "So far, I've used alienated academic, involved pseudo-hippie, educational and social reformer, and one-half of withdrawn simplicity."

The letters betrayed an innocently narcissistic remorse over "my lost youth." She imagined herself as a little girl believing that she was the only person in the universe. If she turned around quickly "everyone else would disappear," the young Rodham wrote. "I'd play out in the patch of sunlight that broke the density of the elms in front of our house and pretend there were heavenly movie cameras watching my every move." She said that she yearned for all the excitement and discoveries of life without losing "the little girl in the sunlight."

What happened to that person? We all grow up, theoretically. But not in such an insanely studied way or with such mediation or accumulated mystique and madness that surrounds people who choose this life. The great Richard Ben Cramer wrote his classic megaprofile compendium of six presidential candidates, *What It Takes*, with the mission of learning not just "what it takes" for someone to run for president, but also "what it takes" to even want such a thing. I spoke to Cramer in 2011, about a year before he died entirely too young of lung cancer. He had come to Washington from his home on the eastern shore of Maryland and was holding court for a group of DC reporters, most of them much younger than him (and me). Even then, near his end, Cramer was marveling at how unnatural the pursuit of running for higher office was for any mortal. The aspiration consumes everything. It also swallows up whole subcultures of people into their aura; self-appointed big deals in small places like Iowa and New Hampshire accruing potent hits of self-worth from the attentions of these supernova figures. Cramer talked about watching George Herbert Walker Bush after he had been elected president in 1988, and how exhausting it was just to watch people responding to him. Even the pro forma encounters of the president's days—a five-second hello in a receiving line—were often one of the most momentous experiences of the other person's life. At those moments, the president is all mystique and icon, and rendered, oddly, invisible—dehumanized—under the specter of his office.

One of my ongoing fascinations is how public people become "different from you and me." I get to see them up close, or up closer, than most. It is a privilege, of course, but also a big challenge to draw human texture from the lobotomized regimens of their bizarre lives. "You really can't ever feel like you're just having a normal day," Hillary Clinton said in her Portland speech. "It can be done, but you never forget you're in that public arena."

As someone who has become known for writing profiles of politicians and media figures (that's what it says on Wikipedia, so it must be true), I occupy a fraught position. It's easy to take for granted how weird this all is—the language of spin, obsequiousness, talking points, lies, and the soundstage artifice of it all. How strange it can be, say, that a man in Girard, Ohio, named James Bunosky, could devote his life to running the campaign of a former congressman, Jim Traficant, who was then confined to a federal prison in White Deer, Pennsylvania ("When your candidate is in jail, it can be a bit of an obstacle," said Bunosky, with a gift for understatement). What inspires such devotion? What leads a six-year-old girl from Topeka, Kansas, Grace Mosier, to become flat-out obsessed with Dick Cheney? She learned the names of the then vice president's dogs and his favorite grade school teachers. A six-year-old!

I admit that I, too, have seen the insides of many green rooms. I have picked at my share of fruit platters and talked professional wrestling with Rick Santorum, just the other day in fact. People are civil with me in general. But let's not for a second get so anaesthetized as to think this is all somehow a normal exercise, or that we're friends. No matter how well public people affect poses of being driven by higher motives, they care more about how they are perceived—the state of their "brand"—than they do about anything else. They are obsessed with "owning their narrative," telling their story as they see fit. Politics, after all, is about people and about control. Those "in the arena" might flatter themselves by saying they are about big and serious things like ideas, policy, and substance—as if a "brand" was just some shallow marketing concept and "people" just a celebrity magazine. But I know as well as anybody that people experience politics as vulnerable and impressionable beings, both as consumers (*What is politician x really like?*) and practitioners (*Did they like me?*). And as someone charged with writing unauthorized profiles that might run counter to preferred narratives, I get that I can be somewhat dangerous to them. How unnerving must it be, in a profession overrun with control freaks, to relinquish control of your story to a demon reporter? What must it be like for them to read such an imperfect verdict of themselves? It is always a little scary and unnerving for me to be part of the transaction, to take these fragile objects in my hands. I get asked a lot, "Why do public people continue to talk to you and for the record?" The implication is that everyone I write about ends up regretting it, a premise that appears not to be true in most cases. My glib answer to people who ask this is something between "Beats the hell out of me" and "Because they believe it's in their self-interest to." Perhaps many politicians are too confident, narcissistic, or delusional to think anyone could render an unflattering portrait of them. Yes, I've been yelled at, snubbed, and accused of committing great injustices against some of the Great Men I've written about. (Even worse, I've also been thanked, sent bottles of wine, and invited to dinner by some of them!) It's a dicey business, I get it. But the highest compliment I hear—and this happens sometimes, too—is people telling me that they learned things about themselves by reading the stories, or learned things about people they thought they knew well.

I also get asked a lot whether I "like" the politicians I write about. When I say yes, which I do more often than not, they are often surprised. But I can't help admire the willingness of public actors to be public actors. Often their high wires make them less boring, and bored, imbuing their days with bigger stakes. Most of these people still talk to me, too, if I still see them around.

"All human beings have three lives," Gabriel García Márquez once said. "Public, private, and secret." Citizens of the green room tend to delineate more finely than most do between the three zones. They know what they want to be public and kept private—and God forbid some unreliable actor breaches the vault where secrets are meant to reside. The green room represents a dynamic synthesis and merging of the various selves. It is a place for public actors to hide in plain sight. In sense, so is politics.

What follows is a collection of dispatches from selected high wires.

Profiles in Courage
(and Self-Delusion)

The Insiders' Insider

April 29, 2010

Before he goes to sleep, between eleven and midnight, Dan Pfeiffer, the White House communications director, typically checks in by e-mail with the same reporter: Mike Allen of *Politico*, who is also the first reporter Pfeiffer corresponds with after he wakes up at 4:20. A hyperactive former Eagle Scout, Allen will have been up for hours, if he ever went to bed. Whether or not he did is one of the many little mysteries that surround him. The abiding certainty about Allen is that sometime between five thirty and eight thirty a.m., seven days a week, he hits "send" on a mass e-mail newsletter that some of America's most influential people will read before they say a word to their spouses.

Allen's e-mail tip sheet, *Playbook*, has become the principal early-morning document for an elite set of political and news-media thrivers and strivers. *Playbook* is an insider's hodgepodge of predawn news, talking-point previews, scooplets, birthday greetings to people you've never heard of, random sightings ("spotted") around town, and inside jokes. It is, in essence, Allen's morning distillation of the Nation's Business in the form of a summer-camp newsletter.

Like many in Washington, Pfeiffer describes Allen with some variation on "the most powerful" or "important" journalist in the capital. The two men exchange e-mail messages about six or eight times a day. Allen also communes a lot with Rahm Emanuel, the White House chief of staff; Robert Gibbs, the press secretary; David Axelrod, President Obama's senior adviser; and about two dozen other White House officials. But Pfeiffer is likely Allen's main point of contact, the one who most often helps him arrive at a "West Wing Mindmeld," as *Playbook* calls it, which is essentially a pro-Obama take on that day's news. (Allen gets a similar fill from Republicans, which he also disseminates in *Playbook*.)

Pfeiffer tells Allen the message that the Obama administration is trying to "drive" that morning—"drive" being the action verb of choice around the male-dominated culture of *Politico*, a three-year-old publication, of which the oft-stated goal is to become as central to political addicts as ESPN is to sports junkies. "Drive" is a stand-in for the stodgier verb "influence." If, say, David S. Broder and R. W. Apple Jr. were said to "influence the political discourse" through the *Washington Post* and the *New York Times* in the last decades of the twentieth century, *Politico* wants to "drive the conversation" in the new-media landscape of the twenty-first. It wants to "win" every news cycle by being first with a morsel of information, whether or not the morsel proves relevant, or even correct, in the long run—and whether the long run proves to be measured in days, hours, or minutes.

In *Politico* parlance, "influence" is less a verb than the root of a noun. *Politico*'s top editors describe "influentials" (or "compulsives") as their target audience: elected officials, political operatives, journalists, and other political-media functionaries. Since early 2007, Allen's "data points," as he calls the items in *Playbook*, have become the cheat sheet of record for a time-starved city in which the power-

and-information hierarchy has been upended. It is also a daily totem for those who deride Washington as a clubby little town where Usual Suspects talk to the same Usual Suspects in a feedback loop of gamesmanship, trivia, conventional wisdom, and personality cults.

Allen refers to his readership as "the *Playbook* community." He appeared wounded one morning in March when I suggested to him that his esoteric chronicle may reinforce a conceit that Washington is a closed conclave. No, no, he protested. *Playbook* is open, intimate. No one even edits it before it goes out, he said, which adds to his "human connection" to "the community." Political insiderdom— or the illusion thereof—has moved from Georgetown salons or cordoned-off security zones to a mass e-mail list administrated by a never-married forty-five-year-old grind known as Mikey.

"He is part mascot and part sleepless narrator of our town," Tracy Sefl, a Democratic media consultant and a close aide to Terry McAuliffe, the former Democratic National Committee chairman, told me by e-mail. "He is an omnipresent participant-observer, abundantly kind, generous, and just unpredictable enough to make him an object of curiosity to even the most self-interested. Everything about him is literary."

Allen darts through the political world much the way he writes *Playbook*: in abbreviated steps, more like chops. You can spot him from far away, his shiny head darting up and often straight down into his BlackBerry. He says he gets two thousand e-mail messages a day, tries to answer all that are addressed to him personally, some while walking. He is always bumping into things.

In 1993, Allen was covering a trial in Richmond, Virginia, for the *New York Times* (as a stringer) and the *Richmond Times-Dispatch* (which employed him). He found a pay phone, darted into the street, and got whacked by a car. Allen composed himself, filed stories for both papers, and then found his way to the hospital with a broken elbow. This is one of the many "Mikey Stories" that Washingtonians share with awe and some concern. A corollary are "Mikey Sightings," a bipartisan e-mail chain among prominent people who track Allen's stutter-stepping whereabouts—his showing up out of nowhere, around corners, at odd hours, sometimes a few time zones away.

He bursts in and out of parties, at once manic and serene, chronically toting gifts, cards, and flower arrangements that seem to consume much of an annual income that is believed to exceed $250,000. Allen—who is childless and owns no cars or real estate— perpetually picks up meal and beverage tabs for his friend-sources (the dominant hybrid around Mikey). He kisses women's hands and thanks you so much for coming, even though the party is never at his home, which not even his closest friends have seen. It is as if Mikey is the host of one big party, and by showing up anywhere in Washington, you have served the *Playbook* community and are deserving of the impresario's thanks (or "Hat Tip" in Playbookese).

Allen also has a tendency to suddenly vanish. But then he will pop up on a TV screen a few minutes later. Or you then learn via e-mail that he is racing through O'Hare or via *Playbook* that he took an excursion to the circus (with "Owen and Grace Gallo, ages three and four, who especially liked: doggies on a slide") or Maine ("where an eagle might grab one of your fish while you're focused on the grill").

Or that it's Mark Paustenbach's birthday, whoever he is.

Allen was the first reporter hired by *Politico*'s founding editors, John F. Harris and Jim VandeHei, when they left the *Washington Post* to start the Web site and newspaper in 2006. He is considered a *Politico* "founding father," in the words of Harris, who, like VandeHei, tends to place great weight and mission onto the organization. Another construct (originating outside *Politico*) is that Harris and VandeHei are God and Jesus—it's unclear who is who—and that Allen is the Holy Ghost. When I mentioned this to Allen recently, he was adamant that it is meant to be facetious and that no one at *Politico* really believes that. Allen, an observant Christian, said the line could be misconstrued. But "Holy Ghost" does seem a particularly apt description of Allen's ubiquity and inscrutability. "I get that what I do is a little elusive, ambiguous," Allen told me. "I try to be a force for good. And I try to be everywhere."

I met Allen on a hot April night at the basement bar of the Hay-Adams hotel, across from the White House. I headed downstairs, and there he was, startling me in a back stairwell, reading his BlackBerry an inch from his wire-rim glasses. As we entered the bar, Allen greeted two Democratic operatives at a corner table and noted that his friend-source Kevin Madden, a Republican consultant, was at that moment on CNN.

Allen's public bearing combines the rumpledness of an old-school print reporter with the sheen of a new-school "cross-platform brand" who has become accustomed to performing on camera. Every time Allen starts to speak—in person or on air—his eyes bulge for a split second, as if he has just seen a light go on. His mannerisms resemble an almost childlike mimicry of a politician—the incessant thanking, deference, greetings, teeth-clenched smiles, and ability to project belief in the purity of his own voice and motivations. He speaks in quick and certain cadences, on message, in sound bites, karate-chopping the table for emphasis. (His work is "joyful, exciting," he says. It is a "privilege" to work at *Politico* with young reporters. "I love this company. I love what I'm doing." And all that.) Over several discussions, Allen repeated full paragraphs almost to the word.

"The people in this community, they all want to read the same ten stories," he said, table-chopping in the Hay-Adams. "And to find all of those, you have to read a thousand stories. And we do that for you."

As a practical matter, here is how Allen's ten stories influence the influentials. Cable bookers, reporters, and editors read *Playbook* obsessively, and it's easy to pinpoint exactly how an item can spark copycat coverage that can drive a story. Items become segment pieces on *Morning Joe*, the MSNBC program, where there are ten *Politico Playbook* segments each week, more than half of them featuring Allen. This incites other cable hits, many featuring *Politico* reporters, who collectively appear on television about 125 times a week. There are subsequent links to *Politico* stories on the *Drudge Report*, the *Huffington Post*, and other Web aggregators that newspaper assigning editors and network news producers check regularly. "Washington narratives and impressions are no longer shaped by the grand pronouncements of big news organizations," said Allen, a former reporter for three of them—the *Washington Post*, the *New York Times*, and *Time* magazine. "The smartest people in politics give us the kindling, and we light the fire."

By "we," Allen is referring to either *Playbook* or *Politico*. But many influentials draw a distinction. They will work to get a little twig into Mikey's kindling and read him faithfully. *Politico*, however, is more fraught.

Nowhere is Washington's ambivalence over *Politico* more evident than in the White House. The Obama and *Politico* enterprises have had parallel ascendancies to an extent: they fashioned themselves as tech-savvy upstarts bent on changing the established order—of politics (Obama) and of how it is covered (*Politico*). They started around the same time, early 2007, and their clashing agendas were apparent early. On the day that *Politico* published its first print edition, Barack Obama's campaign manager, David Plouffe, walked into the campaign's offices and slammed a copy of the new publication on Dan Pfeiffer's keyboard. "This," Plouffe declared, "is going to be a problem."

Politico today remains a White House shorthand for everything the administration claims to dislike about Washington—Beltway myopia, politics as daily sport. Yet most of the president's top aides are as steeped in this culture as anyone else—and work hard to manipulate it. "What's notable about this administration is how ostentatiously its people proclaim to be uninterested in things they are plainly interested in," Harris, *Politico*'s editor in chief, told me in an e-mail message.

That *Politico* has been so vilified inside the White House is itself a sign of its entry into "the bloodstream" (another *Politico* phrase). It is, White House officials say, an indictment of the "Washington mentality" that the city is sustaining *Politico* and letting it "drive the conversation" to the extent it does. In early March, Axelrod was sitting in his West Wing office, complaining to me about the "palace-intrigue pathology" of Washington and why he missed Chicago. "I prefer living in a place where people don't discuss *Politico* over dinner," he said.

But morning is another matter, a solitary, on-the-go cram session in which *Playbook* has become the political-media equivalent of those food pills that futurists envision will replace meals. "*Playbook* is an entity unto itself, far more influential than anything in the rest of *Politico*," Pfeiffer says.

If, for example, Axelrod can't read the papers before rushing off to the White House, he will scroll through *Playbook* during his six-block ride to work and probably be safe in his seven thirty meeting. At this pivotal hour, Allen is the oddball king of a changing political and media order—the frenetic epitome of a moment in which Washington can feel both exhilarating and very, very small.

I should disclose a few things: I have known Mike Allen for more than a decade. We worked together at the *Washington Post*, where I spent nine years and where I came to know VandeHei and

Harris. We all have the same friends and run into each other a lot, and I have told them how much I admire what they have achieved at *Politico*. I like them all.

In other words, I write this from within the tangled web of "the community." I read *Playbook* every morning on my BlackBerry, usually while my copies of the *New York Times* and the *Washington Post* are still in plastic bags. When Allen links to my stories, I see a happy uptick in readership. I have also been a source: after I "spotted" Treasury Secretary Timothy Geithner at an organic Chinese restaurant in my neighborhood last year—picking up kung pao chicken with brown rice ("for Tim")—I dutifully e-mailed Allen with the breaking news.

Playbook is a descendant of political synopses like *National Journal*'s *Hotline*, ABC News's *Note*, and NBC News's *First Read*, all of which still enjoy junkie followings. But nothing of the ilk has embedded itself in the culture of Washington like *Playbook*—to a point where if somebody in Pfeiffer's department is celebrating a birthday, he is sure to send word to Allen so that everybody in the White House will know.

Allen sends out *Playbook* using Microsoft Outlook to a private mailing list of 3,000. A few minutes later, an automatic blast goes out to another 25,000 readers who signed up to receive it. An additional 3,000 or so enter *Playbook* from Politico.com, which adds up to a rough universe of 30,000 interested drivers, passengers, and eavesdroppers to the conversation.

Playbook started three years ago as a chatty "what's happening" memo that Allen sent to his *Politico* bosses. Eventually he started sending it to presidential-campaign officials—the first outside recipient was Howard Wolfson of Hillary Clinton's campaign. Soon Allen would send it to non-*Politico* journalists, White House officials, and, before long, anyone who asked. While most *Playbook* subscribers live around Washington, significant numbers work on Wall Street, in state capitals, and at news and entertainment companies on both coasts. Major retailers (Starbucks) and obscure lobbies (Catfish Farmers of America) pay $15,000 a week to advertise in *Playbook*, a figure that is expected to rise.

Readers describe their allegiance with a conspicuous degree of oversharing. "I definitely read it in bed," Katie Couric told me. "Doesn't everybody read it in bed?" Margaret Carlson, a columnist for Bloomberg News and the Washington editor at large for *The Week* magazine, said in a video tribute to Allen for his forty-fifth-birthday party last June. (For the record, the Republican lobbyist and party hostess Juleanna Glover said in the video that she reads *Playbook* "in my boudoir and while I'm blow-drying my hair.")

"I'd like to thank the Lord for the many blessings he brings me," Allen said at the party. "VandeHei thinks that's a reference to him."

"You don't have to do anything else, just read Mike Allen," Bob Woodward declared in February on *Morning Joe* in one of those statements that jab squarely into the ribs of traditional newspaper purveyors. Allen harbors a deep fondness and knowledge of the newspaper industry he might be helping to kill. Peter Watkins, a former press aide for President George W. Bush, recalls that when he told Allen he was from Davis County, Utah, Allen's instant reply was, "Oh, you must have read the *Davis County Clipper.*"

Part of the appeal and the absurdity of *Playbook* is that it imposes a small-town, small-paper sensibility onto a big, complicated city—Lake Wobegon with power. It is expressed in a dialect of "Sirens," "Shots," and "Chasers" that might as well be Mongolian to 99.9 percent of the electorate. To skim *Playbook* is to experience Washington in the midst of an attention-deficited conversation that can bounce from the Congressional Budget Office's score of the health care bill to news of a "state visit" from Feldman's parents (Jud and Sunny) to an all-caps directive that we all "ask Hari about his new puppy." And members of the *Playbook* community—which includes a former president, two former vice presidents, CEOs, and network anchors—are assumed to know exactly who all these people are.

Allen is a master aggregator, which leads some to dismiss *Playbook* as a cut-and-paste exercise. But that ignores Allen's ability to break news (even if by only fifteen minutes), to cull from e-mail only he is receiving, to get early copies of books and magazines, and to pick out the prime nugget from the bottom of a pool report. He has a knack for selecting the "data points" that an info-saturated clan cares most about and did not know when it went to bed. *Playbook*'s politics are "aggressively neutral," and Allen says his are, too—he refuses to vote.

Just as many sources talk to Woodward because they assume everyone is, the White House will leak early talking points to Allen because they know that, for instance, Dick Cheney seems to have made Allen the go-to outlet for many of his criticisms of the current administration. Like Woodward, Allen can be tagged with the somewhat loaded moniker of "access journalist." Clearly the political and news establishments love him. The feeling is mutual and somewhat transactional. They use him and vice versa ("love" and "use" being mutually nonexclusive in Washington). He seems to know everyone and works at it.

Pfeiffer met Allen a decade ago. Over the years, Allen has sent Pfeiffer e-mail messages about things that he knew interested him (Georgetown basketball), just as Allen has served as a one-man Google-alert service for hundreds of friend-sources around town: news about the Redskins (to the Pentagon spokesman Geoff Morrell), about cuff links (to the Washington lawyer Robert Barnett, who collects them). I heard of a low-level economist who has met

Allen only once or twice and yet receives from him forwarded wire stories about Asian currency.

Before there was e-mail, Allen would do this by fax; before there were fax machines, he would drop off newspaper clips (or entire out-of-town papers) to his friends' doorsteps. "He operates at such a faster speed than any of us and carries on many more relationships than any of us and so many more simultaneous conversations than any of us," Morrell says.

"The most successful journalists have their own unique brand and circle of friends," VandeHei, *Politico*'s executive editor, told me by e-mail. "This is the Facebook-ization of politics and DC. The more friends or acquaintances you have, the more time you spend interacting with them via e-mail and IM, the more information you get, move, and market." VandeHei's conceit seems to equate Allen's circle of friends to a commodity—exactly the kind of mutual back-scratching undercurrent that gives "friendship" in Washington its quotation marks. It also reflects *Politico*'s penchant for placing itself at the vanguard of new media when in fact its business has been heavily sustained by ads in its print edition, distributed free in Washington. "*Playbook* is DC's Facebook," VandeHei concluded. "And Mike's the most popular friend."

Allen spent his childhood in Seal Beach, California, in Orange County, the oldest of four—two boys, two girls. He told me he had an apolitical upbringing but wanted to attend college near Washington. He enrolled at Washington and Lee University in Lexington, Virginia, which he said seemed close to DC on a map. When he got there, Allen told me, he learned that the college was at least a five-hour Greyhound ride from the capital. He has told this story before, just the kind of recurring lore—a fun tale, a bit dubious—that surrounds Allen and that he surely cultivates. Until recently, the dominant spectacle of his cubicle at *Politico*'s Arlington, Virginia, offices was a giant birthday card signed by many members of the *Playbook* community. It featured a color cartoon of Allen as the mythological Sphinx and loomed over the real version as he typed, and typed.

People routinely wonder whether Allen actually lives somewhere besides the briefing rooms, newsrooms, campaign hotels, or going-away dinners for Senator So-and-So's press secretary that seem to be his perpetual regimen. And they wonder, "Does Mikey ever sleep?"

The query tires him. He claims he tries to sleep six hours a night, which seems unrealistic for someone who says he tries to wake at two or three a.m. to start *Playbook* after evenings that can include multiple stops (and trails of midnight-stamped e-mail). He supervises four predawn *Playbook* offshoots—*Pulse* (devoted to health care), *Morning Money* (financial news), *Morning Score* (midterm Congressional races), and *Huddle* (Congress)—often writes multiple stories a week for *Politico*, speaks all over the country, and makes relentless TV and radio appearances. I asked Allen if he slept during the day, and he said no.

Allen has been spotted dozing in public—campaign planes, parties—clutching his BlackBerry with two hands against his chest like a teddy bear. He has also been seen asleep over his laptop, only to snap awake into a full and desperate type, as if momentary slumber were just a blip in the 24/7 political story Mikey is writing. "I once called him with a client," Barnett told me in an e-mail message. "He was sound asleep. I am convinced he did the interview fully asleep. Nevertheless, he got every quote right."

Allen delights in being the cheerfully frantic public man. He refers to himself interchangeably with *Playbook*. "*Playbook* made our CBS hit this a.m. by slipping a Benjamin to a plow driver," Allen wrote to his readers on a snowy February morning. "Thank you, Ray."

No shortage of friends will testify to Mikey's thoughtful gestures, some in the extreme. They involve showing up at a friend's son's baseball game (in South Carolina) or driving from Richmond to New York to visit a fraternity brother and heading back the same night (dropping off the morning New York tabloids to friends in Richmond). When Watkins lost his grandfather, Allen appeared at the funeral in Kaysville, Utah, and filed a "pool report" for Watkins's friends and family.

He attends a nondenominational Protestant church and a Bible-study group. During the George W. Bush presidency, which Allen covered for the *Post*, he drew closer to some people in the administration through worship. "He is one of the most thoughtful people I have ever met," Josh Deckard, a former White House press aide, says. "Philippians 2:3 said, 'In humility, consider others better than yourselves,' and I think Mike exemplifies that better than anyone."

Yet even Allen's supposed confidants say that there is a part of Mikey they will never know or even ask about. He is obsessively private. He has given different dates to different friends for the date of his birthday. I asked three of Allen's close friends if they knew what his father did. One said "teacher," another said "football coach," and the third said "newspaper columnist." A 2000 profile of Allen in the *Columbia Journalism Review* described his late father as an "investor."

It is almost impossible to find anyone who has seen his home (a rented apartment, short walk to the office). "Never seen the apartment," volunteered Robert L. Allbritton, *Politico*'s publisher, mid-interview. "No-man's-land." When sharing a cab, Allen is said to insist that the other party be dropped off first. One friend describes driving Allen home and having him get out at a corner; in the rear-view mirror, the friend saw him hail a cab and set off in another direction. I've heard more than one instance of people who sent holiday cards to Allen's presumed address only to have them re-turned unopened. One former copy editor at *Politico*, Campbell Roth, happened to buy a Washington condominium a few years ago that Allen had just vacated. She told me the neighbors called the former tenant "brilliant but weird" and were "genuinely scared about some fire-code violation" based on the mountains of stuff inside.

Allen is known as a legendary hoarder and pack rat. At the *Post*, enormous piles of yellowing papers, clothes, bags, and detritus leaned ominously above his cubicle. While reporters are rarely neat freaks (I remember hearing rumors about Nixon-era sandwiches that are still being excavated from David Broder's office), Allen's work areas have been egregious. It got so bad at *Time*, where Allen was given his own office, that it became difficult even to open the door. His chair was raised at a crooked angle, as if it were not touch-ing the floor, and the debris rose so high in some places that it blocked a portion of light coming through a picture window. Col-leagues took pictures, as if the place were an archaeological site. It was disturbing to those who cared about Allen, especially after a photo of the office in a seemingly uninhabitable state made the rounds of the press corps and George W. Bush's White House.

Friends and employers have taken on a kind of in-loco-parentis approach to some of Allen's needs—making sure he fills out forms to get his press credentials renewed and encouraging him to slow down. Allbritton says he will sometimes ask Harris and VandeHei: "Are you checking up on Mikey? Is he okay?" Allen's bosses at the *Post* helped him recover some of the thousands of dollars in un-claimed expenses that he accrued during the 2004 presidential cam-paign. Close friends have intervened with him on occasion, worried that he is working nonstop and looking dreadful and that his life appears in disarray. Allen thanks them and tells them not to worry.

I asked Allen about his hoarding and clutter issues, and he

wanted no part of the discussion. He assured me that the Internet had cured him. "Everything is online now," he explained, smiling, never mind that he was terrorizing building-maintenance types long after the Internet was here.

Allen has achieved a merger of life and work, family, and *Playbook*. He is deeply committed to his mother, younger brother, two younger sisters, and eight nieces and nephews scattered on both coasts. They make *Playbook* cameos. He describes Harris and VandeHei as his two closest friends. Both are fiercely protective of Mikey and are students of him. "I've always felt he just, like, operates at levels that I couldn't even begin to fathom with my simple Wisconsin mind," says VandeHei, an Oshkosh native.

A former editor at the *Post* told me that Allen today seems to have taken refuge in his status as a public "brand." He deploys *Playbook* as a protective alter ego. It reminded me of something a senator said to me once—that a lot of politicians are shy, private people and that they enter the business because it allows them to remain shy and private behind a public persona. In a recent phone call, I asked Allen what his hobbies were. He paused, went off the record, and then came back with an unrevealing sound bite. "I'm a well-rounded person," he said, "who is interested in the community, interested in family, interested in sports, interested in the arts, interested in restaurants." I asked him what sports teams he roots for. "I'm not gonna do that," Allen said. "*Playbook* is ecumenical." He allowed that "an astute reader of *Playbook* will notice frequent references to the Packers, Red Sox, and Florida Gators."

At one point, I asked Allen if he would ever consider taking *Playbook* elsewhere. Surely he could sell the franchise for a sum that could easily exceed seven figures. (If *Politico* sells $15,000 in ads a week for *Playbook*, then Allen's newsletter alone brings an estimated $780,000 a year.) He was aghast at the question.

Politico's offices are housed in the same place as Washington's ABC affiliate, owned by *Politico*'s corporate parent, Allbritton Communications. They feel more like a television studio than a newsroom. *Politico* reporters dart to and from their "hits" at the newsroom's TV camera. Kim Kingsley, the *Politico* executive vice president (and a former *Post* colleague of mine) is a tireless promoter of *Politico* stories, its reporters, and its brand.

The publication has clearly exceeded the expectations of its founders and its naysayers. Copies of favorable press articles are framed on VandeHei's office wall, along with keepsakes from *Politico*'s mainstream incursion (a photo of himself moderating a presidential debate on CNN). VandeHei was elected last year to the Pulitzer Prize board.

Harris and VandeHei discussed the idea of starting an all-politics Web site while at the *Washington Post*. Harris, who is forty-six, had distinguished himself as a top-notch White House reporter during the Clinton years, while VandeHei, who previously worked at the *Wall Street Journal* and *Roll Call*, was an aggressive and ambitious beat reporter. Allbritton, the forty-one-year-old scion to a Washington banking and media empire, approached VandeHei in 2006 about running a new Capitol Hill publication. VandeHei told Allbritton about his and Harris's idea, which Allbritton agreed to back. VandeHei's wife, Autumn, coined the name *Politico*.

Harris and VandeHei were bold in trying to lure journalistic "brands." Their "messaging" brimmed with sports analogies and swagger. VandeHei told the *New York Observer* before the site's debut that he had e-mail messages from reporters "begging for jobs" and that *Politico* would "show we're better than the *New York Times* and the *Washington Post*."

Their first target was Allen, an emerging presence on the Web at *Time*. Throughout his career, he has been known as an unfailingly fair, fast, and prolific reporter with an insatiable need to be in the newspaper. "The worst thing you could say to Mike Allen was, 'We don't have space for that story,'" says Maralee Schwartz, the longtime political editor at the *Post*. "It was like telling a child he couldn't have his candy." Allen also struggled to write the front-page analytical stories that were the traditional preserve of newspaper "stars." Harris, who wrote many of these during his twenty-one years at the *Post*, says that the whirling production demands of today's news environment have caught up to Allen's sleepless, space-less peculiarities.

Before I covered politics, I wrote about Silicon Valley. Hearing Harris talk, I was reminded of the engineers at the height of the Web explosion in the 1990s—socially eccentric geniuses who suddenly became the wealthy kings of the culture. Technology had caught up to their wiring. They often worked through several nights straight and never seemed to notice or mind. They were mostly male and single. The real prodigies appeared to achieve total synergy with the machines, just as Allen seems the perfect mental and metabolic match for today's news cycle.

Politico's start-up culture tolerates idiosyncrasies better than more established businesses do, Allbritton told me. "It's like you understand a little more," he said. "We all have the wacky uncle."

VandeHei, who is thirty-nine, reminds me more of a venture capitalist these days. His mind appears to be constantly somersaulting with business models and management philosophies. A boyish-faced Packers fanatic, he is the more emotional and excitable half of the duo known as VandeHarris. He wears a chip on his shoulder plainly about established news organizations, and you sense that he takes the White House's apparent disregard for *Politico* personally.

"The Obama theory seems to be that the *New York Times*, big-name opinion writers, and big shots on network news still largely shape how people think about policy, politics, and news," VandeHei wrote to me in an e-mail message. "It's why White House officials spend so much time on the phone with your reporters (*NYT*)—and yet has had little effect on how the public sees the president."

By any measure, *Politico* employs several top-rank journalists, including the political writer Ben Smith, the congressional reporter David Rogers, and the political reporter Jonathan Martin. Allen has broken some of *Politico*'s biggest stories. He reported that the *Post* was planning to hold paid salons for lobbyists at the home of its publisher, Katharine Weymouth, setting off a firestorm. During the 2008 campaign, he asked John McCain how many homes he owned (eight properties, and it proved a major embarrassment to McCain when he could not immediately answer).

Politico's comprehensive aims can make it goofy and unapologetically trivial at times. A recent item by a congressional blogger for the site consisted of the following: "Lights are out throughout much of the Longworth House Office Building, a denizen tells me. UPDATE: They are back on."

The site's reporters are mostly young, eager to impress, and driven hard. Predawn "Why don't we have this?" e-mail messages from editors are common. Working for *Politico* is "like tackle football," VandeHei reminds people, which might explain why most of *Politico*'s best-known bylines are male. The main players have Little League nicknames (Vandy, JMart), use the same terminology, and, strangely, share the same speech affect. I noticed that at least five of them (Allbritton, Harris, VandeHei, Allen, and Martin), when trying to make a point, tended to elongate their vowels in a half-mouthed midwesternish twang—think Bob Dylan working a wad of chewing tobacco.

In early March, a Web site called Xtranormal featured a spoof about life at the "Politicave," starring computerized automatons of VandeHei and Allen (dressed in a superhero costume). After the VandeHei cartoon addressed Allen as "Mike," Allen replied, "Jim, for the last time, I am not Mike Allen. I am News Cycle Man, here to win the morning!" Allen went on to inform VandeHei about "that unpaid intern who is still crying about when you told her she would never make it in this business if she insists on taking bathroom breaks every day." The spot gave voice to a belief that *Politico*'s cult-like mission demands a freakish devotion that only an action-hero workaholic could achieve. "A page-view sweatshop" is how one *Politico* writer described the place to me.

Several current and former *Politico* employees were eager to relay their resentment of the place to me, though with a few exceptions, none for attribution. "It's not so much the sweatshoppery itself that I minded," said Ryan Grim, a former *Politico* reporter who is now at the *Huffington Post*. "It was the arbitrary nature of how it was applied." Kingsley, the *Politico* executive vice president, e-mailed me an unsolicited defense: "In my experience, the people who whine about working at *Politico* shouldn't be at *Politico*," she wrote. "They likely lack the metabolism and professional drive it takes to thrive here. For those of us who love a fast pace and a tough challenge, this place is a calling, not a job."

Harris readily acknowledges that *Politico* is "not for everybody," and VandeHei said they have begun focusing their recruiting on New York, because "the city produces reporters who are fearless, fast, and ruthlessly competitive."

While journalism breeds a higher-than-average population of bellyachers, turnover was especially high at *Politico* in late March and early April—five reporters and one editor announced they were leaving, including the White House reporter Nia-Malika Henderson (to the *Washington Post*), who had been the only African-American on a staff of about fifty reporters. "The natural order of things" is how Harris describes the departures. He said *Politico* is trying to "mature from start-up mode" in a number of areas, including diversity.

Politico's gold standard is a reporter's "metabolism," measured by speed, proficiency, and the ephemeral currency of "buzz." But *Politico*'s buzz can also derive from provocative headlines placed atop thinly sourced stories. In February, for instance, *Politico* published a story about apparent tension between President Obama and Nancy Pelosi. The story—bylined by Allen and Patrick O'Connor—made its assertions based largely on a single anonymous source and was refuted or seriously played down by two on-the-record sources. Nonetheless, *Politico* played it big on its Web site, under the headline "Family Feud," and multiple stories ensued on cable and online.

More recently, Allen asked in his April 10 *Playbook*: "Good Saturday morning: For brunch convo: Why isn't Secretary Clinton on the media short lists for the Court?" By Monday, the convo had moved from the brunch table to *Morning Joe* (where the host, Joe Scarborough, advocated for her) and *Today* (where the Republican senator Orrin Hatch mentioned her, too). Later that day, *Politico*'s Ben Smith quoted a State Department spokesman who "threw some coolish water on the Clinton-for-Scotus buzz in an e-mail." By then, the cable and blog chatter were fully blown. The White House issued a highly unusual statement that Secretary Clinton would not be nominated. *Politico* then sent out a "breaking news alert," and Smith reported that the White House had "hurriedly punctured the trial balloon." End of convo.

For what it's worth, Philippe Reines, a Clinton adviser, says that he told another *Politico* reporter the previous Friday that the chances of his boss's being nominated were "less than none" and added, "Something being a sexy media story shouldn't be confused with truth."

Political operatives I speak to tend to deploy the word "use" a lot in connection with *Politico*; as in, they "use" the publication to traffic certain stories they know they could not or would not get published elsewhere. I was also struck by how freely VandeHei threw out the word "market" in connection with how newsmakers and sources interacted with *Politico*. "If you want to move data or shape opinion," VandeHei wrote to me by e-mail, "you market it through Mikey and *Playbook*, because those tens of thousands that matter most all read it and most feed it. Or you market it through someone else at *Politico*, which will make damn sure its audience of insiders and compulsives read it and blog about it; and that it gets linked around and talked about on TV programs."

By and large, the most common rap against *Politico* concerns its modeled-on-ESPN sensibility. While Harris and VandeHei say—rightly—that *Politico* has devoted lots of space and effort to, say, the health care debate, many of its prominent stories on the subject followed a reductive, "who's up, who's down" formula. ("No Clear Winner in Seven-Hour Gabfest," read the headline over the main article about President Obama's health care meeting.) Harris and VandeHei have clearly succeeded in driving the conversation, although the more complicated question is exactly where they are driving it.

"I've been in Washington about thirty years," Mark Salter, a former chief of staff and top campaign aide to John McCain, says. "And here's the surprising reality: On any given day, not much happens. It's just the way it is." Not so in the world of *Politico*, he says, where meetings in which senators act like themselves (maybe sarcastic or short) become "tension-filled" affairs. "They have taken every worst trend in reporting, every single one of them, and put them on rocket fuel," Salter says. "It's the shortening of the news cycle. It's the trivialization of news. It's the gossipy nature of news. It's the self-promotion."

Salter asked that if I quoted him, I also mention that he likes and respects many *Politico* reporters, beginning with Mike Allen.

On a recent Friday night, a couple hundred influentials gathered for a Mardi Gras–themed birthday party for Betsy Fischer, the executive producer of *Meet the Press*. Held at the Washington home of the lobbyist Jack Quinn, the party was a classic Suck-Up City affair in which everyone seemed to be congratulating one another on some recent story, book deal, show, or haircut (and, by the way, your boss is doing a swell job, and maybe we could do an interview).

McAuliffe, the former Democratic National Committee chairman, arrived after the former Republican National Committee chairman Ed Gillespie left. Fox News' Greta Van Susteren had David Axelrod pinned into a corner near a tower of cupcakes. In the basement, a very white, bipartisan Soul Train was getting down to hip-hop. David Gregory, the *Meet the Press* host, and *Newsweek*'s Jon Meacham gave speeches about Fischer. Over by the jambalaya, Alan Greenspan picked up some Mardi Gras beads and placed them around the neck of his wife, NBC's Andrea Mitchell, who bristled and quickly removed them. Allen was there, too, of course, but he vanished after a while—sending an e-mail message later, thanking me for coming.

In late March, we met for breakfast at Washington's Mayflower Hotel. He brought with him two recent copies of the *San Jose Mercury News*, because he knew I used to work there, and he had just been in the Bay Area. He became animated when discussing a long-ago reporting job in Fredericksburg, Virginia. His favorite story there was headlined "Hot Dog: A Meal or a Snack?" The county board of supervisors was debating whether hot-dog sales should include a meal tax. "Every single thing that I've written since then," Allen said, "whether it's about a mayor or a governor or senator or president, it all boils down to 'Hot Dog: A Meal or a Snack?' All great questions come from small questions."

Like a lot of reporters, Allen would much rather ask the questions than answer them. He led off with one: "What's the most surprising thing you learned about me?"

It was what I learned about his father, I told him. Gary Allen was an icon of the far right in the 1960s and 1970s. He was affiliated with the John Birch Society and railed against the "big lies" that led to the United States' involvement in World Wars I and II. He denounced the evils of the Trilateral Commission and "Red Teachers." Rock and roll was a "Pavlovian Communist mind-control plot." He wrote speeches for George Wallace, the segregationist governor of Alabama and presidential candidate. "Gary Allen is one of the most popular writers that John Birchites read and believe with a zeal that is nervous-making," wrote Nicholas von Hoffman in a 1972 *Washington Post* column. He wrote mail-order books and pamphlets distributed through a John Birch mailing list.

None of Mike Allen's friends seemed to know any of this about his father, or they were diverting me with other monikers (like "football coach," which he indeed was; Gary Allen coached a Pop Warner team that included Mike, who played center, badly). In an earlier phone interview, Allen said his mother was a first-grade teacher and his dad was a "writer" and "speaker." After I mentioned his father at breakfast, Allen flashed a sudden, teeth-clenched smile that stayed frozen as I spoke. He had described his upbringing to me as nonpolitical. And maybe it was. People who knew Gary Allen, who died of complications from diabetes in 1986, described him as quiet and introspective. "He was more outspoken in his writing," says Dan Lungren, a Republican member of Congress, who represented Orange County back then and knew the family. Lungren, who now represents a district that includes parts of Sacramento, said that the Allens hosted a meet-and-greet at their home for one of his early campaigns.

I asked Mike Allen what it was like being his father's son. "We have a very close family," he said slowly. "I'm very close to all my siblings, and I'm very grateful to my parents for all the emphasis they put on education and family and sports and Scouts." He called his father "a great dad." How did he make his living? "I don't know the details of it," Allen said. He did some teaching, but Allen said he was not sure where or what age groups, whether elementary school or high school or something else. He had an office at home. "To me, he was my dad. So that's what I knew." He says he never read anything his father wrote.

After some fidgety minutes, I asked Allen how he became an Eagle Scout. His eyes softened and stopped blinking as much as they had been, and his voice took on the cadence of solemn recital. He uttered the Boy Scout Law: "A scout is trustworthy," Allen proclaimed, "loyal, helpful, friendly, courteous, kind, obedient, cheerful, thrifty, brave, clean, and reverent."

I asked Allen if I could talk to his siblings. He said he would consider it and maybe set up a conference call but never did. I did not press. It felt intrusive. Nor did I want to overreach for a Rosebud. "Life isn't binary," Allen said a few times at breakfast, in the context of whether a hot dog is a meal or a snack and later in the context of what his father was like. But I could not help being struck by the contrast between father and son.

Gary Allen's writings conveyed great distrust of the established order. He saw conspiracies in both parties, despised Richard Nixon and Henry Kissinger for their internationalism and the "establishment media" for enabling the "communist conspiracy." Mike Allen traverses politics with a boyish and almost star-struck approach toward the assumed order. He is diligent in addressing leaders by proper titles, ranks, "Madam Speakers" and "Mr. Presidents" (a scout is reverent). Friends said he seemed particularly enthralled to be covering the White House during the Bush years and was spotted at all hours around the briefing room and press area.

Allen views *Playbook* as a respite from the chaos and invective of the daily news cycle. And at the end of our discussion about his father, he made a point of ending on a sweet and orderly data point. After Gary Allen died, at fifty, many of his former Pop Warner players filled the church in tribute. Allen said he recalled no talk of his father's political work at the memorial, but he will never forget one detail: a giant blue-and-gold floral arrangement in the shape of a football was placed onstage, a gift from the kids on Gary Allen's team, the Phantoms.

One of the few times I can recall Allen stepping out of his friendly scoutmaster persona in *Playbook* was when he dismissed a Sunday column by the public editor in the *New York Times* as "a bit of a snore." The column was about how reporters should not use the *Times* to, among other things, plug their friends. "Okay, then!" Allen wrote to conclude the item.

Allen clearly plugs his friends in *Playbook*—quoting from press releases announcing their new jobs ("Taylor Griffin Joins Hamilton Place Strategies as Partner"), referring to pal Katie Couric as a "media icon," reporting that the model car built by Ethan Gibbs, the six-year-old son of Robert Gibbs, finished second in the Cub Scouts' Pinewood Derby. Isn't part of the function of *Playbook* to plug Mike Allen's friends? "I wouldn't agree with that," Allen told me. "*Playbook* is to serve its audience and community, and we serve them by giving them information they need and want. If it were the way you describe it, people wouldn't read it." Recognition of a friend's milestone can also be a data point. People in this tiny world care if two of their own (say, the Democratic operatives Phil Singer and Kim Molstre) have a baby ("Introducing Max George Singer," *Playbook*, March 18).

Allen's focus is customer service. He wants to "spread joy" as the Holy Ghost of the Almighty News Cycle. "I am fortunate," he keeps saying. (Hat Tip: God.)

In early March, I was meeting with Harris in his office when Allen walked in. He welcomed me, thanked me for coming, and returned to his desk to finish a story or six. I visited his cubicle, but Allen was gone. His work area was notable for its lack of clutter—there were a few small stacks of magazines and newspapers and a tray of mint Girl Scout cookies on the top of his terminal. To the left of his desktop was a picture of Allen standing upright and asking President Obama a question at a White House news conference.

In the days leading up to a photo shoot for this article, Allen's work area became spotless, surfaces shining, befitting News Cycle Man. The poster of the cartoon sphinx had been removed. I kept asking Kingsley, "Who cleaned up Mikey's room?" but neither she nor Allen would say. All great questions come from small questions. And some just hang there, until they vanish.

Chris Matthews, Seriously
(O.K., Not That Seriously)

April 13, 2008

Whenever Chris Matthews says something he likes, which happens a lot, he repeats it often and at volumes suggesting a speaker who feels insufficiently listened to at times. "Tim Russert finally reeled the big marlin into the boat tonight," Matthews yelled—nine times, on and off the air, after a Democratic debate that Russert moderated with Brian Williams in late February at Cleveland State University. Matthews believed that Russert (the fisherman) had finally succeeded in getting Hillary Clinton (the marlin) to admit that she was wrong to vote in favor of the Iraq War Resolution in 2002. "We've been trolling for that marlin for, what, a year now?" Matthews said to Russert.

Comparing Hillary Rodham Clinton to a big flopping fish will do nothing to stop criticism—from Clinton's presidential campaign, among others—that Matthews and his network, MSNBC, have treated the former First Lady unfairly. But this didn't keep Matthews from bludgeoning the marlin line to death in the post-debate "spin room." "Russert caught the marlin; he got the marlin,"

Matthews shouted to a school of downcast reporters who had been hanging on every canned word of Clinton's chief campaign strategist, Mark Penn.

The spin room is a modern political-media marvel whose full-on uselessness is perfectly conveyed by its name, but Matthews appeared in his element. He wore a dreamy smile, walking around, signing autographs. As he went, Matthews seemed compelled to give his "take," which is how he describes his job each night at five and seven, eastern time, on *Hardball*—"giving my take."

Someone from Matthews's staff mentioned that the office of Senator Larry Craig, the Idaho Republican who got in trouble for his "wide stance" in an airport men's room, had been looking for interns. "Ha!" Matthews exploded, a trademark outcry. "Guess what, Mom and Dad, I just got an internship with that senator from Idaho, you know the one.

"Ha!

"Did you get a load of Lou Rawls's wife?" Matthews said as he left the spin room. Apparently the Reverend Jesse Jackson was introducing the widow of the R&B singer at the media center. "She was an absolute knockout," Matthews declared. It's a common Matthews designation. The actress Kerry Washington was also a "total knockout," according to Matthews, who by one a.m. had repaired to the bar of the Cleveland Ritz-Carlton. He was sipping a Diet Coke and holding court for a cluster of network and political types, as well as for a procession of random glad-handers that included, wouldn't you know it, Kerry Washington herself. Washington played Ray Charles's wife in the movie *Ray* and Kay Amin in *The Last King of Scotland*. She is a big Obama supporter and was in town for the debate; more to the point, she said she likes *Hardball*. Matthews grabbed her hand, and Phil Griffin, the head of MSNBC who was seated across the table, vowed to get her on the show.

"I know why he wants you on," Matthews said to Washington

while looking at Griffin. At which point Matthews did something he rarely does. He paused. He seemed actually to be considering what he was about to say. He might even have been editing himself, which is anything but a natural act for him. He was grimacing. I imagined a little superego hamster racing against a speeding treadmill inside Matthews's skull, until the superego hamster was overrun and the pause ended.

"He wants you on because you're beautiful," Matthews said. "And because you're black." He handed Washington a business card and told her to call anytime "if you ever want to hang out with Chris Matthews."

Then a young Irish-looking woman walked up shyly and asked if he was "Mr. Matthews." "Ah, an Irish girl has come to my aid," Matthews said, placing his hand gently on the woman's shoulder. She was in law school and said her name was Margaret Sweeney. "I went out with a Sweeney once, a nurse," Matthews said, taking her hand. This Sweeney attends law school at Cleveland State, "where Russert went," Matthews told her, before starting again on the marlin thing.

The post-debate tableau at the Ritz was another media-political bazaar, minus the riffraff of the spin room. This is about as glitzy as you'll get on a snowy night in Cleveland at one a.m. The Ohio congresswoman, Stephanie Tubbs Jones, came over from the next table to visit with Matthews, along with the former Ohio congressman Dennis Eckart, and a guy who told Matthews he ran for attorney general in Ohio and a bunch of suited money people and the actor Timothy Hutton and some fancy Hollywood director. "This is all sort of like a big play world," Griffin, the MSNBC chief, said, surveying the room. "You have all these politicians and media people and Hollywood celebrities in here. It sort of embarrasses me. It feels a little incestuous."

(A disclaimer that advances this notion of incestuousness: I have been a guest on *Hardball* on occasion, but probably not more than a half dozen times over the years. The *New York Times* also has a partnership with NBC in which the news organizations coordinate some aspects of their political coverage, posting politics-related stories and videos on each other's Web sites. And Matthews and I have the same book agent, for what that's worth.)

"People are a little impressed with themselves," Griffin went on to say, continuing his commentary about the scene. "It's a bit of an echo chamber." Matthews is central to that echo chamber—at the Ritz, as in the 2008 presidential campaign. He is, in a sense, the carnival barker at the center of it, spewing tiny pellets of chewed nuts across the table while comparing Obama to Mozart and Clinton to Salieri. At one point, Matthews suddenly became hypnotized by a TV over the bar set to a rebroadcast of *Hardball*. "Hey, there I am—it's me," he said, staring at himself on the screen. "It's me."

There is a level of ubiquity about Chris Matthews today that can be exhausting, occasionally edifying, and, for better or worse, central to what has become a very loud national conversation about politics. His soothing-like-a-blender voice feels unnervingly constant in a presidential campaign that has drawn big interest, ratings, and voter turnout. He gets in trouble sometimes and has to apologize—as he did after suggesting that Hillary Clinton owed her election to the Senate to the fact that her husband "messed around." He is also something of a YouTube sensation: see Chris getting challenged to a duel by former Georgia governor Zell Miller; describing the "thrill going up my leg" after an Obama speech; dancing with (and accidentally groping) Ellen DeGeneres on her show; shouting down the conservative commentator Michelle Malkin; ogling CNBC's Erin Burnett. And he has provided a running bounty of material for Media Matters for America, a liberal media watchdog, which has devoted an entire section of its Web site ("The Matthews Monitor") to cataloging Matthews's alleged offenses, especially against Hillary Clinton and women generally.

In addition to doing *Hardball*, Matthews is the host of a Sunday-morning show on NBC, *The Chris Matthews Show*; has been a staple of the network's coverage of presidential debates; and has helped moderate two of them. He is also a frequent guest on NBC and MSNBC news shows and an ongoing spoof target on *Saturday Night Live*. It can be difficult not to hear Darrell Hammond's long-running impression of Matthews when Matthews himself is speaking. Matthews, for his part, says he loves the Hammond impression and sometimes catches himself "doing Hammond doing Matthews." If parody is an emblem of pop-culture status—signifying a measure of permanence—Matthews belongs on any Mount Rushmore of political screaming heads.

Matthews is as pure a political being as there is on TV. He is the whip-tongued, name-dropping, self-promoting wise guy you often find in campaigns, and in the bigger offices on Capitol Hill or K Street. ("Rain Man," NBC's Brian Williams jokingly called Matthews, referring to his breadth of political knowledge.) He wrote speeches for Jimmy Carter, worked as a top adviser to Tip O'Neill, ran unsuccessfully for Congress himself in his native Philadelphia at twenty-eight. In an age of cynicism about politics, Matthews can be romantic about the craft, defensive about its practitioners, and personally affronted when someone derides Washington or "the game." He can also be unsparing in his criticism of those who run afoul of his "take." "I am not a cheerleader for politics per se," Matthews says. "I am a cheerleader for the possibilities of politics."

This election season, MSNBC has placed great emphasis on politics, devoting 28 percent of its airtime to the subject last year (compared with 15 percent for Fox News and 12 percent for CNN, according to the Project for Excellence in Journalism). The thrilling

2008 presidential campaign has been a boon, and in the first quarter MSNBC's prime-time audience rose 63 percent over the previous year (compared with 12 percent for the Fox News Channel and 70 percent for CNN, though MSNBC still draws many fewer viewers overall). As Matthews is clearly a signature figure on the network, and one of the most recognizable political personalities on the air, this has been something of a heyday for him.

Yet for as basic as he has become to the political and media furniture, Matthews is anything but secure. He is of the moment but, at sixty-two, also something of a throwback—to an era of politics set in the ethnic Democratic wards of the '60s and the O'Neill-Reagan battles of the '80s. And he is a product of an aging era of cable news, the late '90s, when *Hardball* started and Matthews made his name as a battering critic of Bill Clinton during the Monica saga.

Cable political coverage has changed, however, and so has the sensibility that viewers—particularly young ones—expect from it. Matthews's bombast is radically at odds with the wry, anti-political style fashioned by Jon Stewart and Stephen Colbert or the cutting and finely tuned cynicism of Matthews's MSNBC co-worker Keith Olbermann. These hosts betray none of the reverence for politics or the rituals of Washington that Matthews does. On the contrary, they appeal to the eye-rolling tendencies of a cooler, highly educated urban cohort of the electorate that mostly dismisses an exuberant political animal like Matthews as annoyingly antiquated, like the ranting uncle at the Thanksgiving table whom the kids have learned to tune out.

Nothing illustrated Matthews's discordance with the new cable ethos better than an eviscerating interview he suffered through last fall at the hands of Stewart himself. Matthews went on *The Daily Show* to promote his book *Life's a Campaign: What Politics Has Taught Me About Friendship, Rivalry, Reputation, and Success*. The book essentially advertises itself as a guidebook for readers wishing to apply the lessons of winning politicians to succeeding in life. "People don't mind being used; they mind being discarded" is the title of one chapter. "A self-hurt book" and "a recipe for sadness," Stewart called it, and the interview was all squirms from there. "This strikes me as artifice," Stewart said. "If you live by this book, your life will be strategy, and if your life is strategy, you will be unhappy."

Matthews accused Stewart of "trashing my book."

"I'm not trashing your book," Stewart protested. "I'm trashing your philosophy of life."

Matthews told me that the interview was a painful experience. Not only did Stewart humiliate him, but the interview exposed an essential truth that people by and large don't want to hear advice from politicians, a breed that, in many ways, has defined Matthews's value system. "I think Stewart was right in that he caught the drift of anti-politics," Matthews said.

So has Olbermann, the host of MSNBC's *Countdown*. While Matthews is clearly a stalwart on the MSNBC menu, he is hardly a flavor of the month, or the year. Olbermann is. *Countdown*, on at eight, is getting good ratings, usually second in its slot to *The O'Reilly Factor* on Fox News. Olbermann draws considerably more viewers than Matthews—about one million a night, compared with 660,000 for the seven p.m. broadcast of *Hardball* (which typically runs third in its time slots after Fox News and CNN but is up in the ratings this year). There is a view within the TV industry that MSNBC is positioning itself as the younger, edgier, left-tilting cable network, and no one there embodies this ideal better than Olbermann. NBC executives have been promoting him heavily, and three network officials asked me why I was writing about Matthews and not Olbermann.

Part of this can be viewed purely through a bottom-line lens. Matthews's contract expires next year, and NBC officials clearly would like to renew it for considerably less than the $5 million a year he is making now. Whether it's a formal talking point or not, NBC officials seem bent on conveying the message that they could get the same ratings, or better ones, for considerably less money.

But the broader issue involves whether Matthews is a man trapped in a tired caricature. And it touches on the future of his archetype in general—in other words, whither the cable blowhard? The "What happens to Chris?" question—a hot topic at NBC these days—infuses the Matthews story with a kind of "lion in winter" urgency, if not poignancy. It also goes to the core of how Matthews sees himself, how cable news is changing, and how Americans perceive of and consume their politics.

The morning after the Cleveland debate, Matthews was walking through the airport to catch his flight home to Washington. People kept squinting at him, double-taking, stepping in and out of his monologue.

"I like the fact that people don't think of me as famous, but that they know me," Matthews said. "They come up to me and say, 'Chris, what do you think?' There's no aura. It's a different kind of celebrity. People assume they have a right to talk to me. They want to know my take."

A woman picked Matthews out of the security line and declared herself a fan. "Don't tell me, you're a liberal NPR-listener type," Matthews said, reducing said fan to a psychographic niche (though warmly).

She described herself as "just an old lady going to Florida."

"Who are you voting for?" Matthews asked.

"Hillary," she said, adding in a whisper, "but I don't want her to win."

"Hey, what's your name?" another person in line asked him.

"I'm Chris Matthews."

"Oh, yes, we watch your show every night."

"Thanks," Matthews said, wondering aloud to me whether it would be possible for someone to watch his show every night and not know his name.

The security agent working the metal detector told Matthews that he had seen him at this airport before, and Matthews volunteered that he was in Cleveland a few years ago to speak at the Case Western Reserve University graduation. "But they didn't give me an honorary degree," Matthews said. "Can you believe that? I spoke at the graduation and didn't get an honorary degree?" He gets a lot of honorary degrees, by the way—nineteen, if you're counting, and guess who is counting?

As we approached the airport gate, Matthews mentioned that he and his wife, Kathleen, have been contemplating a trip to Damascus. It's something they have wanted to do for a long time. But he worries that he might make an inviting target for a kidnapper. "I can imagine getting some big-name media figure would be a big propaganda catch for them," Matthews said. "You can imagine what the neocons would say if I were kidnapped. They'd be like, 'See, Matthews, terrorism isn't so funny now, is it?'"

There is a level of solipsism about Matthews that is oddly endearing in its self-conscious extreme, even by the standards of television vanity.

"Did you see me on the *Today* show?" Matthews asked when I called him one afternoon in early March. "I quoted F. Scott Fitzgerald. I think I'm the only guy around who quotes F. Scott Fitzgerald on the *Today* show."

A few days later, Matthews greeted me with a report that he was up at six a.m. that day he did *Today*; did *Morning Joe*, MSNBC'S morning political program; taped the Sunday *Chris Matthews Show*; then talked to a bunch of people in Pennsylvania, his home state, about the primary. He's big into the Pennsylvania primary, talks a lot to "Eddie Rendell," and urged me repeatedly to call the Pennsylvania governor's office and "talk to Eddie Rendell about me."

"By the way, have you figured me out yet?" Matthews said at the end of another phone conversation the following day. "You gotta understand, it's all complicated. It's not like Tim."

Tim—as in Russert, the inquisitive jackhammer host of *Meet the Press*—is a particular obsession of Matthews's. Matthews craves Russert's approval like that of an older brother. He is often solicitous. On the morning of the Cleveland debate, Matthews was standing in the lobby of the Ritz when Russert walked through, straight from a workout, wearing a sweat-drenched Buffalo Bills sweatshirt, long shorts, and black rubber-soled shoes with tube socks. "Here he is; here he is, the man," Matthews said to Russert, who smiled and chatted for a few minutes before returning to his room. (An MSNBC spokesman, Jeremy Gaines, tried, after the fact, to declare Russert's outfit "off the record.")

Matthews has berated Russert to several people at NBC and has told friends and associates that Russert is like John F. Kennedy while he is more like Richard Nixon. Kennedy was the golden boy while Nixon was the scrapper for whom nothing came easily. It's an imperfect comparison, certainly (Matthews is Irish Catholic, for starters, and Russert is not charismatic by any classic Kennedyesque definition), but it does offer a glimpse into how Matthews perceives himself, especially in relation to Russert. It's also worth noting that Nixon was obsessed with Kennedy, and Kennedy could be dismissive and disparaging of Nixon.

A number of people I spoke with at NBC said that Russert can be disdainful of Matthews, whose act he often sees as clownish. They also told me that Russert believes Matthews is something of a loose cannon who brings him undue headaches in his capacity as NBC's Washington bureau chief. This friction was immortalized in notes revealed during the trial of Scooter Libby. Mary Matalin, an adviser to Vice President Dick Cheney, was quoted as having suggested that Libby call Russert to complain about Matthews's rants against the White House's Iraq policy. "Call Tim—he hates Chris," Matalin supposedly told Libby. Russert denies that he felt this way then or now. "I've always had a very good relationship with Chris," he told me. "We do different things." Matalin, for her part, insists that she doesn't remember ever saying that Russert "hates Chris."

Regardless, Matthews has an attuned sense of pecking order— at MSNBC, at NBC, in Washington, and in life. This is no great rarity among the fragile egos of TV or, for that matter, in the status-fixated world of politics. But Matthews is especially frontal about it. In an interview with *Playboy* a few years ago, he volunteered that he had made the list of the Top 50 journalists in DC in the *Washingtonian* magazine. "I'm like thirty-sixth, and Tim Russert is number one," Matthews told *Playboy*. "I would argue for a higher position for myself."

He wanted to feel part of the "first team," he added. "You can be on the second team at twenty-five or thirty-six. But at some point you say: No, this is my opportunity, my life. I want to be on the first team."

Matthews, the second oldest of five boys, often talks about birth order and sibling rivalry. One day when I was with him, Matthews kept calling his son Thomas for his twenty-second birthday. "You always have to pay special attention to the middle one," Matthews said. "They need to know you're thinking of them."

Matthews and his brothers deploy the standard line about how their crowded family dinner table made for nightly battles over food and the right to be heard. It is also clear that MSNBC's political dinner table is getting crowded. NBC views MSNBC as a major source of potential growth and is encouraging its big-name talents— Russert, Brian Williams, and, from time to time, Tom Brokaw—to appear as guests on the cable channel. It makes for crammed sets, limited airtime, and a lot of personalities to keep happy on important campaign nights.

Friends say Matthews is wary of another up-and-comer, David Gregory, who last month was given a show at six o'clock, between airings of *Hardball*. It is a common view around NBC that Gregory is trying out as a possible replacement for Matthews. Before the flight from Cleveland to Washington took off, an NBC staff member noted that Matthews, Russert, and Andrea Mitchell were all on board, and if the plane were to crash, it would devastate the network's talent pool. Matthews quipped that Gregory was outside the plane arranging for just that. ("I hadn't heard that," Gregory told me. "I'm quite sure he was joking.")

Matthews is also aware that little brother Keith Olbermann has become the signature talent of MSNBC. Matthews seems less than thrilled with "co-anchoring" MSNBC's election coverage with him, as he has done on many nights during this campaign. When Olbermann is on the same set, Matthews appears different—restrained, even shrinking. According to people at NBC, Matthews has not been shy in voicing his resentment of Olbermann. Nor, according to network sources, has Olbermann bothered to hide his low regard for Matthews, although when I spoke to him, Olbermann denied any personal animosity toward Matthews and told me that he appreciates his "John Madden–like enthusiasm for politics."

But Olbermann does acknowledge that their on-air marriage has been rocky. Stylistically, Olbermann is scripted and disciplined while Matthews is free-form. While Olbermann is a natural anchor, Matthews struggles with its basic mechanics—staying on time, not talking into breaks. "There is a sense at times that we are always joining Chris Matthews already in progress," Olbermann told me. Matthews has been on ten years, he went on to say, "and he has no idea when it stops and starts. My responsibility sometimes is to grab the wheel when he doesn't hold it." Matthews has also called their joint appearances *Hardball*, which annoys Olbermann and which he has not been shy about correcting on the air. "'No, this is not *Hardball*,' I will say, and in those instances, a correction is appropriate."

Sometimes during commercial breaks, Matthews will boast to Olbermann of having restrained himself during the prior segment. "And I reward him with a grape," Olbermann says.

Chris Matthews loved politics from a young age—starting at around five, his brothers say. He spent a lot of time with his grandfather Charles Patrick Shields, a Democratic committeeman from the working-class North Philadelphia neighborhood of Nicetown. Shields's "office" was a neighborhood newsstand. "He was a good man of the parish," Chris's younger brother Jim told me. Chris revered him. "I think Tip O'Neill reminded Chris a little of Grandpa," Jim added, meaning they both fit the urban-ethnic prototype of the backslapping operator from the neighborhood.

Matthews's father, Herb, was a court reporter and worked all the time. Chris spent his early childhood in a row house, before the family moved to Somerton, a leafy neighborhood at Philadelphia's northeast tip. The boys went to Catholic schools and took family trips to a summer house on the Jersey shore. The family generally voted Republican. Chris loved John F. Kennedy in 1960, but wound up falling harder for Nixon by the end and cried when he lost. "We weren't a huggy family—we had our fracases—but we basically got along," Jim Matthews, now the Republican chairman of the board of commissioners in Montgomery County, Pennsylvania, told me.

Matthews attended Holy Cross in Worcester, Massachusetts. He studied hard and engaged in long, loud political debates in the cafeteria. His political allegiance evolved from Barry Goldwater to Eugene McCarthy ("just like Hillary," he says). He also nurtured a passionate affair with television. He loved Johnny Carson, particularly his persona as a wide-eyed Nebraskan, awed that movie stars were actually talking to him. "Carson was great company," Matthews says. "He was big company. Best company in the world." He identifies with this. "Now, I am people's company," he told me. "Do you know that women come up to me all the time and say, 'My husband watched you until the end, until he died'?" (Also, Matthews added, Carson "had babes on the show.")

After graduating from college in 1967, Matthews went on to the University of North Carolina to pursue a doctorate in economics, but he left in 1968 to join the Peace Corps. The following year, he was posted in Swaziland, in southeast Africa, where he taught business skills to villagers and rode around on a little Suzuki motorcycle. "He often wore a necktie," recalls Fred O'Regan, a fellow volunteer.

"I remember we were out hitchhiking once," O'Regan told me. Matthews started arguing about Nixon and Vietnam. "It was just like watching his show today. Chris would ask a question, then he would answer it himself and then the person was invited to comment on Chris's answer to his own question."

Matthews returned after two years and in 1974 ran for Congress in northeast Philadelphia. He lost in the Democratic primary, but it started what became an exhaustive job search that landed him on Capitol Hill and then in the White House as a speechwriter for President Carter. He parlayed the White House job into a series of positions on Capitol Hill that would culminate at the side of Speaker Tip O'Neill during the 1980s. Matthews was essentially his media and message guru, such as they were in those days. He would help the lumbering, untelegenic speaker do battle with Ronald Reagan. "Chris was an important bridge for my father between the old and the new media world," said Rosemary O'Neill, the daughter of the late speaker. "You always knew Chris was there. He was a big personality, even then. He was never hiding behind the ficus trees."

Matthews's 1988 book, *Hardball*, distilled lessons from his life in politics and became a best seller. It also could be read as a how-to guide to social and career climbing in Washington. "It's Not Who You Know; It's Who You Get to Know" is the title of the first chapter and has been something of a mantra for Matthews throughout his ascent.

After O'Neill retired in 1987, Matthews was offered a columnist's job at the *San Francisco Examiner*. He earned $200 a week for his twice-weekly column and envisioned himself a big-city scribe like Jimmy Breslin, who could walk into a bar and have people give him grief about his column. But San Francisco wasn't one of those newspaper cities. "It looks like an eastern city," he says. "But it's pretty hard for people to read newspapers when they're riding a bike."

Still, the column—at the *Examiner* and then at the *San Francisco Chronicle*—gave him an affiliation that helped get him on TV. He appeared on *CBS This Morning* and *Good Morning America* and begged himself onto the political shout fests like *The McLaughlin Group*. Fox News's Roger Ailes gave Matthews his first show, *In-Depth*, on an obscure network called America's Talking. *Hardball* had its debut in 1997, on CNBC, and was catapulted by the Clinton-Lewinsky scandal. Matthews built an instant following, and loathing. In his book about the media's conduct during the Monica saga, Bill Kovach, the founding chairman of the Committee of Concerned Journalists, anointed Matthews as part of a "new class of chatterers who emerged in this scandal . . . a group of loosely credentialed, self-interested performers whose primary job is remaining on TV."

Matthews is clearly an acquired taste, and some of his most devoted followers are Washington media figures and politicians. "The things people complain about I actually like," says Roger

Simon, the chief political columnist for *Politico* and an occasional guest on *Hardball*. "His interruptions are invariably a reaction to something you just said, which indicates that he is, in fact, listening." Simon calls Matthews "a major political force" whose shows are closely monitored by campaigns and journalists. "I know when I go on the show, I get comments, I get e-mails," Simon told me. "He drives conversations."

If Matthews has an overriding professional insecurity, it is being confined to the pigeonhole of cable blowhard. The insecurity is well founded, since this is how many people view him. "The shorthand for Chris in the gossip columns is always 'blabbermouth' or 'cable yakker' or something," said Nancy Nathan, the executive producer of *The Chris Matthews Show*. "It's not fair or accurate. But it's obviously out there."

Matthews takes great pride in *The Chris Matthews Show*, as if its select Sunday-morning time slot, just before *Meet the Press*, confers him a spot on the coveted first team. "We envision viewers watching up on the West Side of New York," Nathan told me. "They've been to Zabar's. They have their bagel, juice, coffee. These are smart people who want smart analysis. We like to think we're a complement to *Meet the Press*."

When I asked Matthews about the bloviator stigma, he dismissed it as jealousy or at the very least ignorance among those who don't know him or who don't regularly watch his Sunday show or who have not read his books or who are not aware that he is a student of history and film or that he is on the board of trustees of the Churchill Center or that he has received—did he mention?—nineteen honorary degrees. (Breaking honorary-degree news: Matthews told me in late March that he expects to be up to at least twenty-two later this spring.)

He also mentioned—more than once—that he has heard that

the historian David McCullough watches *Hardball* every night and that "Arthur Schlesinger watched *Hardball*" and that sometimes "Joan Didion watched *Hardball* with her husband, John Gregory Dunne, before he died."

Matthews envisions his role in this presidential campaign to that of Eric Sevareid and Walter Cronkite in 1968. "Your job is to illuminate, illuminate the game," Matthews says. He faces a nightly challenge to "bring to life" the unfurling of history. Matthews says he wants to be synonymous with this campaign, like Howard Cosell was with Muhammad Ali.

"Imagine bullfighting without Hemingway," he says. "I can't."

Is Matthews comparing himself to Hemingway?

"No way," he says. "Don't you, don't you [expletive] do that."

Matthews fashions himself a blend of big-think historian and little-guy populist. Steve Capus, the president of NBC News, who is also from Philadelphia, says that Matthews has internalized the "inferiority complex" of his native city. Matthews says that although he's now six-feet-three, he was little as a child and has always viewed himself as "a short guy."

"I don't think people look at me as the establishment, do you?" Matthews asked me. "Am I part of the winners' circle in American life? I don't think so."

But he attends many of the same events they do. He is diligent about showing up at the city's tribal rites—hotel dinners, book parties, tributes. He is dutiful about traveling to family weddings, funerals, graduations, and first communions. "I place a high premium on showing up," Matthews says. "It's the Woody Allen thing.'"

It's important to be around. When our plane from Cleveland landed in Washington, Matthews learned that William F. Buckley Jr. had just died. Matthews appeared stricken, though he barely knew Buckley. He said he would attend the funeral.

Washington has no dearth of events honoring Matthews himself. Serial bashes seem to follow every Matthews milestone. Within a few weeks last fall, Matthews was feted at the Georgetown home of the socialite and Democratic fund-raiser Elizabeth Bagley to mark the publication of *Life's a Campaign*. He was toasted at a bigger tenth-anniversary party for *Hardball*, which doubled as a book party for *Life's a Campaign*, at Decatur House in Washington.

"I don't go where the politicians go," Matthews told me, though he is grateful when they show up, and he keeps track ("Teddy was at the Decatur House," he said, meaning Kennedy). As I began researching this article, Jeremy Gaines, the MSNBC spokesman, gave me the names of about a dozen people that Matthews recommended I speak to, all famous—everyone from Nancy Pelosi to Marvin Hamlisch. But gatekeepers for more than one of these people expressed confusion as to why Matthews would refer me to them. "Please keep us out of this," pleaded a spokesperson for one prominent politician whom Matthews had recommended via Gaines.

For someone so steeped in the ego manglings of politics and television, Matthews can be spectacularly thin-skinned. He sulks at mild put-downs and lashes out at critics (though rarely holds grudges). At one point, I teased him gently about his tendency to repeat things—it was the item about how Arthur Schlesinger, Joan Didion, and David McCullough all watched *Hardball*. It seemed to deflate him. He sunk in his chair. "It's tough, it's a rough cut," Matthews said of criticism. "I'm not completely Nietzschean about this. That what doesn't kill me makes me stronger? I've always wondered about that. I'm not sure that's true at all."

When I asked his wife, Kathleen, how he takes criticism, she told me: "He hears it; he absorbs it. Then he comes home and wrestles with it."

The 2008 campaign has provided Matthews with much to wrestle with. He has been attacked, repeatedly, for his perceived pro-Obama/anti-Clinton perspective—a bias he disputes. He notes that he and the former First Lady like to "kid around" when they see each other and that he did a memorably tough interview with an Obama surrogate, State Senator Kirk Watson of Texas, who failed— despite Matthews's grilling—to identify a single legislative accomplishment by Obama. "That was an iconic moment," Matthews said of the Watson interview.

Still, it's hard to watch Matthews and conclude that he has been anything less than enthralled by Obama and, at the very least, is sick of Clinton. The antipathy dates back some time. Just before the start of Clinton's first campaign for the Senate in 2000, Matthews said: "Hillary Clinton bugs a lot of guys, I mean, really bugs people—like maybe me on occasion. . . . She drives some of us absolutely nuts." During this campaign he has repeatedly referred to her sense of entitlement and arrogance. Meanwhile, David Shuster, a correspondent for MSNBC who appears frequently on *Hardball*, was suspended for two weeks earlier this year for asking whether the Clinton campaign had "pimped out" Chelsea Clinton by enlisting her to court celebrities and superdelegates.

By contrast, Matthews has called Obama "bigger than Kennedy" and compared the success of his campaign to "the New Testament." His reviews of Obama's speeches have been comically effusive at times, as when he described "this thrill going up my leg" after an Obama victory speech. ("Steady," Olbermann cautioned him on the air.)

"I love Chris, but he definitely drank the Obama Kool-Aid," Ed Rendell, the Pennsylvania governor and a Clinton supporter, told me.

In a recent interview on *Morning Joe* with Governor Bill Richardson of New Mexico, who had just endorsed Obama, Matthews described the "stunning picture" of a Latino governor (Richardson) standing with an African-American candidate and how inspiring it was for so many voters. "That is where we should be putting our focus, not on the feelings of the Clintons, about what people owe them and their sense of entitlement," Matthews said.

Richardson tried to say something, but Matthews just kept going. "We've got to stop talking about this as if this were a sitcom," Matthews continued. "We had eight years of the sitcom. . . . It's a sitcom, and it's gotta end." He lamented that four thousand people are dead in Iraq "because of decisions made by politicians like the Clintons."

Mika Brzezinski, a co-host of *Morning Joe*, then asked Matthews whether he was endorsing Obama.

"Why would you say that?" Matthews said, looking dumbfounded.

It can be amusing if slightly painful to watch Matthews's facial expressions and body language on the set of *Hardball* when others are talking; he will, at times, bounce in his seat like a Ritalin-deprived second-grader who is dying to give an answer but has been admonished too many times for interrupting. He appears to go through the same pained exercise in his own home. Indeed, as I learned at Sunday brunch there, the degree to which the cadences of the Matthews dining room mimic *Hardball* is striking.

Kathleen Matthews had invited me over. "The queen would love to receive you," Chris said on the phone by way of extending the invitation. Matthews's effusiveness toward women certainly extends to his wife of nearly twenty-eight years, a longtime local news anchor in Washington who now works in communications and public affairs for Marriott International. "Everyone who meets Kathy thinks she's a monumental figure," Matthews promised.

The Matthewses have three children—two sons and a daughter—and Chris is quick to boast about all of them, often in terms that convey an acute case of status consciousness. "Caroline is at Penn, Thomas is an actor at NYU, and Michael went to Brown,"

Matthews told me on multiple occasions. Kathleen "graduated from Stanford," he mentioned one day, adding that "she had a 3.7 there." That was thirty-three years ago.

Chris gave directions to his white-frame Victorian house in Chevy Chase, Maryland, built in 1885. "Right across from Tommy Boggs's house," he said, referring to the Washington lobbyist, son of the former House majority leader. The Matthews house is sun-lit, art-filled, and cozy, with three Mercedes of various sizes and degrees of wear in the driveway. I arrived at eleven a.m., just as Matthews was leaving.

"I promised a bunch of Koreans I'd get my picture taken with them, so that's where I'm going," he explained. "I'll be right back."

The morning had been a small fiasco at the Matthews home. Chris and Kathleen had overslept, and instead of waking at ten a.m., as they typically do on Sundays—in time for *The Chris Matthews Show*—they woke at ten thirty (and Russert!), and then Chris had to run off to this photo thing he had forgotten about.

So Kathleen made lattes in the kitchen while Caroline—home on a break from Penn—sat at an island-table spread with Sunday newspapers. She is finishing her freshman year and active in the Obama campaign. Kathleen, meanwhile, contributed $2,200 to the Clinton campaign.

Chris returned after twenty minutes, and Kathleen served seafood pasta in the dining room. When he realized the pasta was whole wheat, Chris helped himself to seconds.

After we finished eating, I placed a tape recorder on the table, which would later yield many sequences of indecipherable cross-talk, along with long, loud monologues from Chris. "We all talk about the Clintons," Matthews said at the conclusion of a diatribe about the national obsession with Bill and Hillary. "I have never been at a party where it doesn't become a topic. Who are we gonna talk about? Bob Dole? John Kerry? Al Gore?"

Kathleen added, "Also, we've had so much time with them. We've watched them in this fishbowl."

Chris: "I find it very hard to do."

Kathleen: "With the Obamas, we can't even speculate."

Chris: "I watched the DLC convention in 1991."

Kathleen: "And even McCain."

Chris: "I sort of get him. We went out with the McCains for dinner one night."

Kathleen: "Chi-chi Vietnamese."

Chris: "Here's the thing about the Clintons."

The conversation moved to what Matthews calls "the sexist thing," or what Media Matters calls Matthews's "history of degrading comments about women, in which he focuses on the physical appearances of his female guests and of other women discussed on his program." This would include Matthews loudly admiring the conservative radio host Laura Ingraham ("You're great-looking, obviously—one of God's gifts to men in this country"), Elizabeth Edwards ("You've got a great face"), Jane Fonda ("You also dazzle us with your beauty and all the good things"), CNBC's Margaret Brennan ("You're gorgeous"), and Erin Burnett ("You're beautiful. . . . You're a knockout"), among others. The Burnett episode was especially remarked upon. In the video Matthews instructed Burnett to "get a little closer to the camera." As Burnett became confused, Matthews persisted: "Come on in closer. No, come in—come in further—come in closer. Really close." It was, at the minimum, uncomfortable to watch.

Matthews says the notion that he is sexist has been pushed unfairly by blogs, women's groups, and, to some degree, the Clinton campaign. His remark that Clinton benefitted because her husband "messed around" triggered much outrage from the Clinton team. Matthews eventually apologized in a rambling on-air explanation, but he hardly sounds contrite now. "I was tonally inaccurate but factually true," he told me. I had asked him earlier if he was forced into the apology. "Oh, yeah, of course I was forced into that," he said, laughing. "No, no, no . . . Phil [Griffin] asked me to do that."

Matthews vigorously denies the broader charge that he demeans women on the air. "I don't think there's any evidence of that at all," he said at brunch. "I've gone back and looked. Give me the evidence. No one can give it to me. I went through all my stuff. I can't find it." I mentioned Erin Burnett, and the name landed like a brick on the dining-room table.

"Ask Kathy, she might have a view," Matthews said.

Kathy began to give her view, but Chris interrupted. "She was doing peek-a-boo style," he said of Burnett. "She was doing in and out of the camera, and I said, 'Can you get any closer to the camera?' And she said, 'What are you kidding about—is there something wrong with the way I look?' And I said, 'No, you're a knockout.'"

Anyway, as Kathleen was saying: "I think it's pure Chris appreciating a good-looking woman. And from her standpoint it was embarrassing because she wasn't sure what to do with it."

Her husband jumped in and added that before the Burnett interview, he had "made a decision to do a whimsical Friday-night show."

"I guess the bottom line is, What does it show?" Kathleen said. "Is it disrespect for women? Objectifying women?"

"It's a show," Chris replied.

"Or does it show appreciation for a pretty woman?" Kathleen said. "I think that's the question." It was unclear exactly where Kathleen stood on this question. "I think his greatest worry," Kathleen said, "is that I might watch it on TV and scream at him." It wasn't clear in this case whether she did or not.

"It's a show," Chris said again, interrupting. "It's a show. That's my basic response."

He bemoaned political correctness. "We'll, we're just going to have to survive this era," Matthews said, sighing.

He looked down at the tape recorder. "We're taping all this, aren't we? I'm giving you a lot of stuff here."

It had now been more than three hours at the Matthews home without a commercial. Chris drove me to a subway stop. "Don't talk to anyone who hasn't known me thirty years," he instructed, not for the first time. That, he said, will show readers that Chris Matthews hasn't changed, that he has always been the way he is. The implication, also, is that it would be hard to change him now.

I visited Matthews at NBC's Washington bureau on the night of the Mississippi primary. He would be broadcasting a special edition of *Hardball* after the returns came in. Since Mississippi was a smaller primary, none of the NBC first team would be cluttering the set, and it would be Matthews's show, with help from his regulars—Eugene Robinson of the *Washington Post*, Chuck Todd of NBC, and Howard Fineman of *Newsweek*.

Matthews was scheduled to do a taped interview with Obama. When I arrived, he was sitting in his office with a bunch of *Hardball* staff members arrayed around his desk. Matthews can be temperamental and sometimes explosive, but his employees evince ease in his presence. They were thinking of questions for Matthews to ask Obama. Professor Orlando Patterson of Harvard had written a column in that day's *New York Times* suggesting that Hillary Clinton's three a.m. phone-call ad was not meant to evoke fear of terrorism but rather crime. "Is this an ad about 9/11 or an ad about 911?" Matthews said. "Ha!" He loved this line. We would hear it again.

"Hey, you haven't looked around in here, have you?" he asked, gesturing toward me. He was already up and leading a quickie tour. "Did you know that Holy Cross gave me a chair?" Matthews said. "I was excited. I thought it was going to be something like, the Distinguished Chris Matthews Chair of So-and-So at Holy Cross." But no, he said. He received an actual chair from the college, emblazoned with the school logo. The chair is now in the middle of the office. And, for what it's worth, it's lovely, made of solid wood. "But I was disappointed, I have to admit," Matthews said.

He taped the Obama interview, which went smoothly if uneventfully. *Hardball* began. During a cut-in, Dan Abrams, the host of the previous hour, mentioned that the Clinton campaign was going after delegates who were already committed to Obama. Matthews pounced: "They do that for the reason North Koreans dig tunnels underneath the DMZ at the thirtieth parallel [*sic*]. They get people jittery on the other side. That's why they do it. They can't get through those tunnels. They can have the tunnels to scare people, but they ain't going through the tunnels."

It was vintage Matthews, as was the scene while his interview with Obama played, without volume, on a monitor. Staring at the screen, Matthews squinted, cocked his head, and leaned forward. "Have you noticed," he said to no one in particular, "that my head looks about four times as big as Obama's?"

Later, I talked to Matthews about his TV franchise. He's clearly proud of it, but also restless. He worries that "the suits" at NBC want him out. He has been openly contemplating "the second act" in a career that has already featured several.

"I have a lot of options," Matthews told me. "I'm a free man starting next June." There has been long-running speculation that Matthews could be a candidate to replace Bob Schieffer, whenever he retires, as the host of CBS's Sunday morning show *Face the Nation*.

The more intriguing notion is that Matthews could challenge Senator Arlen Specter, who is up for reelection in Pennsylvania in 2010. This has been rumored before, but Matthews has been particularly obsessed with Pennsylvania of late, devoting hours on and off the air to the state's upcoming Democratic primary, staying in close contact with the state's party apparatus. "I talked to Eddie Rendell today," Matthew told me on the phone a few weeks ago, urging me again to call the Pennsylvania governor.

My phone call with Matthews also yielded the following: His recent appearance on *Ellen* is getting "all kinds of pickup." He had dinner the previous night with Nancy Reagan in Beverly Hills. The film rights for his book on Kennedy and Nixon were optioned. He is speaking at Harvard in May.

I asked him about the Senate rumors. He thinks Specter has hung on way too long, he said, but running would require Matthews to give up a career he loves. Still, "I get a great feeling when I go home," he told me. "Is Thomas Wolfe right? Can you go home again?

"Really, you should talk to Eddie Rendell."

The Heart of Politics:
One Woman, Two Senators,
and Presidential Ambitions:
The Washington Tale of
John Kerry and Teresa Heinz

June 2, 2002

Teresa Heinz is getting up a full head of rage while her husband, Senator John Kerry, fidgets.

They are in the living room of their Georgetown home, where Heinz has lived ever since her late first husband, John Heinz, came to Washington in 1971 as a Republican congressman from Pennsylvania. In the front entrance, the first things a visitor sees are two framed photos of Teresa Heinz cuddled with tall, smiling men with big heads of brown hair: in one is John Kerry, in the other John Heinz.

She still calls John Heinz "my husband" and doesn't always correct herself—"my late husband"—even when Kerry is around. She still wears the blue sapphire engagement ring that Heinz gave her.

But John Heinz's enduring presence in Teresa's life is best

revealed when someone slights his memory. Which, at least indirectly, is why she and Kerry are now in mid-bicker.

"That guy does not deserve diplomacy," says Heinz. She is referring to Senator Rick Santorum, the Pennsylvania Republican who offended her in 1994 during his campaign for John Heinz's old Senate seat. She won't elaborate on what Santorum said to earn her enmity, only that she won't speak to him again.

"He's changed," Kerry mumbles, trying to keep this from becoming an on-the-record spectacle. The Massachusetts Democrat tries to add that he gets along with his colleague, but Heinz interrupts. "Sweetie, I know," Kerry says, talking over her, "I'm just saying . . ." He exhales a long, loud sigh.

Just a few minutes earlier, Kerry, fifty-eight, was saying how much he admires his wife's candor. And Heinz, sixty-three, was saying that while she can be opinionated, she can also be tactful. But sometimes she can't help herself, especially when the matter involves John Heinz, who was killed in a plane crash in 1991.

Every time Heinz raises her voice, Kerry tries to play down his wife's agitation, which only inflames her more. A Yankee stoic, he gently suggests that his wife and Santorum get together.

"No, I don't want to get together with him, John," she snaps. "I don't have to do certain things."

"Well."

"Okay? I don't have to be that politic."

Heinz speaks in a high, breathy voice and sharply accented English—she grew up in colonial Mozambique, where her first language was Portuguese.

In 1995 she married Kerry, and today they are perhaps America's most compelling political couple not named Clinton or Bush.

Their story packs all the qualities that captivate Washington—money, romance, and ambition—with the bonus of mingling the big legacy of one senator with the big plans of another. The Heinz-

Kerry marriage is a delicate merging of public families, large profiles, and political missions. It is a story that belies the shorthand of so much Washington narrative, a union of shared grief, hard work, frequent tensions, and, ultimately, of love that filled shared voids.

Kerry officially says he is undecided on whether he'll run for president in 2004. But he's acting like a candidate—raising money, careening to Jefferson–Jackson dinners, attending picnics in Iowa. Friends and colleagues say the once desperate edges of Kerry's ambition have been smoothed by age, experience, stature, and the settled domestic life that had eluded him for much of his Senate career.

But there remains a baseline reserve to Kerry that can leave him difficult to embrace. He is dismissive on matters self-analytic and has a politician's bent for evading dicey matters or framing them in tidy certainties.

Part of Heinz's charm is that she has no patience for this. When Kerry is asked about the nightmares that haunted his sleep for years after he returned from Vietnam, he shrugs. "I don't think I've had a nightmare in a long time," he says. But then Heinz begins to mimic Kerry having a Vietnam nightmare.

"Down! Down, down!" she yells, patting her hands down on her auburn hair.

"I haven't gotten slapped yet," she says. "But there were times when I thought I might get throttled."

Kerry quivers his right foot and steers the discussion to the counseling programs he has supported for Vietnam veterans. Asked if he has been in therapy himself, he non-answers. "It doesn't bother me anymore, I just go back to sleep."

Heinz presses him. "Not therapy for the dreams, therapy for the angst," she says, and looks quizzically at him, awaiting an answer. Kerry shakes his head no. This is not your father's political couple, though you wonder, at this moment, if Kerry wishes it were.

"Barbara Walters time," Kerry says when he is asked about an observation from Heinz that the "shells" around him have softened in recent years. Nor does he relish the personal issues that a presidential run highlights, "the kind of crap that's so light and trivial."

"I keep thinking of [Winslow] Homer watercolors," Heinz exclaims, jumping in. She spins a notion of how politics is driven by fast decisions, black-and-white perceptions, and the "immediacy of pictures." In fact, she says, political characters comprise the "nuance of a Homer watercolor," better animated in a palette of grays and beiges than in black and white.

Kerry checks his watch and dashes off to a Senate vote. He kisses his wife on the forehead as he leaves, and she calls after him to take his lozenges.

Kerry is classically drawn as How a Senator Should Look: he is six-feet-four and slim, with a helmet of brownish-silver hair, high and knobby cheekbones, and a surgically enhanced chin—not cosmetic surgery, contrary to speculation. (The operation, says Kerry press secretary David Wade, was to correct "a malocclusion," a bad bite that caused a clicking in his jaw.)

The second of four children, John Forbes Kerry was born in Colorado, the son of an Army pilot who later worked for the Foreign Service across Europe. At St. Paul's School in New Hampshire, Kerry's classmates recall a driven student who was thrilled—even obsessed—with the idea that he shared initials with his political idol, JFK. He graduated from Yale and volunteered for the Navy during Vietnam. For his service, he was awarded a Silver Star, a Bronze Star, and three Purple Hearts.

Kerry has always been at his best in unsettled, improvisational settings, like the jungle warfare of Vietnam, the Don Imus radio show, or the pickup ice hockey games he plays in at the Fort Dupont rink in Anacostia. There he is "John," profane and earthy, his guard down, his Boston accent more pronounced. After one shift, an exhausted Kerry skates off the ice and offers this early-morning rejoinder to no one in particular: "It's time to barf!"

Being the junior senator to Ted Kennedy and, before that, the lieutenant governor to Michael Dukakis is not a résumé that will thrill swing voters. But Kerry's aides duly tout his mainstream bona fides: his membership in centrist Democratic groups, his love of hunting, the four years he spent as a prosecutor, his close friendship with Senator John McCain, and his defeat of popular Republican governor William Weld in the 1996 Senate race.

But Kerry's ace credential is Vietnam. His combat heroism could spring him from liberal pigeonholes, just as his dissent has long endeared him to a generation of antiwar activists—the kind who still vote in Democratic primaries.

Kerry commanded a Navy Swift Boat that patrolled the Mekong Delta. His crew recalls Kerry as brainy and extremely aggressive, "a good leader and a bit of a hard-charger," says Del Sandusky from Elgin, Illinois.

Two years after Kerry returned to the United States, he appeared before Senator William Fulbright's Foreign Relations Committee in 1971. "How do you ask a man to be the last man to die in Vietnam?" Kerry said in the speech's enduring sound bite. "How do you ask a man to be the last man to die for a mistake?" After Kerry spoke, committee member Claiborne Pell (D-R.I.) expressed his hope that the young man would return to the Senate one day as a member.

In his political career, Kerry has been hampered by an air of self-seriousness. He speaks in lecturing cadences and slopes his long face downward when he's addressing someone. "My dad has a knack for coming off as stiff and insincere," says daughter Vanessa Kerry, twenty-five. "Sometimes I see him speaking in that uptight way that he does and I think, Who is this guy?"

John Kerry is no backslapper. To compensate, he can seem like he's playacting the role of ebullient pol. In a series of interviews this spring, Kerry repeats the same lines, same stories, same observations—not uncommon for a politician—but to do so with the same person, within a few days of each other, suggests a mode of rote showmanship.

He has always had difficulty with the political art of shrouding ambition in nonchalance. He has been dubbed "Liveshot" by some in the Boston press for his zealous pursuit of TV cameras. As Kerry prepares for 2004, he could be suspect, oddly enough, because many people assume running for president is something he has always wanted to do. This is a peculiar stigma, given his profession, but one that affixed itself to Kerry decades ago. In a *60 Minutes* report on Kerry's leadership of Vietnam Veterans Against the War in 1971, Morley Safer asked him if he wanted to be president. Kerry, who said no, was twenty-seven.

On a recent afternoon, Kerry was in his Russell Building office, sitting on a wing chair with his legs crossed next to a fireplace. The office is decorated with a watercolor painted by Ted Kennedy and framed five- and one-dollar bills that Eugene McCarthy contributed to his first campaign. Kerry's computer screen is filled with a smiling photo of . . . John Kerry.

Asked about the perception that he desperately wants to be president, Kerry shakes his big head. If he wanted to be president so badly, Kerry wonders testily, then why is he the only Democrat in his Senate class who has not run?

"Sometimes in the past, I was a little bit defensive about" wanting to be president, he says. "Al Gore ran in 1988. Do people throw that at Al Gore? He ran in 1988, I didn't. He's run four times for national office, I haven't run once."

He ticks off a list of other Senate Democrats who have run for president: Tom Harkin, Bob Kerrey ("and Bob Kerrey came to the

Senate after me"), Paul Simon. "Jay Rockefeller went out and explored it.

"But I said no. I said no."

"If you interviewed one hundred senators, you could get most of them to admit to wanting to be president," says longtime Senate staffer Cliff Shannon, who includes in that group his boss for fifteen years, H. John Heinz III.

John Heinz was born in Pittsburgh and raised in San Francisco, the only child of parents who divorced when he was three. He graduated from Yale and, between his first and second years at Harvard Business School, went to work at a bank in Geneva, with an eye to one day working for the food empire that his great-grandfather founded in 1869. There he met the daughter of a Portuguese doctor, Maria Teresa Thierstein Simões Ferreira, who was attending the interpreting school of the University of Geneva. (She is fluent in five languages.) They were married in 1966, lived in Pittsburgh, and moved to Washington when Heinz was elected to Congress in 1971.

John Heinz would become the most popular politician in Pennsylvania, a centrist Republican who won six elections for the House and Senate between 1971 and 1988. His aides had begun holding events around the country to stoke his national profile. He never mentioned his presidential aspirations to Teresa. Others did, though, and her stock response was "Over my dead body."

A presidential campaign would only disrupt her desire for a semi-normal family life. She was more engaged in issues than many Senate spouses, but she viewed her role primarily as a wife and mother. By most accounts, John and Teresa Heinz had a devoted marriage, although it was not without difficulty.

Charming, driven, and impatient, John Heinz had a knack for applying the pointed questioning style that he honed in Senate hearing rooms to his home life. He would grill his wife about the food she was cooking, his three boys about school, Social Security, whatever came up at the dinner table. Teresa would jump in. "I would say, 'Jack, this is your family. We're just stupid. We're just normal. We don't know.'"

John and Teresa Heinz were married twenty-five years. "It's a beautiful time of a marriage," she says. "The things that used to rattle you and make you upset all of a sudden become endearing. And you never knew it could happen." They were starting to think about grandchildren.

"And then, whoa, it's gone," she whispers. "That was so unkind. That was so unkind."

One second, she was a Senate wife, downstairs in her Georgetown home, in the den where the kids used to play. She got a phone call and learned that John Heinz's plane had collided with a helicopter over a Lower Merion, Pennsylvania, schoolyard.

Suddenly, she was political widow, principal heir to a half-billion-dollar fortune, and head of the billion-dollar Howard Heinz Endowment.

Republicans in Pennsylvania were urging her to take over John Heinz's vacated Senate seat. She almost did, but it was too soon, and there was too much else to do.

She was zooming through her life in a manic fog. A year later, when the logistics thinned, the magnitude of her loss came pouring in. Heinz was fighting with her boys, particularly the youngest, Christopher. He was the closest of the three to his father. "If you wish that I was dead instead of your father, that's quite normal and don't feel guilty about it," Teresa Heinz recalled saying to him. "But just don't make me pay the price for it." (Christopher Heinz, now twenty-nine, declined to comment.)

She saw a psychiatrist who prescribed Prozac. It eased the paralysis, she says, not the sadness. She began devoting much of her time, energy, and money to issues that John Heinz worked on in the

Senate. In a sense, Teresa says, keeping John Heinz's issues alive was a way to keep the senator alive.

Pittsburgh mayor Tom Murphy calls her "Saint Teresa" for her charitable work, much of which was concentrated in that city. She has become one of the nation's foremost philanthropists, able to spin unscripted policy yarns on the environment, women's health issues, pension planning, and other causes the Heinz Foundation has taken on.

Teresa first met John Kerry at a Washington Earth Day event in 1990. They were introduced by John Heinz, who served with Kerry on the Senate Banking Committee. They were friends in the way that everyone in the Senate is a good friend, but they were more cordial than close.

Kerry had been unhappily single for most of his time in Washington. His election to the Senate in 1984 came two years after his separation from his wife, Julia Thorne. They were separated six years and divorced in 1988.

His separation and divorce were "awful in every regard," Kerry says. He had two young daughters, Alex and Vanessa. He spent hours on the phone helping them with homework. He spent every weekend in Boston. "Trying to make it all work, trying to be a senator, trying to be a father, trying to hold those pieces together, I found challenging."

Kerry had been a prodigious but reluctant dater, linked in gossip columns to many women, often much younger. He hated the scrutiny. "If you have one date, and you go to a restaurant, and somebody sees you, boom, you're going out," Kerry says. "There's no early test." He became a "Senate hermit."

Then came Teresa Heinz. "There was a real void in John's life," says Bruce Droste, a close friend. "He was a lonely person. She was a lonely person, too."

Kerry renewed his acquaintance with Heinz at the Earth

Summit in Rio de Janeiro in 1992. They met again at a Washington dinner party a few months later and, after a long conversation, Kerry invited her on a walk to the Mall that ended at the Vietnam Veterans Memorial.

Kerry and Heinz began dating late in 1993 and announced their engagement in November 1994. They lived together four months and married on May 26, 1995, on the Nantucket estate where Teresa and John Heinz used to spend their summers. Heinz was escorted down the aisle by her three sons, met by Kerry and his daughters on the porch.

There was family friction. It centered particularly on Teresa Heinz and the Kerry daughters. Little dustups—Alex or Vanessa calling after Teresa's bedtime, showing up unannounced when there was company—would escalate. The macro issue was that all parties expected to be Kerry's first priority. He would always drop everything for Alex and Vanessa, who were eighteen and twenty-one at the time of the marriage. But if Heinz expected something from Kerry and didn't get it, she would become wounded.

"I'm a real needy person," Heinz says, "and that's because of loss. . . . It's like when you say to a child you're going to do something and you don't, they're very threatened. For me, it's a loss."

Several of Heinz's intimates have died in crashes: her husband, her sister (at nineteen), her grandmother, and godfather. She lost her father and John Heinz's father within four years of her husband's death. Teresa Heinz always learned the news by phone and, it seemed, when she was alone. As she reflects on her life in her O Street NW home, the phones ring constantly, an unnerving background echo to the grief she is discussing.

Heinz frequently invokes her repeated disappointments. "It's hard," she says, referring to her relationships with Kerry's daughters. "When they want their father, they want their father, same as I want their father when I want their father, because I don't have much."

All parties point out that such tensions are normal in such family mergers. "We're not trying to play Ozzie and Harriet or something," John Kerry says.

"I still think everyone is still finding their own comfort with one another," says David Thorne, Kerry's close friend and the twin brother of his first wife. "You have a lot of strong-willed, strong-minded people trying to reach some combination with each other."

Vanessa and Alex have grown close to Heinz's sons, Chris, André, and John Heinz IV. "Strong characters sometimes, you know, adjust at different rates, and in different ways," Kerry says. "I think the family and the kids are very affectionate with one another."

Yes, they have all "grown" as a family, Heinz says, but she won't abide explanations that are too clean. "Like everything else, you go forward two steps, you go backward one," she says.

Heinz was reluctant to embrace parts of her new husband's life. She never considered taking the name Kerry (she eventually added it to her own during John Kerry's presidential campaign in 2004), never cast a vote for him (she remains registered, as a Republican, in Pittsburgh), and still spends much of her time in the four homes she shared with John Heinz in Washington, Idaho, Nantucket, and Pittsburgh. They are all adorned with multiple photos of John Heinz, whom she still calls "the love of my life," and their telephone numbers contain the digits "57," the traditional number of Heinz food varieties. (Heinz and Kerry own a mansion together on Boston's Beacon Hill.)

"The cliché is that time heals everything," says David Garth, the media consultant who was a friend of John Heinz and remains close to Teresa. "But that doesn't seem entirely true in this case."

Teresa Heinz says Kerry knew what he was getting when he married her. "I am sentimental, loyal," she says. "I love my husband"—she means John Heinz—"I am in love with my husband, and I have three kids." Kerry has plenty for himself, she says. He has his daughters, his mother, three siblings, dozens of cousins. "When I go to Boston, he has family and friends and everything," she says. "I have to make everything up. He's got all his classmates he went to school with, they're all in America. I have no classmates. I have no cousins."

The shared life of Kerry and Heinz is an ongoing and delicate balance between past and present. It made for some uneasy scenes. In January 1997, Kerry and Heinz hosted a reception for a group of Kerry supporters and campaign workers, many of them in town for the second Clinton inauguration. The reception drew more people than expected and Heinz was furious, according to two staffers who were present. When the guests left, she vowed to Kerry that they would not hold such a reception again. Kerry tried to calm her, saying that inviting people to their home was part of the political process.

"This isn't your house, John," she said, according to a former staffer who heard the discussion. "This is my house."

The Kerry-Heinz marriage has invited crude assumptions from the outset. The most cynical is that he needs the fortune she inherited from John Heinz to be president. To that, Kerry says he won't spend any Heinz money on a campaign—and Heinz says she won't make it available—unless, in her words, an opponent engages in "character assassination" against her or Kerry. As an example, Kerry says that if he is attacked in the way that McCain was attacked by George W. Bush before the South Carolina Republican primary in 2000, he would not hesitate to tap "other resources."

Friends of Kerry say that Heinz has kept him on edge, a necessary function, as he can be prone to a kind of mental cruise control. "John needs a kind of tension to be at his best," says Thomas Vallely, a Vietnam veteran and close Kerry friend. "Part of him needs the high-wire act."

Over two long interviews, Teresa Heinz is by turns effusive and harsh, warm and slightly bitter, solemn and melodramatic. And she is always, unfailingly, smart, original, and provocative. She hits on the following things: the excessive drinking of a Massachusetts politician, the miscarriage suffered by one senator's wife, her own miscarriage, and the Boston TV reporter who is an "unhappy, lonely man." She speaks of how her oldest son, John IV, started "hating her" two years ago, when his daughter was born. (He declined to comment.) She also talks about how shy she is.

You wonder how Teresa Heinz's "shyness" would play in the blitz of a presidential campaign, and how the relative peace that Kerry and Heinz have achieved would be sustained in such a pressured environment.

Kerry says his wife is a huge campaign asset, someone who "raises things up a little bit," who brings freshness to the dialogue.

Some aides worry that her bluntness could become a problem, though they won't say it for attribution. The topic of how to "handle Teresa" has been raised in several conversations within Kerry's political circle, the aides say, including at least one discussion where Kerry was present. The conclusion is that it would be futile to try.

Heinz says as much. She has no intention of subverting her hard-won wisdom to the on-message orthodoxies of a campaign. "I don't want to be perfect, I want to be engaged," she says. "But that makes a lot of people uncomfortable."

The bright face of John Heinz smiled down onto a cozy gathering of his family and friends. He filled a big video screen at the Heinz Awards at the Folger Theatre, the signature event of the Heinz family foundation's year.

Teresa Heinz, who spends hours each year on the ceremony's smallest details, presents the five $250,000 awards and is the night's featured speaker. She gulps water. She speaks in a small, mumbly voice. In a two-and-a-half-hour ceremony, there is no mention of John Kerry, who is sitting slightly hunched in the second row, separate from the rest of the family.

When Teresa Heinz is asked if such an elaborate tribute to her first husband might be difficult for the second, she shrugs, as if the question had never crossed her mind. "No, he's a tall guy, he's gotten enough attention," she says of Kerry. "Just when you love one child, you love your next child. You might have a predilection for one because you get along better, but you'd give your life for any of them."

Teresa Heinz walks away from the stage as the program concludes, and Kerry slaps triceps several feet away. Heinz is engulfed by her children and by old family friends who congratulate her on a perfect tribute to her husband. She squeezes hands, gives long hugs, and soaks in the assurance that the legacy of John Heinz abides in the room, just as John Kerry is declared "our next president" by a guest waiting to shake his hand.

How John McCain Turned His Clichés into Meaning

December 18, 2013

When I walk into John McCain's office a week before Thanksgiving, he is not at all happy—and seems to be enjoying it quite a bit.

He is sampling none of the usual flavors of upset we tend to associate with the Arizona senator: not the "McCain is bitter" or "get off my yard" varieties, not even the "deeply troubled" umbrage that politicians of all stripes love to assume. Here is a man, instead, who is gleefully seizing an opportunity for outrage.

"I am very angry," McCain says through a smiling grimace. He hands me a photocopied compilation of old quotes from the Senate majority leader, Harry Reid, from back when Democrats were in the minority and Republicans were threatening to enact a rule—the so-called nuclear option—that would require only a fifty-one-vote majority to confirm most presidential and judicial nominations. Turns out Reid believed this was a bad idea when the Republicans were in charge but was a good one now, and McCain is packing bullet points.

"I'm going to go kick the crap out of Harry Reid," he keeps announcing as we walk from his office to the Capitol. Once on the Senate floor, McCain approaches Reid, puts his hands on the majority leader's shoulders, smiles, and says something I can't make out from the visitors' gallery above. Reid smiles back, says a few words in reply, and places his hands on McCain's sides. It looks as if they are dancing.

Minutes later, McCain stands to address the chamber. He is, as advertised, very, very unhappy. Today is a "black chapter in the history of the Senate," he says, referencing something Reid said back in 2008, as a way of pointing out his hypocrisy. He then goes on to explain that this is as "historic" a vote as he can remember casting and that he feels great "sorrow" for the harm done to the institution on this "sad day."

After McCain leaves the floor, I ask him what he said to Reid before his speech. "I said, 'Harry, I'm going to go kick the crap out of you.' Then he said, 'John, I would expect nothing less.'" McCain grins big to conclude this dark chapter in the history of the United States Senate.

J ohn McCain is a cliché.

It is not his fault, or not entirely. Many of us become walking self-caricatures at a certain point, and politicians can be particularly vulnerable, especially those who have maneuvered their very public lives as conspicuously as McCain. They tell and retell the same stories; things get musty. They engage in a lot of self-mythologizing, and no one in Washington has been the subject and the perpetrator of more mythmaking than McCain: the maverick, the former maverick, the curmudgeon, the bridge builder, the war hero bent on transcending the call of self-interest to serve a cause greater than himself, the sore loser, old bull, last lion, loose cannon, happy warrior, elder statesman, lion in winter . . . you lose track of which McCain cliché is operational at a given moment. He does, too. "I think I was the brave maverick when I was taking on Bush," McCain told me, "and then I was the bitter old man when I was criticizing Obamacare."

Critics will take their shots, he says, it comes with being "in the arena." That cliché isn't McCain's—it's the self-consoling Teddy Roosevelt line that politicians are always trotting out. "It's not the critic who counts" but "the man who really was in the arena."

McCain has another favorite Teddy Roosevelt phrase, "the crowded hour," which I have heard him invoke several times over the years. It comes from a poem by the English writer Thomas Mordaunt, and TR used it to famously describe his charge on San Juan Hill. In McCain's philosophy, "the crowded hour" refers to a moment of character testing. "The 'crowded hour' is as appropriate for me right now as any in a long time," McCain told me as we walked through the Capitol. In some respects, this is just a function of public figures' tendency to overdramatize the current moment and their role in it. But five years after losing to Barack Obama, after enduring the recriminations between his splintered campaign staff and rogue running mate, Sarah Palin, and after returning to the Senate and falling into a prolonged funk, McCain finds himself in the midst of another crowded hour, maybe his last as an elected leader.

Along with his Senate Tonto, Lindsey Graham of South Carolina, McCain has been the most ardent critic of the White House's foreign policy in pretty much every hot spot in the world. "Obama drives him crazy," Graham told me. He seemed to be speaking generally, but McCain said he was referring strictly to foreign policy, on which he believes Obama has been a disaster. (He recently referred to Secretary of State John Kerry as "a human wrecking ball.") Either way, Obama has also been a gift to McCain, in that there is part of him that loves being driven crazy. "He operates on outrage, which is genuine, and he seems happiest when there's friction around," says Mark Salter, McCain's former Senate chief of staff and a longtime adviser.

McCain also finds himself in the thick of the latest "fight for the soul of the GOP" against the Tea Party right, a cohort that arguably would not have the influence it has if McCain had not chosen Palin as his running mate. They are represented in the Senate by McCain's junior colleagues Ted Cruz of Texas and Rand Paul of Kentucky—or "wacko birds," as McCain has referred to their far-right ilk. Once the most disruptive figure in his party, McCain now fashions himself a grown-up voice for civility, pragmatism, and the best traditions of the Senate—albeit one who tosses around names like "wacko birds" and "human wrecking ball." The paradox of this is not lost on him. "It just goes to show you," McCain told me, "that if you live long enough, anything is possible."

Now seventy-seven, which makes him only the ninth-oldest member of the Senate, McCain looks as if he has not aged a day since conceding to Barack Obama on the night of November 4, 2008. He resists suggestions that he has tried on different personae to suit the political moment, but he certainly understands the laws of political reinvention. On a wall next to his office desk hangs a group photo that includes David Petraeus, the decorated general who quit as head of the CIA last year after admitting to an extramarital affair with his "biographer" Paula Broadwell. I ask McCain what Petraeus is up to these days. "Oh, he's off doing that rehabbing. Speeches, teaching, maybe a book, that kind of thing. You know, there are second acts in American politics."

This raises the obvious question of which act McCain himself is on. "I've probably gone through about twenty-five, twenty-six," he says. "Something like that."

I have known McCain for about a decade. He was always fun to hang around with, for obvious reasons, back when he used to refer to the media as "my base" and called his 2000 presidential campaign bus the Straight Talk Express. The novelist David Foster Wallace described McCain, flatteringly, as someone who "acts somewhat in the ballpark of the way a real human being would act." (By contrast, Wallace quoted a CNN sound tech describing Al Gore as "amazingly lifelike.") Central to that human quality, Wallace and many others have noted, was the fact that McCain has survived three plane crashes, cancer, public disgrace, and, above all, five and a half years of torture in a North Vietnamese POW camp. As Bob Dole is said to have put it, "You spend five years in a box, and you're entitled to speak your mind."

Friends of McCain's say that his loss in '08, and the ridicule he suffered in the wake of it, was traumatizing in itself. "John has had two defining events in his life," Senator Tom Coburn, Republican of Oklahoma, told me. "The first was his imprisonment, and the second was his failure to win the presidency."

For a long time after the election, his colleagues in the Senate treaded lightly around McCain. They described conversations over policy disagreements ending in personal attacks. Other senators would come to Lindsey Graham to ask what was up with McCain. "Give it time," Graham says he would tell them. He tried to serve as an intermediary between McCain and old friends like John Kerry, with whom McCain became enraged for what he considered an excessive assault against him in a 2008 convention speech after McCain defended Kerry four years earlier from attacks by fellow Vietnam veterans. "I felt like Match.com," Graham said. "It took a while for John to learn to let go."

It had been nearly six years since I'd spoken to McCain. The *New York Times* is not his favorite newspaper, to say the least. The flash point was an article the paper published in February 2008, which some readers took to imply that he'd had an intimate relationship with a Washington lobbyist, Vicki Iseman. Both parties denied a romantic involvement, and Iseman sued the *Times*. (Iseman ultimately dropped the suit after the *Times* agreed to print a note to readers saying the story was not intended to imply a romantic relationship.) The report was widely criticized, and McCain distanced himself from the paper's reporters. "I will never forgive the *New York Times* for what they did," McCain told me in October. He agreed to talk to me, he says, because he knew me before "that story" ran. I have a preexisting condition.

After his screed on the floor against Harry Reid, McCain hurries back to his office for a scheduled sit-down with a group of dignitaries from Australia. "I love the Aussies!" he declares to me outside his office door, then swings it open and is met with a faceful of them. "Sorry I'm late," he tells them. "I was just up on the floor kicking the crap out of the Democratic leader." They all sit down, and McCain mentions that Congress's approval ratings are now so low "we're down to paid staffers and blood relatives." He drops this line so often that probably the only people on the planet who haven't heard it are in Australia. Everyone laughs, and McCain adds that he recently received a call from his 101-year-old mother, and she's not happy with Congress, either. "So now we're down to just paid staff," he says, to genuine belly laughs. A few minutes later, McCain wants to talk about Fiji, the archipelago in the South Pacific where he says he used to vacation with his family. "They are lovely, gentle people," McCain says of the Fijians, "even though they used to eat each other."

On that note, McCain goes off to be interviewed by Wolf Blitzer of CNN from a remote studio on the Hill.

Blitzer, whose arching dome of white hair rests in perfect symmetry with the anchor desk's Capitol backdrop, greets McCain off the air. "Woof, woof," McCain says to the host while someone fastens on a microphone. Then he howls and grins and prepares to discuss the day's "outright hypocrisy."

It is well entrenched in the McCain mythology that he finished nearly last (894th out of 900) in his class at the Naval Academy and never set out to be a great American hero, let alone a politician. He fell into the role—out of an airplane. Politics caught him. He ran for the House in 1982 and then the Senate in 1986. Even then, he conveyed a sense that he didn't need or especially want this job, but over the years he became essential to the scenery: the Sunday shows, the Senate fights, the high-level globe-trotting. The arena suited and needed and defined McCain. He often parks himself in a hallway at the Capitol and waits for reporters to surround him. He is proud to hold the record for most appearances—sixty-nine—in the sixty-six-year history of *Meet the Press* and also to have more Twitter followers than anyone in the Senate (1.85 million badges of his relevance— nearly four times as many as the next Republican colleague, Marco Rubio). You can call this vanity, self-celebration, whatever—if it were a crime, the Capitol would be empty. But in McCain's case, it's also proof that he was present and accounted for, which is perhaps no small thing when you spent a good portion of your life expecting to die in a POW camp. In McCain's worldview, anonymity equals absence.

"I think the biggest fear John has is not being relevant," Graham told me. "He worried after he lost the election in 2008. He worried, Okay, I'm done, nobody wants to deal with a loser." McCain has a favorite line, one of his hundreds, which he attributes to the late Texas senator John Tower: "Don't let your coattails hit you in the ass," Tower told him once. "Keep moving." To McCain, "keep moving" is both a credo and a coping strategy, a balm of perpetual motion and high demand. He likes to provide unprompted recitations of his packed schedule. I was sitting with him in his office in October, shortly after the government shutdown ended. He was, as he often is, fresh off a regimen of morning TV interviews—CNN, *Squawk Box*. "I did a bunch last night, too," he volunteered.

Even when sitting still, McCain projects stir-craziness. Lengthy Senate hearings can be a challenge for him. He was recently busted in a photograph playing video poker on his iPhone during a hearing on Syria. ("Scandal!" he tweeted. "Caught playing iPhone game at 3+ hour Senate hearing—worst of all, I lost!")

Sometimes McCain will express his need to "keep moving" with a more exasperated, even plaintive construction: "Can't we just move on to something else?" he will say, particularly when people ask him, as they still do, about Sarah Palin's continued presence on the national stage—or on Facebook. Friends and colleagues who respect him for his many virtues and heroic résumé also acknowledge that his role in the unleashing of Palin is an unfortunate part of his legacy. Surely McCain regrets the association, right? He is a man of seriousness, someone who becomes emotional when talking about the need for a more aggressive United States presence in Syria. And then Palin hops onto Facebook and quips that the United States should just stay out of Syria and "let Allah sort it out." People close to him say that he bristles at these things and that he wishes Palin had consulted him about some of the endorsements she has made of Republican primary challengers but that he will never go public with any of his regrets. "Good luck trying to get that out of him," his daughter Meghan McCain told me, laughing.

McCain has always been unrestrained in his expressions of remorse. He spent much of the 1990s doing extravagant penance for his role in the Keating Five savings-and-loan mess. This led to the reformed campaign-finance crusader incarnation, which led to his first presidential campaign. After dropping out of the Republican primaries in 2000, he returned to South Carolina and grandly apologized for not calling for the removal of the Confederate flag from the statehouse. "I chose to compromise my principles," he said at the time. "I broke my promise to always tell the truth." When it comes to Palin, though, he fidgets slightly in his office chair and meets me with a defiant stare. He reaffirms his allegiance to Palin, saying that she was unfairly attacked in 2008 and that "the liberal-left feminists" felt threatened by her. "Look, it's been five years," McCain says. "Can't we move on?"

Sure, except that Ted Cruz, whose upset win in the Texas Republican primary last year was propelled by the former Alaska governor's endorsement, has not been shy about announcing to the world that "I would not be in the US Senate today if it were not for Sarah Palin."

McCain is sick of talking about Cruz. "We have a cordial relationship," he insists, which in the Google translation of political code is something between minimal tolerance and abject disgust. Cruz is an upstart, whose goal seems to be to position himself to run for president in 2016. He appears indifferent to the traditional markers of Senate experience and prestige—passing bills, leading committees, dutifully winning the respect of colleagues. "You know, it's a funny thing about Cruz," McCain says, and then stops himself. "No, actually, it's not funny. It aggravates me more than anything else"—the way Cruz called his fellow Republicans a bunch of wimps and talks about "how we've been around too long." Cruz is the Senate's modern-day maverick, it would seem, while McCain has become one of the institution's fiercest traditionalists.

When I read Cruz's quote about owing his success to Palin, McCain shrugs. Palin has suggested, too, that she might support Tea Party primary challengers to the Senate Republican leader, Mitch McConnell, in Kentucky and to Lindsey Graham in South Carolina, whom McCain has likened to a son. "Oh, I pray she wouldn't do that," he says of Palin's supporting Graham. "And you know, I find it hard to believe that she would." He points out that Palin has never said anything critical about him, that she campaigned in Arizona for him in 2010. And then he adds, again: "I've moved on. What's the statute of limitations on this issue?"

McCain's cell phone rings, and it's Joe Lieberman, the former senator from Connecticut who was McCain's first choice to be his running mate in 2008, until his advisers convinced him that the Republican base would go full wacko bird if he picked a pro-choice Democrat. McCain answers the phone by saying, "I love you, Joey." He speaks loudly, the way that people tend to on cell phones, or when they might be speaking for the benefit of a third party. "Joey, Joey, where have you been?" After a minute or so, he tells Joey he's with someone and will call him back.

"Funny story about Lieberman," he says to me. The Israeli ambassador in Washington honored him after he left the Senate. "Everyone was saying Joe's the most wonderful guy, the usual crap you hear," McCain says. "So I got up, I was the last guy, and I say: 'I'm here to announce that I'm converting to Judaism. Because for all these years with Joe, I've had to eat that crappy salmon. I had to ride the damn Shabbat elevator. I've observed Shabbat to a point where I couldn't even ride in a goddamn car. I've had all of the bull associated with this religion, and I've gotten not a single benefit. So I'm converting to Judaism.'"

Lieberman then stood up and announced that before McCain could convert, he must first have a proper bris. In the retelling, McCain pronounces it "brits"—which is how he pronounced it when he told me this story a week earlier.

A few days later, I join McCain in Arizona, where he is scheduled to host two town meetings and is expecting hostile incoming from the local Tea Party brigades. After missing my flight to Phoenix, I caught the last plane of the night to the general vicinity (Las Vegas), then drove five hours through the pitch-black desert to meet up with McCain at dawn. Those five hours were filled with the sound of incessant grievance across the radio dial—about President Obama and about RINOs (Republicans in Name Only) like McCain, who are just as responsible for the socialist, lawless, porous-bordered dystopia our once great nation has become. Captive exposure to these voices in the dark, over endless miles, makes you wonder how anyone to the left of Ted Cruz has ever been elected to anything. It also brings into relief how grueling it must be to oppose the most fervent sector of his own party. "I'm really not psyched about going back to Arizona to do another Tea Party election," Meghan McCain told me. "I honestly don't know how much more of that I can hear."

Yet John McCain seems characteristically energized by the prospect—as evidenced by his recent barrages against the Tea Partiers. As disastrous as the shutdown was for their party, many Republicans in the Senate greeted the humiliation with glee, and McCain was a particularly ebullient leader of this "I told you so" caucus. "It didn't take a goddamned rocket scientist to see how this was going to turn out," he said, and then switched metaphors. "When the rainstorm came, we were all wearing cardboard shoes."

His first stop of the day in Arizona is an early-morning radio interview with a conservative host, Barry Young on KFYI in Phoenix. McCain eats a Sausage McMuffin in the passenger seat of an SUV driven by an aide, Michelle Shipley, who at one point makes a wrong turn and has to spin around in a parking lot. As she gets us headed down the correct street, McCain exhales an exaggerated sigh. "Every once in a while a blind hog will unearth an acorn," he says. (Shipley giggles and seems not to mind being likened to a blind hog.)

Young's show is focused heavily on the disastrous rollout of Obamacare. He and his sidekick, Michele Larson, joke about calling the Obamacare 800 number and repeatedly play a busy signal over the air. McCain mentions that help with the law is available in 150 languages. "I would like mine in Urdu," he says, and then he quotes Dana Milbank of the *Washington Post*, who compared the president's pitch for Obamacare with late-night ads for the Ginsu knife. "If you call within the next twenty minutes, you'll get fifty percent off!" McCain says. "And you'll lose weight!"

He also has news of his own to make. He mentions to Young that he's thinking about running for reelection in 2016. This is a different message from the one he sent over the summer, when he said that he didn't want to be one of those old geezers hanging around the Capitol. He repeats this status update during a commercial to everyone in the studio. "I'm thinking about running again," he says, and makes eye contact with me to make sure I caught it. "Couldn't we assume that you were considering this already?" I ask. "Aren't you also thinking about retiring?" McCain shrugs.

Back on the air, Young asks if McCain has just said that he was considering another run for Senate.

"If some wild-eyed journalist hears this and wants to run with it and says that John McCain has announced on the air that he may run for another term in the Senate—that would not be wrong?"

"That would not be wrong," McCain says.

I ask McCain if I can tweet the momentous information he has just relayed. He nods.

"Just so I'm clear," I ask, "are you 'considering' running? Or can I say 'strongly considering' it?"

"I am very much considering it," McCain says.

That settled, we get back in the car to cover about two hours of Interstate 10 between Phoenix and Tucson. Shipley is again driving—also texting and e-mailing, balancing her iPhone against the wheel with her leg at high speeds. This would seem hazardous both from a safety and a public-relations standpoint, but McCain doesn't seem to care at all. He even tells Shipley to tweet a few things for him while she drives—about how the town meetings would be "spirited" and so forth. He takes a phone call from Meghan and tells her that Jay Leno wants them to come on his show together in January; it will be a blast. He calls "Lindsey, my boy," and reads him a *Wall Street Journal* article about Saudi Arabia. Calls Tom Coburn, tells him he did a great job on *Meet the Press* a few days earlier. Calls Senator Kelly Ayotte of New Hampshire, one of his new favorites. After each call, McCain repeats the name of the person he was just talking to. He likes to advertise his friendships, cataloging the names of colleagues he is close to, whom he has been impressed with, and whom "we take traveling with us"—a reference to the Senate delegations he and Graham lead around the world. He prizes his role as ringleader and is fiercely selective about who gets to be part of the bipartisan "gangs" he is always organizing.

Colleagues approach him "pretty much every day," he says, about joining the gangs. As with many things in politics, there is an element of middle-school cliquishness about this. I ask what happens if he does not want someone in his group. "Sometimes we just get together and don't tell anybody else," he says. Or, in the case of an international trip, they won't publicize it until they land in Ukraine or wherever.

Gestures seem to matter more to him than they used to—things that people say about him, compliments they pay. "For somebody who seems to be gruff, he's one of the most sensitive people I've ever met," Graham told me of McCain. "In a good way and a bad way." McCain has many Washington friends—meaning he will promiscuously address people as "my friend" or colleagues as "my good friend from Texas" or whatever. (Cruz, naturally, tells me that he is "proud to count John McCain as a friend.") But for as social an organism as McCain is, he puts up a forbidding barrier. "There's no such thing as friends," he told me. "There's me and Joe and Lindsey, but it's rare. I can count on one hand the number of real friends I have, or maybe two hands."

When he's not on the phone en route to Tucson, McCain keeps

reading news headlines ("Sebelius calling in sick!") and e-mails aloud. He reads an item about a poll, just out, about how only 12 percent of Americans believe that the rollout of Obamacare has gone smoothly. "Just goes to show you," McCain says, "that you can probably get 12 percent of Americans to say pigs can fly." He learns that Liz Cheney, waging a primary challenge in Wyoming against his colleague Mike Enzi, referred to McCain as a "liberal," which sparks an animated commentary from McCain—not against Cheney but about Enzi: "Have you seen that Geico ad?" he says. "Mike Enzi looks exactly like the guy in that Geico ad. He talks like him, too. It's the damnedest thing!"

We enter the city limits of Tucson, which McCain notes is the birthplace "of that singer who used to go out with Jerry Brown, 'Blue Bayou'"—Linda Ronstadt. In the parking lot of the community center where the town meeting will be held, Shipley brushes McCain's hair and sprays on a ton of hair spray. "We might very well have some fireworks in here," McCain says again on the way into the town meeting. He has been priming me for a raucous assembly all morning. But the crowd inside is small and subdued: forty-seven people in the room—three of them babies, three cops, fourteen staff people, and a trickle of media. The questions are pro forma and polite. McCain trots out the "paid staff and blood relatives" line. He vows to keep "doing God's work in the city of Satan." He is back on the road in less than an hour and appears slightly deflated by the reception. He assures me things will be rowdier in Phoenix.

To pass the time on the drive back, I engage McCain in a game of hypothetical-question roulette: If he were a young man living in Arizona today, not a politician, would he register to vote as an Independent? "I would think about it," he says, but then catches himself and reasserts his faith in "the party of Lincoln and Ronald Reagan." Would he consider supporting an Independent presidential candidate if Ted Cruz were the Republican nominee? "No, because I have to respect the process." Would he support his friend Hillary Clinton in a head-to-head against Cruz? "I will support the Republican ticket," he says, then adds, "With all due respect, that is a foolish question, my friend."

The Phoenix town meeting is also lightly attended—about fifty people—but does yield fireworks. One Tea Party guy hits McCain on immigration, and a sizable man who claims to have family in the Jordanian army becomes volcanic on the subject of US policy in Syria, then engages in a shouting match with a man across the room. He keeps accusing McCain of "insulting my intelligence," and McCain asks the man repeatedly, "Are you done?" He calls the man rude, which really sets him off, and a few security jumbos have to escort the guy out of the room. McCain solicits the next question as if nothing happened, but his face remains bright red, and he looks slightly shaken and very much alive.

He invites me to an actual arena that night: in Glendale, Arizona, where the Calgary Flames of the NHL were in town to play the Phoenix Coyotes. This is not the most fabled rivalry in sports, but McCain says he will watch any sporting event ("I'd pay to see the Bedwetters play the Thumbsuckers"). He is a big fan of the Coyotes. There are supposedly other Phoenix Coyote fans, too, though not many of them come to home games. McCain's twenty-five-year-old son, Jimmy, drives us to the arena. Cindy McCain is in the front seat, and I'm in back with the senator, who is desperate to hear the pregame show on the radio. Silence makes him nervous. He keeps barking out call numbers to Cindy, but no luck. He checks the Coyotes app to find information about the show (McCain talks incessantly about his new Coyotes app), and Cindy continues to hunt around the radio dial, except when she is bracing herself for a crash, which happens on three separate occasions during Jimmy's gun-and-slam death ride through the greater Phoenix sprawl. When we arrive, miraculously without incident, the McCains engage in a spirited debate about which parking lot to use. Jimmy takes a few wrong turns; Cindy tells him to slow down and asks why he's going this way or that way, until finally Jimmy snaps and says, "Mom, you make it seem like which parking-lot entrance is the most important thing in the world!" In fact, it's not, he tells her. "I had a woman almost OD in front of me at a strip club this afternoon. Now, *that's* something serious."

"Why were you in a strip club this afternoon?" Cindy asks. Jimmy says he was making a delivery for the family beer distributorship. The woman will be fine, Jimmy reports. His father chuckles in the back.

The arena is ringed with palm trees popping out of the concrete and named for a company I've never heard of. Twenty minutes before face-off, the concourse is as placid as Penn Station on a Sunday morning. The celebrity politician walks a few feet ahead of the rest of us. He carries himself with a full and rightful expectation that people will recognize him, and he greets anyone that meets his glance. "Thank you for your service, Senator," many say. He gets this a lot, he says, "usually right before they unload on me."

In the elevator, we meet a big, handsome guy in a suit who looks like a hockey player and, sure enough, turns out to be an inactive member of the Flames. McCain asks him where he's from. Minnesota. "Where are you from?" he asks McCain. "Oh, I'm sort of from all over," McCain tells him. When the player gets off the elevator and I mention to McCain that the guy had no idea who he was, the senator seems slightly amused and even a bit disoriented. "It happens sometimes," he says.

The seats are about half filled, and the arena is quiet enough during the game to hear the players shouting to each other. Fans are periodically instructed to howl like Coyotes, which McCain does in the same way he greets Wolf Blitzer. The home-team Bedwetters beat the visiting Thumbsuckers 4–2, and McCain heads home happy, except when Cindy can't find the postgame show on the radio, and Jimmy is nearly killing us again.

I'm sure you've noticed, I never talk about my experiences in prison," McCain said to me on the Sunday after Thanksgiving. "I've known too many professional heroes in my life." We were speaking by phone after a weekend he spent at his vacation home in Sedona, and he was getting ready to leave on a weeklong tour of Libya and Saudi Arabia. He would be joined by two staff members but no Lindsey, no entourage, and no other members of the Senate.

For as much as McCain's POW story has been told, the details never fail to astound: the two badly broken arms, a shattered knee, and multiple gashes after parachuting from a shot-down plane into the hands of an enemy mob; how he received no treatment for his wounds for four days, his captors hanging him by his broken limbs and beating him repeatedly; how they offered to release McCain early because of his famous father (who was about to take over as commander of US forces in the Pacific), but he refused to leave, not wanting to give his enemies a propaganda win or risk demoralizing his fellow prisoners.

In his book about five Naval Academy graduates, *The Nightingale's Song*, the journalist Robert Timberg described what McCain looked like after two months of imprisonment—weighing less than 100 pounds, with collapsed cheeks and atrophied limbs. "His eyes, I'll never forget," McCain's cell mate, Bud Day, told Timberg. "They were bug-eyed like you see in those pictures from the Jewish concentration camps. His eyes were real pop-eyed like that."

Day, a decorated fighter pilot, died in July at age eighty-eight. "He was the bravest man I ever knew," McCain said after his death. He and Day had notable disagreements over the years: Day was part of the Swift Boat Veterans for Truth, who campaigned against John Kerry in the 2004 presidential campaign. McCain condemned the group for their attacks against Kerry. "Like a lot of heroes, everything was black and white with Bud," he told me. "That's how you survive."

In captivity, McCain said many of his fellow POWs would search for omens that their release was imminent. "People would say, 'Hey, there's a carrot in my soup, so that must mean we're going home,'" he said. "Bud used to say to them: 'Right, guys. We'll be going home one day, but it sure as hell won't be because we found a carrot in the damn soup.'"

McCain says he has learned forgiveness, which is essential to maintaining forward motion. "He seems to be thinking about his life," Meghan McCain told me. "He just said to me, 'I watched an interview with myself on CNN and thought, Who is that old man that's staring back at me on the TV?'" McCain agrees that he is in a reflective mode. His friends are dying off and longtime colleagues are retiring, and he himself is weighing whether to run again. He fears growing too old in the Senate, as he believes many of his colleagues did—he mentions Robert Byrd and Strom Thurmond. But he has also spoken about his father and grandfather, both decorated Navy men who died not long after they retired. "My grandfather actually flew home from the peace-signing on the *Missouri* and died," McCain says. "I have seen people age dramatically when they go into retirement." If he seeks reelection and wins, McCain would be eighty-six at the end of that term. He is in line to become chairman of the Senate Armed Services Committee if Republicans win a majority next November.

Last April, Harry Reid convened the Senate for a special lunch in the Kennedy Caucus Room to commemorate the fortieth anniversary of McCain's release from prison. McCain appreciated the gesture, and nearly all of his colleagues were present. He spoke through tears at times and without notes. He talked about the kindness he encountered in prison as well as the cruelty. That was striking to the people there, but more so that he spoke about his experience at all. "John told a lot of little poignant stories," Susan Collins of Maine told me. "When John was tied up in such a painful position, he talked about the one guard who would loosen the bonds. He told the story of being out in the yard on Easter, and how one of the guards drew a little cross in the sand, just to acknowledge the holiday, and then rubbed it out so no one would get in trouble." Collins has spent more than a hundred hours on airplane trips with McCain, she says, and has never heard him tell these stories.

McCain points out that he was thirty-one when he became a prisoner of war. He was a formed human being, he says, as opposed to someone like Bob Dole, who sustained crippling wounds in World War II at age twenty-one. "That's obviously going to be a transformational experience," he said. "For me, prison was obviously a testing period, but certainly not something that changed me." He also made a point of reminding me that his "performance" in prison was lacking. He did sign a confession, McCain noted. It followed sustained torture. "You think to yourself, If I get into a situation like that, they'll never get me down," he said. "And you know, they did. It took a lot of pain, but they did." He still feels shame over it, he said.

I had a meeting with McCain in his office the day after Nelson Mandela's memorial, which McCain said he was invited to but "couldn't justify" attending because there was too much going on in Washington. This could be construed as a slap at Cruz, who was the only senator who did attend. I asked him what he thought about Cruz's going—trying to bait him, yes. (I was a blind hog seeking an acorn.) But McCain wasn't playing. "Would it help you if I called Cruz a wacko bird again?" he said. As the conversation veered to topics like jail soup, his own mortality, and the death of yet another friend, McCain began jiggling his leg. "If you stay really busy, you don't get nostalgic," he told me earlier, and it felt as if that was what was happening now, that he was physically willing the introspection away. An aide was waiting with a bunch of logistical questions for McCain about a trip to Kiev he was scheduled to take in a few days. Across the Hill, John Kerry was about to brief a group of senators about Iran. When I asked McCain one final question about the aftermath of 2008, he said, "You find out who your friends are after something like that." He projected no bitterness, only the restlessness of someone who had another place to get to in a hurry. "Do you mind if we walk?" he asked.

Clinton Proudly Talks
of Scars While Keeping
Her Guard Up

December 9, 2007

I n July 2000, Hillary Clinton stood on a stage at the University of Arkansas and struggled to keep her composure. Her voice was unusually soft that day, her words seemingly unfiltered.

"Diane, you were the awesomest," Mrs. Clinton said, referring to Diane Blair, a political science professor whose eulogy she was giving. "You were the best person that one could have as a friend."

Mrs. Blair, who died at sixty-one, was described as the sister Mrs. Clinton had always wanted. She practically moved into the White House in 1993 to ease Mrs. Clinton's transition to Washington, and returned at the end, during the Monica Lewinsky scandal. She sent Mrs. Clinton recipes (though the First Lady did not cook), bird-watching manuals (though she cared little for birds), vitamins (with a note signed "Nurse Diane Fuzzy Wuzzy"), and cards.

"Whenever you have trouble coping, just think of Snow White," one note said. "She had to live with seven men."

The crowd laughed when Mrs. Clinton read that at the memorial service, and she smiled along. Her eyes stayed dry, another triumph of her self-possession. Still, her face was puffy and her jaw slightly clenched, as if any breach of emotion could start a deluge.

That was a glimpse of a "softer" Hillary Clinton, billed as the "real Hillary" by legions of loyalists, the person so often encased in armor.

Mrs. Clinton's surrogates lament that the engaging, generous, and vulnerable woman on the stage would seem alien to many Americans.

Perhaps more than any other candidate, Mrs. Clinton faces an unusual challenge in her quest for the presidency. After a political lifetime of public battles, suspicions, and humiliations, she must prove she is not too hardened to inspire, or too wary to truly lead.

The scar tissue she has accumulated over the years is central to Mrs. Clinton's political identity. She catalogs her wounds with an air of pride and defiance. Invoking a mantra attributed to Eleanor Roosevelt, Mrs. Clinton likes to say that women in politics "need to develop skin as tough as a rhinoceros hide."

"I joke that I have the scars to show from my experiences," she said in an interview.

"But you know, our scars are part of us, and they are a reminder of the experiences we've gone through, and our history. I am constantly making sure that the rhinoceros skin still breathes. And that's a challenge that all of us face. But again, not all of us have to live it out in public."

Critics say that Mrs. Clinton's repeated invocations of her "battles" and "scars" unfairly suggest victimhood, obscuring her own history of picking fights, jettisoning friends, and vilifying adversaries. She was recently criticized for the relish with which she vowed to confront her main rival for the Democratic nomination, Senator Barack Obama.

"Well, now the fun part starts," Mrs. Clinton said.

Others cast her as someone whose ambitions have led her to become a completely political construct. Her campaign, for example, has been lauded as deft and disciplined, but also derided, in the words of the columnist Al Hunt, as "joyless, humorless, and lacking in heart and soul." A popular YouTube parody this year portrayed Mrs. Clinton and her supporters as mechanized drones.

Aides often describe her as "the most famous person nobody knows," a conceit that both condemns those who have mischaracterized Mrs. Clinton and acknowledges how inscrutable she can be.

Mrs. Clinton has always been easier for many people to follow than to know, and people around her tend to speak of her in tones of distant awe, suggesting that they are more acolytes than friends. People who have known her well acknowledge her shell. "Hillary is a person who feels herself very vulnerable, and her response is to make herself bulletproof," said Nancy Pietrafesa, a classmate of Mrs. Clinton's at Wellesley College.

Friends and others say that Mrs. Clinton's wariness has been buttressed by years of scrutiny and ego mangling. She has seemingly spent much of her waking life weathering public storms, each known by shorthand: Gennifer, Paula, Monica, Cookies and Teas, Travelgate, Filegate, Pardongate, Troopergate, Whitewater, Cattle Futures, Impeachment. Among other things, she has also been accused of having a grating voice and bad taste in clothes.

"She's been attacked every day for the last fifteen years," said Jim Blair, Diane Blair's husband. "What else are they going to say or find about her?"

Ann Henry, a friend from Arkansas, recalled that in the early 1980s, when Mrs. Clinton was being assailed over her efforts to overhaul the state's education system, she took Mrs. Henry to a store in Little Rock to buy bath salts.

"At the end of every day, Hillary said she liked to give Chelsea a bath and wash off all of that day's dirt and let it flow down the drain," Mrs. Henry said. "That's essentially her approach. Get dirty, then wash it all off and move on."

Mrs. Clinton said it is a constant challenge to protect herself emotionally and still connect with the people she yearns to serve. "It's not easy, and I don't think it's ever been easy," she said. "You go out into public, and no one, whether you're running for office, or going to work for a newspaper, or running a subway car, you never are open with every nerve ending."

The Reverend Ed Matthews, a Methodist pastor in Little Rock, who ministered to Mrs. Clinton in Arkansas and in the White House and attended Mrs. Blair's memorial service, has seen Mrs. Clinton at vulnerable moments. But Mr. Matthews acknowledges that her public bearing can at times "cause people to wonder how open she would be to my needs and feelings."

"I think there has been a natural steeling process that has gone on," he said. "I don't think she has intended to be a harder person. 'Cautious' might be a better word."

Growing up in the Chicago suburb of Park Ridge, Illinois, Mrs. Clinton learned early the virtue of a sturdy spine and stiff upper lip. Her father, Hugh Rodham, who owned a small drapery-making business, was spare in his praise, if not his spankings. He was "a tough and gruff man," as Bill Clinton described him in his eulogy. When his only daughter brought home stellar grades, Mr. Rodham suggested that she "must go to an easy school."

Dorothy Rodham, who had survived a harsh childhood, pushed her own three children to stand up for themselves. In one oft-told story, Mrs. Rodham encouraged Hillary—then four—to "hit back" against a bullying neighbor.

"She later told me she watched from behind the curtain as I squared my shoulders and marched across the street," Mrs. Clinton wrote in her memoir, *Living History*. "I returned a few minutes later, glowing with victory."

Now eighty-eight, Mrs. Rodham lives in Washington with Mrs. Clinton, who describes her mother as her hero and role model, if not a confidante. Mrs. Rodham told the author Gail Sheehy in 1998: "We don't sit down and have those mother-daughter discussions about how she relates to her husband, her daughter, or anything else as far as her personal life is concerned. We don't talk about deeply personal things."

In high school and then college, Hillary Rodham worked with and was friendly with many, but had few intimates, a pattern that has continued throughout her life. People remember her as fun, focused on politics and student government, and not given to confidences.

"Whatever Hillary may have been going through, and I don't imagine it was too major, she seemed more comfortable being in the role of counselor," said Hardye Moel, a friend from Park Ridge.

In a letter to a high school friend, John Peavoy, when she was at Wellesley, Mrs. Clinton expressed a preference for "worrying about other people and the state of the world" rather than facing the "opaque reality" of her own self.

Mrs. Clinton had a difficult adjustment after following her eventual husband, Bill Clinton, to Arkansas, partly because it marked a transition into being a public figure. "Bill genuinely likes being with people; Hillary does not," said Ms. Pietrafesa, who was a close friend of Mrs. Clinton when they were in their twenties but has not spoken to her in many years.

She was a reluctant campaigner, recalled Rudy Moore, a former campaign manager and chief of staff to Mr. Clinton when he was governor. "I didn't sense that getting out and pressing the flesh was something that she liked at all," he said. Mrs. Clinton was thin-skinned and took criticism hard. Her response was often to buckle down and lash out.

Her defensiveness was partly due to her direct manner and doubting nature. In Arkansas, Mrs. Clinton was perceived as the cold realist to Bill's more sanguine softie. "She was much more inclined to see people's dark sides," Mr. Moore said. "She had a more practical view of what people's motives could be."

She also discovered what life in the political fishbowl could be like. Stories about her husband's extramarital dalliances were widely circulated in Arkansas political circles, from their earliest days in the state. ("It's nothing she didn't know when they were dating," Mr. Blair said.)

Mrs. Clinton said that Washington was much more of a shock than Arkansas, though. So Diane Blair's company in early 1993 was especially helpful. The two women had met two decades earlier, kindred spirits who had moved reluctantly to Arkansas (Mrs. Blair, who attended Cornell, grew up in Washington). Mrs. Clinton, pregnant with Chelsea, stood as "best person" to Diane at her wedding to Jim Blair in 1979; Bill Clinton, then the governor, presided (in top hat and tails).

In Washington, the two friends would don baseball caps and take long walks to escape the prison sanctuary of the White House. The travails of Mr. Clinton's first term—the political blundering, controversies over the Clintons' financial dealings, and rampant criticism in the news media—had already begun. Jim Blair played a part in another dustup when it was revealed that he had helped Mrs. Clinton make nearly $100,000 in profits from trading in commodities futures.

"It was during that time when they were already kind of under siege that Hillary and I grew closer," Mrs. Blair said in an oral history at the University of Arkansas archives. (In addition to her teaching position, Mrs. Blair served as chairwoman of the Corporation for Public Broadcasting in the Clinton administration.)

To the outside word, Mrs. Clinton seemed variously combative or stoic. But friends said she suffered in private, crying and blaming herself. Mr. Matthews, the Methodist pastor, visited Mrs. Clinton at the White House in 1994 and recalls her sitting at her desk, saying plaintively how difficult a time she was having.

Worse, friends said, was a sense of betrayal. She felt deeply wounded by Webb Hubbell, who resigned as associate attorney general after it was disclosed that he had padded billing records at the Rose Law Firm in Little Rock, where Mrs. Clinton had worked. The 1993 suicide of Vince Foster, a close friend and former law partner who was working as deputy White House counsel, shattered her. And she seethed for months after publication of *The Agenda*, Bob Woodward's inside account of the administration based on a torrent of leaks. Mr. Clinton's relationship with Monica Lewinsky was the ultimate betrayal.

It was "the most devastating, shocking, and hurtful experience of my life," Mrs. Clinton wrote in her memoir. She worried that the ordeal would turn her into "the brittle caricature some critics accused me of being."

Mr. Matthews recalled sitting with Mrs. Clinton at a White House prayer breakfast shortly after Mr. Clinton confessed to the affair. "I don't know what I'm going to do," she whispered to him as he knelt before her.

She turned to Mrs. Blair, who traveled frequently to Washington to comfort Mrs. Clinton and confront the president, calling him an "idiot," among other things. ("I think Diane was angrier than Hillary was," Jim Blair said.)

From others, Mrs. Clinton mostly resisted overtures of support, saying she did not want to get people in trouble in case they were contacted by the news media or issued subpoenas. Longtime friends received most un-Hillary-like form letters in response to their "Hang in there" notes.

After Mrs. Clinton helped thwart Republican efforts to oust Mr. Clinton from office, friends say she found solace by initiating her own run for elected office. She was not shy about invoking her embattled past during her Senate campaign in New York.

"My policy for the last eight years has largely been to absorb whatever insult, whatever charge, whatever accusation anybody said and not respond because they are so outrageous and so unfair," she said in a news conference. "I've been accused of everything from complicity in murder to, you know, you name it."

As a presidential candidate, other than frequent reminders of her "scars," Mrs. Clinton's tone has, until recently, been different. Her campaign has strived to create a cozier, more welcoming feel (more girlfriend than warrior princess, campaign events billed as "conversations"). Mrs. Clinton has remained strenuously on message, perpetually on guard.

Her discipline has been viewed as an asset by political strategists but with some frustration by admirers who have found her straitjacketed by the data-driven and market-tested sensibilities of her pollsters. Surveys show that Mrs. Clinton is the candidate seen as most likely to say what she thinks voters want to hear rather than what she truly believes.

"I understand where they're coming from," Mr. Matthews said of those who find her overly staged. "I would just say to them, 'I wish you knew the Hillary I think I know.'"

Few have seen that more-open Hillary Clinton in public in recent years, which is what made her eulogy for Diane Blair so remarkable.

During her tribute, Mrs. Clinton donned a pair of Mrs. Blair's giant round glasses. She talked of Mrs. Blair's love of moose (yes, the animal), needlepoint, and dressing up as Richard Nixon for Halloween. She recalled how the two friends once played tennis with very bouncy balls, made in Korea. "We made up words that we assumed were Korean and screamed them at one another," Mrs. Clinton said.

It was left to Bill Clinton to bring the service to its emotional peak. He talked of Jim Blair's devotion to his wife at the end of her life, how he had never seen such a "more beautiful expression of love."

When he spoke of Mrs. Blair, Mr. Clinton wept. "I felt about her as I have rarely felt about anyone," he said. His wife, Diane Blair's best friend, held steady.

In the '60s, a Future Candidate Poured Her Heart Out in Letters

July 29, 2007

They were high school friends from Park Ridge, Illinois, both high achievers headed east to college. John Peavoy was a bookish film buff bound for Princeton, Hillary Rodham a driven, civic-minded Republican going off to Wellesley. They were not especially close, but they found each other smart and interesting and said they would try to keep in touch.

Which they did, exchanging dozens of letters between the late summer of 1965 and the spring of 1969. Ms. Rodham's thirty dispatches offer a rare, unfiltered look into the head and heart of a future First Lady and senator and would-be president. Their private expressiveness contrasts with the ever-disciplined political persona she now presents.

"Since Xmas vacation, I've gone through three and a half metamorphoses and am beginning to feel as though there is a smorgasbord of personalities spread before me," Ms. Rodham wrote to Mr. Peavoy in April 1967. "So far, I've used alienated academic, involved pseudo-hippie, educational and social reformer, and one-half of withdrawn simplicity."

Befitting college students of any era, the letters are also self-absorbed and revelatory, missives from an unformed and vulnerable striver who had, in her own words, "not yet reconciled myself to the fate of not being the star."

"Sunday was lethargic from the beginning as I wallowed in a morass of general and specific dislike and pity for most people but me especially," Ms. Rodham reported in a letter postmarked October 3, 1967.

In other letters, she would convey a mounting exasperation with her rigid, conservative father and disdain for both "debutante" dorm mates and an acid-dropping friend. She would issue a blanket condemnation of the "boys" she had met ("who know a lot about 'self' and nothing about 'man'") and also tell of an encounter she had with "a Dartmouth boy" the previous weekend.

"It always seems as though I write you when I've been thinking too much again," Ms. Rodham wrote in one of her first notes to Mr. Peavoy, postmarked November 15, 1965. She later joked that she planned to keep his letters and "make a million" when he became famous. "Don't begrudge me my mercenary interest," she wrote.

Of course, it was Hillary Rodham Clinton who became famous, while Mr. Peavoy has lived out his life in contented obscurity as an English professor at Scripps College, a small women's school in Southern California, where he has taught since 1977. Every bit the wild-haired academic, with big silver glasses tucked behind bushy gray sideburns, he lives with his wife, Frances McConnel, and their cat, Lulu, in a one-story house cluttered with movies, books, and boxes—one of which contains a trove of letters from an old friend who has since become one of the most cautious and analyzed politicians in America.

When contacted about the letters, Mr. Peavoy allowed the *New York Times* to read and copy them.

The Clinton campaign declined to comment.

The letters were written during a period when the future Mrs. Clinton was undergoing a period of profound political transformation, from the "Goldwater girl" who shared her father's conservative outlook to a liberal antiwar activist.

In her early letters, Ms. Rodham refers to her involvement with the Young Republicans, a legacy of her upbringing. In October of her freshman year, she dismisses the local chapter as "so inept," which she says she might be able to leverage to her own benefit. "I figure that I may be able to work things my own way by the time I'm a junior so I'm going to stick to it," she writes.

Still, the letters reveal a fast-eroding allegiance to the party of her childhood. She ridicules a trip she had taken to a Young Republicans convention as "a farce that would have done Oscar Wilde credit." By the summer of 1967, Ms. Rodham—writing from her parents' vacation home in Lake Winola, Pennsylvania—begins referring to Republicans as "they" rather than "we."

"That's no Freudian slip," she adds. A few months later, she would be volunteering on Senator Eugene McCarthy's antiwar presidential campaign in New Hampshire. By the time she delivered her commencement address at Wellesley in 1969, she was citing her generation's "indispensable task of criticizing and constructive protest."

But in many ways her letters are more revealing about her search for her own sense of self.

"Can you be a misanthrope and still love or enjoy some individuals?" Ms. Rodham wrote in an April 1967 letter. "How about a compassionate misanthrope?"

Mr. Peavoy's letters to Ms. Rodham are lost to posterity, unless she happened to keep them, which he doubts. He said he wished he had kept copies himself. "They are windows into a time and a place and a journey of self-discovery," he said in an interview. "This was what college students did before Facebook."

The letters are Mr. Peavoy's only link to his former pen pal. They never visited or exchanged a single phone call during their four years of college. They lost touch entirely after graduation, except for the thirty-year reunion of the Maine South High School class of 1965, held in Washington to accommodate the class's most famous graduate, whose husband was then serving his first term in the White House.

"I was on the White House Christmas card list for a while," Mr. Peavoy said. Besides a quick receiving-line greeting from Mrs. Clinton at the reunion, Mr. Peavoy has had just one direct contact with her in thirty-eight years. It was, fittingly, by letter, only this time her words were more businesslike.

In the late 1990s, Mr. Peavoy was contacted by the author Gail Sheehy, who was researching a book on the First Lady. He agreed to let Ms. Sheehy see the letters, from which she would quote snippets in her 1999 biography, *Hillary's Choice*. When Mrs. Clinton heard that Mr. Peavoy had kept her old letters, she wrote him asking for copies, which he obliged. He has not heard from her since.

"For all I know she's mad at me for keeping the letters," said Mr. Peavoy, a pack rat who says he has kept volumes of letters from friends over the years. A Democrat, he said he was undecided between supporting Mrs. Clinton and Senator Barack Obama.

Ms. Rodham's letters are written in a tight, flowing script with near-impeccable spelling and punctuation. Ever the pleaser, she frequently begins them with an apology that it had taken her so long to respond. She praises Mr. Peavoy's missives while disparaging her own ("my usual drivel") and signs off with a simple "Hillary," except for the occasional "H" or "Me."

As one would expect of letters written during college, Ms.

Rodham's letters display an evolution in sophistication, viewpoint, and intellectual focus. One existential theme that recurs throughout is that Ms. Rodham views herself as an "actor," meaning a student activist committed to a life of civic action, which she contrasts with Mr. Peavoy, who, in her view, is more of an outside critic, or "reactor."

"Are you satisfied with the part you have cast yourself in?" she asks Mr. Peavoy in April 1966. "It seems that you have decided to become a reactor rather than actor—everything around will determine your life."

She is mildly patronizing if not scornful, as she encourages her friend to "try-out" for life. She quotes from *Doctor Zhivago*, "Man is born to live, not prepare for life," and signs the letter "Me" ("the world's saddest word," she adds parenthetically).

Ms. Rodham becomes expansive and wistful when discussing the nature of leadership and public service, and how the validation of serving others can be a substitute for self-directed wisdom. "If people react to you in the role of answer bestower then quite possibly you are," she writes in a letter postmarked November 15, 1967, and continues in this vein for another page before changing the subject to what Mr. Peavoy plans to do the following weekend.

Ms. Rodham's dispatches indicate a steady separation from Park Ridge, her old friends, and her family, notably her strict father. She seethes at her parents' refusal to let her spend a weekend in New York ("Their reasons—money, fear of the city, they think I've been running around too much, etc.—are ridiculous") and fantasizes about spending the summer between her sophomore and junior years in Africa, only to dismiss the notion, envisioning "the scene with my father."

While home on a break in February of her junior year, Ms. Rodham bemoans "the communication chasm" that has opened within her family. "I feel like I'm losing the top of my head," she complains, describing an argument raging in the next room between—"for a change"—her father and one of her brothers.

"God, I feel so divorced from Park Ridge, parents, home, the entire unreality of middle class America," she says. "This all sounds so predictable, but it's true."

Ms. Rodham has been described by people who knew her growing up as precocious, and in the letters she is scathingly judgmental at times. She spent the bulk of one letter on a withering assessment of dorm mates.

"Next me," Ms. Rodham says wryly. "Of course, I'm normal, if that is a permissible adjective for a Wellesley girl."

In other notes, she speaks of her own despair; in one, written in the winter of her sophomore year, she describes a "February depression." She catalogs a long, paralyzed morning spent in bed, skipping classes, hating herself. "Random thinking usually becomes a process of self-analysis with my ego coming out on the short end," she writes.

Another recurring theme of Ms. Rodham's musings is the familiar late-adolescent impulse not to grow up. "Such a drag," she says, invoking the Rolling Stones, a rare instance of her referring to pop culture.

Her letters at times betray a kind of innocent narcissism over "my lost youth," as she described it in a letter shortly after her nineteenth birthday. She wrote of being a little girl and believing that she was the only person in the universe. She had a sense that if she turned around quickly, "everyone else would disappear.

"I'd play out in the patch of sunlight that broke the density of the elms in front of our house and pretend there were heavenly movie cameras watching my every move," she says. She yearns for all the excitement and discoveries of life without losing "the little girl in the sunlight."

At which point, Ms. Rodham declares that she has spent too

much time wandering "aimlessly through a verbal morass" and writes that she is going to bed.

"You'll probably think I'm retreating from the world back to the sunlight in an attempt to dream my child's movie," she says.

The letters contain no possibly damaging revelations of the proverbial "youthful indiscretions," and mention nothing glaringly outlandish or irresponsible. Indeed, she tends toward the self-scolding: "I have been enjoying myself too much, and spring and letter-writing are—to the bourgeois mind—no excuses!"

She reports in one letter from October of her sophomore year that she spent a "miserable weekend" arguing with a friend who believed that "acid is the way and what did I have against expanding my conscience."

In a previous letter from her freshman year, she divulges that a junior in her dorm had been caught at her boyfriend's apartment in Cambridge at 3:15 a.m. "I don't condone her actions," Ms. Rodham declares, "but I'll defend to expulsion her right to do as she pleases— an improvement on Voltaire."

Ms. Rodham's notes to Mr. Peavoy are revelatory, even intimate at times, but if there is any romantic energy between the friends, they are not evident in Ms. Rodham's side of the conversation. "P.S. thanks for the Valentine's card," she says at the end of one letter. "Good night."

Her letters contain no mention of any romantic interest, except for one from February 1967 in which Ms. Rodham divulges that she "met a boy from Dartmouth and spent a Saturday night in Hanover."

Ms. Rodham skates earnestly on the surface of life, raising more questions than answers. "Last week I decided that even if life is absurd why couldn't I spend it absurdly happy?" she wrote in November of her junior year. She then challenges herself to "define 'happiness,' Hillary Rodham, acknowledged agnostic intellectual liberal, emotional conservative."

From there, she deems the process of self-definition to be "too depressing" and asserts that "the easiest way out is to stop any thought approaching introspection and to advise others whenever possible."

The letters to Mr. Peavoy taper off considerably after the first half of Ms. Rodham's junior year; there are just two from 1968 and one from 1969.

"I'm sitting here at a stolen table in a pair of dirty denim bell-bottoms, a never-ironed work shirt, and a beautiful purple felt hat with a purple polka-dotted scarf streaming off it," she writes in her final correspondence, March 25, 1969. A senior bound for law school, she betrays exhaustion with the times, a country at war, and a culture in tumult. "I'm really tired of people slamming doors and screaming obscenities at poor old life," she says, and describes the sound of chirping birds amid the "soulless academia" that she will inhabit for just a few more weeks as an undergraduate.

Being Glenn Beck

October 3, 2010

Glenn Beck was sprawled out on his office couch a couple of weeks ago, taking—as self-helpers like to say—an inventory. "I think what the country is going through right now is, in a way, what I went through with my alcoholism," he told me. "You can either live or die. You have a choice." Beck, who is forty-six, was in the Midtown Manhattan offices of his production company, Mercury Radio Arts, which is named for Mercury Theatre, the company created by Orson Welles. He had just finished his three-hour syndicated radio show and was a few hours away from his television show. It was a Wednesday afternoon in the middle of September, and Beck had just returned from a week's vacation in the Grand Tetons followed by a quick hop to Anchorage, where he and Sarah Palin appeared at an event on September 11.

Beck has a square, boyish face, an alternately plagued and twinkle-eyed demeanor that conjures (when Beck is wearing glasses) the comedian Drew Carey. He is six-feet-two, which is slightly jarring when you first meet him, because he is all head and doughiness on television; I never thought of Beck as big or small, just as someone who was suddenly ubiquitous and who talked a lot and said some really astonishing things, to a point where it made you wonder—constantly—whether he was being serious.

At some point in the past few months, Beck ceased being just the guy who cries a lot on Fox News or a "rodeo clown" (as he has described himself) or simply a voice of the ultraconservative opposition to President Obama. In record time, Beck has traveled the loop of curiosity to ratings bonanza to self-parody to sage. It is remarkable to think he has been on Fox News only since January 2009.

In person, Beck is sheepish and approachable, betraying none of the grandiosity or bluster you might expect from a man who predicted "the next Great Awakening" to a few hundred thousand people in late August at the Lincoln Memorial or who declared last year that the president has a "deep-seated hatred for white people or the white culture." He wore a blue dress shirt tucked into jeans and brown loafers, which he kicked off as soon as he sat down. He showed little interest in the results from primary elections held the day before— upsets in Delaware and New York for Tea Party candidates whose followers often invoke Beck and Palin as spiritual leaders and even promote them as a prospective presidential ticket in 2012.

"Not involved with the Tea Party," Beck told me, shrugging. While many identify Beck with a political insurgency—as Rush Limbaugh was identified with the Republican sweep of 1994—to believe that the nation suffers from "a political problem" comically understates things, in his view. "I stand with the Tea Party as long as they stand for certain principles and values," Beck told me. He is a principles-and-values guy.

Beck talks like someone who is accustomed to thinking out loud and inflicting his revelations in real time. He speaks in the language of therapy, in which he has been steeped through years of twelve-step programs and the Mormon-affiliated addiction-treatment center he and his wife run in the New York, New Jersey, and Connecticut region. As he lay on his office couch, he recalled a very low moment. It was back in the mid-1990s. He was newly divorced, lying on the olive green shag carpet of a two-bedroom apartment in Hamden, Connecticut, that smelled like soup. It had a tiny kitchen, and his young children slept in a bed together when they visited on weekends. "It was the kind of place where loser guys who just got divorced wind up," Beck said. "You'd see a new guy come in, you'd say hello and he'd walk in alone, and you'd be like, 'Yeah, I understand, brother.'"

Beck understands, brother. Communists in the White House are bent on "fundamentally transforming" the country; progressives speak of putting "the common good" before the individual, which "is exactly the kind of talk that led to the death camps in Germany," as he said on his show in May. Or, as he said in July of last year, "Everything that is getting pushed through Congress, including this health care bill," is "driven by President Obama's thinking on . . . reparations" and his desire to "settle old racial scores." It sounds harsh, maybe, but this is the rhetoric of crisis and desperation, and so much of the population is too blind drunk to recognize the reality—which is that the country is lying on an olive green shag carpet on the brink of ending it all. "Some have to destroy their family and their job and their house and their income," Beck told me. "Some don't get it, and they die."

Some do get it, and they revere Glenn Beck.

While the right has traditionally responded to its aggrieved sense of alienation with anger, Beck is not particularly angry. He seems sorrowful; his prevailing message is umbrage born of self-taught wisdom. He is more agonized than mad. He is post-angry.

Beck rarely speaks with the squinty-eyed certainty or smugness of Rush Limbaugh or his fellow Fox News hosts Bill O'Reilly and Sean Hannity. He often changes his mind or nakedly contradicts himself. "When you listen and watch me, it's where I am in my thinking in the moment," Beck told me. "I'm trying to figure it out as I go." He will sometimes stop midsentence and recognize that something he is about to say could be misunderstood and could cause him trouble. Then, more often than not, he will say it anyway.

In the middle of his analogy to me about his own personal crash and the country's need to heal itself, Beck looked at his publicist with a flash of alarm about how I might construe what he was saying. "He is going to write a story that I believe the whole country is alcoholics," he said. And then he went on to essentially compare his Restoring Honor pageant at the Lincoln Memorial to a large-scale AA meeting. "When I bottomed out, I couldn't put it back together myself," Beck told me. "I could do all the hard work. I could do the twelve steps. But I needed like-minded people around me."

He needed support, just as responsible Americans need it now to reinforce the principles and values that the founders instilled and that, he says, have since decayed. "You need people to be able to reach out and connect and say, 'Let me help hold you when you're stumbling, and you hold me when I'm stumbling, because what we're going through now is a storm of confusion.'" Fans approach Beck and give him hugs. Do people feel they can hug Limbaugh?

There is something feminine about Beck—the soft features, the crying on the air, the reflexive vulnerability. It sets him apart from the standard, testosterone-addled rant artists of cable and talk radio. Women tune in to Beck's radio show more heavily than they do to other conservative commentators, says Chris Balfe, the president and chief operating officer of Mercury, which employs more than forty people. And Beck's television show is on at five p.m. Eastern, traditionally a slot with more women viewers. (On a typical day,

Beck's show is recorded on more DVRs than any other cable-news program.) But Beck also appeals to a more traditionally female sensibility. "He works through things in real time," Balfe told me. "Maybe he'll come back tomorrow and say, 'You know what, I've given this some thought, and here's what I'm thinking now.'" Or maybe he'll come back sooner. Within a few sentences of proposing Obama's "deep-seated hatred for white people," he added this caveat: "I'm not saying that he doesn't like white people."

Beck's staff and loyalists love to compare Beck with Oprah Winfrey. Balfe was the first to say it to me, adding the requisite faux apology. As Winfrey does, Beck talks a great deal about himself and subscribes to the pop-recovery ethic. "Part of Oprah's appeal is that people see her as a real person," says Joel Cheatwood, the Fox executive who initially brought Beck to CNN's *Headline News* and then to Fox. "She has struggled with her weight; she is open about it. Glenn is not a pretty boy. He comes off as a regular guy who has also been open about his struggles." (Beck dabbled in Pilates recently, he disclosed on radio.)

The presumed Oprah parallel is corporate as well as stylistic. Beck, like Winfrey, has a knack for making best sellers of books he mentions on the air. He publishes a magazine, sells more than a million dollars in merchandise, and speaks of an array of possible multimedia ventures. Beck's magazine, *Fusion*, is so named because it is a "fusion of entertainment and enlightenment." Beck himself is a study in fusions. He blends TV-ready empathy with push-the-edge conservative talk, as well as self-doubt with the self-absorbed grandeur of a man whose hard-won recovery grants him the power to speak from the steps of the Lincoln Memorial.

Beck is constantly admitting his weaknesses and failures, which he wields as both a crutch and a shield. "Maybe Glenn's transparency is what keeps him out of trouble," says Robert Beath, Beck's drama teacher at Sehome High School in Bellingham, Washington.

Beath, who was fond of Beck as a teenager, said Beck appears to now think that his revelations grant him license. "When he says, 'I am not perfect,' he seems to escape accountability for his various points of view. Yet he expects others to be accountable for their point of view without seeming to allow them the 'I am not perfect' exception."

That's where the Winfrey comparison falls apart. You could never imagine her joking about poisoning the Speaker of the House or talking about choking the life out of a filmmaker or fantasizing about beating a congressman "to death with a shovel" (as Beck did for Nancy Pelosi, Michael Moore, and Charles Rangel, respectively). Beck invites extreme reactions from both directions.

"He has a spiritual connection to us; you can hear his heart speaking," Susan Trevethan, a psychiatric nurse from Milford, Connecticut, told me at the Restoring Honor rally. "I believe he has been divinely guided to be here in this place," she said. "He is doing the research. He is teaching us."

Or if you prefer: "Even the leather-winged shouting heads at Fox News look like intellectual giants next to this bleating, benighted Cassandra," wrote the *Buffalo Beast*, in naming Beck one of the fifty most loathsome people in America in 2006. (Number twenty-four then, but in January he made it to number one.) "It's like someone found a manic, doom-prophesying hobo in a sandwich board, shaved him, shot him full of Zoloft, and gave him a show."

The Mercury Radio Arts headquarters are a museum to Beck's quirks, aspirations, successes, and self. Poster-size color photos of Beck, taken by his personal photographer, George Lange, dominate the lobby. One features Beck wrapped up head to toe in yellow police tape; another has him dressed and made up like a rodeo clown. The offices evoke the self-image of a multimedia entrepreneur and would-be titan: portraits of Orson Welles, Ronald Reagan, and Walt Disney hang on the walls. Balfe, the chief executive, keeps a massive red-and-blue "Capitalism" poster above his desk—hand-painted by Beck.

Next door to Balfe's office is Beck's, which is spacious, sunfilled and arrayed with family photos, books, and a yellowed copy of the *Boston Post* with the headline "Woodrow Wilson Is Dead." His computer flashes with alternating screen savers of his second wife, Tania, and his four children—two from each marriage—along with photos of landmarks like Pike Place Market in Seattle, near where Beck grew up.

Beck can be difficult to get to. He is acutely conscious of his personal safety. He feels targeted. Security guards trail him on the street. He wears bulletproof vests at public events. He wanted to build a six-foot barrier around his estate in New Canaan, Connecticut, running him afoul of local zoning ordinances. The barrier would not stop those who would do him harm, Beck's lawyer told New Canaan's zoning commission, but it would slow them down. "It will stop anything people send into the property, whether photographs or bullets," the lawyer said, according to the *New Canaan Advertiser*.

Beck says he trusts very few people. He gives few interviews. I first spoke to him by phone, a few days after the rally in Washington. He sounded thrilled—on the phone, as he did on the air that week—with how everything went on August 28. But he never seems far from the precipice of something. It is all precarious.

"I said to someone the other day," Beck told me, "I am as close today to a complete and total collapse as I was on the first day of recovery." He calls himself a "recovering dirtbag." There were many days, he said, when he would avoid the bathroom mirror so he would not have to face himself. He was in therapy with "Dr. Jack Daniel's."

He smoked marijuana every day for about fifteen years. He fired an underling for bringing him the wrong pen. He once even called the wife of a radio rival to ridicule her—on the air—about her recent miscarriage.

"You get to a place where you disgust yourself," Beck told me. "Where you realize what a weak, pathetic, and despicable person you have become."

Beck grew up in Mount Vernon, Washington, about fifty miles north of Seattle. He was an unfocused student with discrete passions and talents who could have benefited from a more stable home environment—and a prescription. His love affair with radio began, he says, when his mother gave him an album set of radio classics that included Welles's *War of the Worlds*. He was eight and spent much of his free time honing his radio voice into a tape recorder.

Bill and Mary Beck, Glenn's parents, owned a bakery in Mount Vernon that eventually closed. The couple divorced when Glenn was thirteen, and Mary Beck, who battled alcoholism, drowned a few years later along with a male companion on a boating expedition in 1979 on a bay near Tacoma. Beck deemed her death a suicide (though local newspapers and government records called it an accident, according to Salon.com's Alexander Zaitchik). Beck was fifteen then, and he says the episode sank him into decades of misery, chemical dependence, and misanthropic behavior that played out on and off the air at a procession of FM stations across the country—morning-DJ jobs in markets like Provo, Utah; Phoenix; Corpus Christi, Texas; and New Haven, where he hit bottom.

I asked Beck if he could pinpoint the moment he decided to change his life. "Here's something I haven't told anyone before," Beck said. "When my mother was at her worst, she was dating a guy who was abusive. He was a big Navy guy, too." It was right at the end of her life. Glenn got between his mother and the man during an ugly fight. "I just came in and stood between them and said, 'Get out of our house.'" The man left, but he came back a few days later and begged forgiveness. "When I sobered up, I remember looking back to that point," Beck told me. "Something I learned still kind of plays a role." He went on to say: "One of the phrases I use is: You need to be who you were born to be, not the people we have allowed ourselves to become. Don't let life and the world shape us. That's not who we are."

I asked Beck how he knew that his mother's death was a suicide. The man who drowned with her was that same abusive boyfriend, he said. Either the two of them jumped overboard at the same time, or Mary fell in and the Navy man jumped in to save her—and that was unlikely. Why? Beck said he been out on a boat with the boyfriend before, and the man preached to him never to jump in and save somebody who is drowning. It only endangers the would-be rescuer. Throw in a life preserver instead. Plus, the Navy man's clothes were found neatly folded, along with his wallet and watch.

At just twenty-one, Beck took a job as a morning-drive impresario in Louisville. His show, *Captain Beck and the A-Team*, included the usual antics of the genre: juvenile jokes, pranks, impersonations, sound effects, and fat jokes about a news reader for a rival station—anything to fill the four hours.

By most accounts, Beck succeeded; but by his own, he was miserable. "There was a bridge abutment in Louisville, Kentucky, that had my name on it," Beck wrote in his 2003 book, *Real America: Messages from the Heart and Heartland*. "Every day I prayed for the strength to be able to drive my car at 70 mph into that bridge abutment." He says he contemplated only violent suicides ("like the bridge abutment thing and putting a gun in my mouth while listening to Nirvana"). He attributes his inability to off himself to cowardice and stupidity—qualities that also suited him to his tour of morning zoo America. "I hated people," Beck wrote, "because I hated myself."

By the mid-nineties, Beck had been married, divorced, ponytailed, and seemingly at a dead end. He joined Alcoholics Anonymous, reluctantly attending his first meetings in a church basement in Cheshire, Connecticut. The olive-green-carpet episode was formative but not a singular turning point. "It was more a point of recognition," Beck told me. "Are you going to stand or are you going to grow up? Are you going to succeed or fail, live or die? What is it going to be? There weren't any angels or the sky opening up." He embarked on a period of "searching" and self-education. The process was largely haphazard. He tells of walking into a bookstore and loading up on books by a hodgepodge that included Alan Dershowitz, Pope John Paul II, Carl Sagan, Nietzsche, Billy Graham, and Adolf Hitler. "The library of a serial killer," he called it. He even enrolled at Yale, with a written recommendation from an alum who was a listener at the time, Senator Joe Lieberman. He took one class, early Christology, but says he "spent more time trying to find a parking space" than in class and quickly dropped out.

Beck met Tania in 1998. She walked into the New Haven radio station where he was working to pick up a Sony Walkman she won in a contest. They began dating. He wanted to marry, and she agreed, but only on the condition that they find a religion together. They shopped around, attended services, and eventually settled on Mormonism—inspired in part by Beck's best friend and radio sidekick, Pat Gray, who himself is Mormon. Beck, who was brought up Roman Catholic, has called his faith "the most important thing" in his life.

By the late 1990s, Beck had come to despise the FM zoo format. He was becoming more spiritual, more engaged in news and current affairs, and more opinionated on the air about his political views (generally conservative then, though not as much as now—he favored abortion rights at the time). He was a connoisseur of talk radio and yearned to break into the genre.

Beck moved to Tampa, Florida, in late 1999—leaving his two daughters back in Connecticut—to host his first talk-radio show, an afternoon slot on WFLA. "I may have made the biggest mistake of my life in taking this job," Beck recalls saying during his first segment on the air. "Because I've just made a pact that I was going to leave my children in Connecticut and move to Florida, and it's killing me. I may have traded my children for this job."

Beck's radio show was heavily political but not exclusively. It was more stream of consciousness—veering in unforeseen directions, as reflected in the first segment. "I found it to be a very *Seinfeld*-like radio program," says Kraig Kitchin, the former president of Premiere Radio Networks, who signed Beck to a national-syndication deal. "There was one main plot streaming through the program and two or three subplots."

Joel Cheatwood, then the executive director of program development for CNN and *Headline News*, heard Beck's radio show in late 2004, when Beck was on the air in Philadelphia, and said he believed that the host could translate to television. Cheatwood, a controversial innovator of television news, pioneered the flashy "if it bleeds, it leads" local-news formats. He persuaded Beck to join *Headline News* in 2006. As with his first stint in Tampa, Beck had early doubts. "Glenn had been on the air for about three weeks," recalled Cheatwood, who has one of the most thrillingly sculptured waves of slicked-back hair I have ever seen. "He came into my office and said something like, 'This is kind of a disaster,' and he was right." Beck struggled to adapt his radio persona to the regimented bites of television. "It was all over the board," Cheatwood says of the early *Headline News* show.

Beck compares his free-associative radio orientation to the real-time oversharing ethic of today's culture. "My life is what I think our children are going through with Facebook," he told me. "They're putting things up there, because they're living their life, and everybody's doing it." Eventually Beck learned to harness his talent to the demands of television, at least somewhat. His best-known episode at *Headline News* was a November 2006 interview with Keith Ellison, a Democrat from Minnesota, who had just become the first Muslim elected to the House. "I have to tell you, I have been nervous about this interview with you," Beck told Ellison to break the ice. "Because what I feel like saying is, 'Sir, prove to me that you are not working with our enemies.' And I know you're not. I'm not accusing you of being an enemy, but that's the way I feel, and I think a lot of Americans will feel that way." Groups complained, Beck expressed regret for "a poorly worded question," and Jon Stewart played the clip on *The Daily Show.* "Finally," Stewart said, "a guy who says what people who aren't thinking are thinking."

B eck was lured to Fox News by the prospect of more viewers and a recruiting pitch by Cheatwood—who had since moved there—and the network's president, Roger Ailes. He began his Fox News show the day before Barack Obama's inauguration.

People watch Beck in remarkable numbers, at least by the standards of his time slot on cable news—he averages more than two million viewers, whether the topic is a Founding Father, an obscure president, or a little-known White House administrator.

"If you were in an imaginary meeting for a TV show," Bill Shine, Fox News' programming director, says, "and someone said: 'I have an idea. Let's spend a month talking about the Founding Fathers and get a bunch of pictures of Benjamin Franklin and hang them up,' you'd be like, 'What?' But it works." Beck fashions himself a kind of self-teaching populist for the Internet age. His characteristic chalkboard lends his show an air of retro-professorial authority, despite the fact that Beck did not attend college and says that before September 11, 2001, "I didn't know my butt from my elbow." He recommends books. He recently started "Glenn Beck University," a special collection of "classes" on GlennBeck.com to go with Beck's daily tutorials. Pat Gray said Beck was "America's history professor."

"Beck offers a story about the American past for people who are feeling right now very angry and alienated," says David Frum, a former speechwriter for President George W. Bush and editor of the conservative Web site Frum Forum. "It is different enough from the usual story in that he makes them feel like they've got access to secret knowledge."

Beck's Fox News show intersperses history with weeping laments, melodramatic calls to faith, and vehement attacks on "progressives." He also mixes in campy stage props and laughs straight from the morning zoo playbook. One moment, he is giving an impassioned plea for the would-be builder of Park51, the Islamic community center planned for a location not far from the World Trade Center site, to build elsewhere; the next moment, he is discussing possible names for a hypothetical Islam-friendly gay bar next door ("Turban Cowboy," "You Mecca Me Hot").

"I find it riveting to watch," says Anita Dunn, the former White House communications director whom Beck railed against prodigiously on the air last year after she named Mother Teresa and Mao Zedong as her "favorite political philosophers" (she says she was joking about Mao) in a commencement address. "There is that edge where you are always thinking, Is he going to totally lose it on camera?" Dunn told me.

The ethos of Beck's program is extreme doom and pessimism. In a lead-in to Beck's show, Shepard Smith referred to his fellow host's studio as "the Fear Chamber." This is another departure from the Limbaugh formula. "Rush is basically of a quite optimistic creed," Frum says. "It's the Reagan creed: America's best days are still to come. If we maintain the free-enterprise system, we're all going to be richer and more united and stronger. With Beck, there is no optimism."

On Fox News in early September, Beck stood in a mock doorway painted gold. When the country's economic system reaches "the point of insanity," he said, it is wise to invest in gold. "Gold prices are climbing," Beck said, a point buttressed throughout the hour by advertisements from gold dealers. On the other side of the golden doorway is where things get really scary, he said. Who knows what dark, apocalyptic things are there? "Is it bullets?" Beck wondered. "Is it whiskey? Is it cigarettes?"

Beck often speaks of—and is teased about—his "bunker," where he will retreat after the social fabric rends and the economic system collapses. Some of his most devoted advertisers include companies that could thrive in a period of total collapse—makers of emergency power generators, for instance, or "survival seeds" (allowing citizens to grow their own food).

I asked Beck if he actually had a bunker. No, he said, there is no bunker. He does keep a great deal of food in reserve, although he says that predates his fear that the world would melt down. Food storage is a tenet of his Mormon faith, he said. It is for when tough times come.

"Am I actively engaged in survival training?" he told me. "No. Should I be? Maybe."

. . .

Beck performs more than twenty live stage shows a year as part of what has become a growing multimedia and merchandising empire that, according to Forbes, earned $35 million between June 2009 and June 2010. At the end of July, I paid $147 for a ticket to see him and Bill O'Reilly perform together at a theater in the round in Westbury, New York, on Long Island—part of Beck and O'Reilly's "Bold and Fresh" tour. The theater drew an orderly suburban procession of khaki-wearing, Camry-driving Caucasians who say they want their country back. The woman next to me complained that her large oil can of Heineken and a pretzel cost sixteen dollars. Air Supply played the venue a few days earlier.

Beck and O'Reilly each spoke solo for about forty minutes, followed by a conversational duet by the two Fox News hosts. The sets mingled stand-up comedy with political rants and, in Beck's case, a history sermon. It included a call for America to return to the spirit of "divine providence" that the founders intended—before it was perverted by Manifest Destiny in the mid–nineteenth century. "We've lost our way since Andrew Jackson," said Beck, who wore an unlaced pair of black Chuck Taylor sneakers. "Manifest Destiny is 'Get out of my way, I'm on a mission from God.' That's where we went wrong. We must humble ourselves."

Later, Beck and O'Reilly did a riff about Chelsea Clinton's wedding, which was being held that night.

"What are the odds of Hillary Clinton inviting me to her daughter's wedding?" O'Reilly asked Beck.

"What are the odds we have a Communist revolutionary in the White House?" Beck replied, to loud applause.

A recurring theme of the evening was Beck and O'Reilly talking about how despised they are by venomous critics bent on silencing them. Both wear this "constant abuse" proudly, although, unlike

O'Reilly, Beck will betray vulnerability, even woundedness. "They want to destroy you, get you off the air," O'Reilly told Beck. "And I want to know if that bothers you?"

"It bothers me when I walk down the street with my children," Beck said, "and my college-age daughter is holding my hand, and someone says something horribly vicious. And my daughter hears them, cries, and says to me, 'Dad, all I wish is that people will remember that you are a dad occasionally as well.'" (This was several weeks after Beck apologized for doing an extended imitation of then eleven-year-old Malia Obama on his radio show. "Daddy," Beck said, mimicking the president's daughter, "why do you hate black people so much?")

Beck seemed to draw more fans than O'Reilly, despite O'Reilly's home-field advantage on his native Long Island. "He is a modern-day prophet doing God's work," a man named Lee Hein told me. He resides in Hawaii, where he wakes at three a.m. to hear a live stream of Beck's radio show on the Internet. Hein, a plumbing contractor, recently purchased three copies of Beck's novel *The Overton Window*, five copies of his book *Glenn Beck's Common Sense*, and three copies of *Arguing with Idiots*. He likes to give the books out to educate his friends.

Several people at Beck's events described themselves as "students of history" or "historians." When I asked one if he was affiliated with a school or college, he said: "Yes. Glenn Beck University."

When Beck meets his fans, he does so with the gusto of a public figure engaging his constituents. People he meets often give him presents and notes. He signs autographs, poses for photos. He has perfected the Everyman shtick that presidential candidates spend years trying to master in places like Iowa. No doubt, someone loyal to Beck will read that and say, 'No, no, it's not a shtick.' Like many famous performers, Beck is described by friends and supplicants as someone who is authentic and real, that what you see is what you get. (It's usually their public-relations person who says this.)

On the Thursday night before his Saturday bar mitzvah at the Lincoln Memorial, Beck walked around the Kennedy Center for the Performing Arts in anticipation of a *Divine Destiny* event he would host the next night. *Divine Destiny* featured music, speeches, and testimonials from a procession of prominent spiritual teachers—priests, pastors, rabbis, Chuck Norris.

Free tickets to *Divine Destiny* were triple hot, like the concert passes Beck used to give away to the twenty-third caller on the morning zoo. People lined up outside in hopes of getting tickets. Beck came out to say hello. Tania Beck handed out pizza. Beck wore a blue baseball cap, pink shirt, and thick-rimmed glasses. He looked like a square dad checking in on the kids at a sleepover. "Do you smell the pizza?" he asked. People greeted him with shrieks, whoops, and gasps.

"Are you the first in line?" Beck asked a man with a crew cut and wispy beard from Fayetteville, Arkansas.

"Yes, sir," the man said.

Beck had a special prize for the man. "I haven't given this to anybody," Beck said. It was a Badge of Merit, an award Beck modeled on the Purple Heart–like token that George Washington bestowed for meritorious conduct (for, say, valor in a war or the commitment required to score free tickets).

Beck hugged his way through the line. People were moved, some tearful. "It's such an honor," a woman said softly, hugging him. "God bless you, man," a guy in a Dallas Cowboys shirt said. "Thank you for giving us a voice," another woman added.

"We hate Woodrow Wilson," another woman called out. This is like a secret handshake among Beck followers, who have heard his diatribes about the evils of our twenty-eighth president, a father of the Progressive Era. "I hate him," Beck affirmed for the Woodrow Wilson–hating women at the Kennedy Center. "I hate that guy."

A mother asked him to pose for a photo with her and her autistic child who, the mother says, watches Beck every day. Like Palin, Beck has a special-needs child—a daughter, Mary, who has cerebral palsy—and he often hears from parents who have dealt with similar circumstances.

Beck then stopped and addressed a section of the line. "Do you guys know what's going on here tonight?" Beck asked them.

"Magic," answered a woman in an orange T-shirt. "Miracles."

"There are twenty-four hundred seats," Beck explained. "Most of them will be pastors and priests and rabbis. And it's the beginning."

He started to cry.

"It's the beginning of the . . ." He choked up, making it hard to make out his words.

"It's going to be neat," he finally mustered.

Beck seems able to cry on cue. He says he is a softie who is prone to crying during television commercials. He is an emotional person, Balfe says, which speaks to his sincerity and the reason that people are so quick to identify with him.

As Beck worked the Kennedy Center, his every move was captured by a videographer who was with him during his trip to Washington. I watched the intimate event from my desktop—it was linked on GlennBeck.com and available to premium "insider extreme" subscribers ($9.95 a month). It was one of the many times I found myself wondering whether this was real, part of the show, or some fusion of both.

. . .

On the air and in person, Beck often goes on long stretches that are warm, conciliatory, and even plaintive. He says he yearns for the cohesion in the country after September 11, 2001, and will speak in paragraphs that could fit into Barack Obama's plea for national unity in his speech at the 2004 Democratic National Convention. "There's a lot we can disagree on, but our values and principles can unite us," Beck said from the Lincoln Memorial.

But "standing together" can be a tough sell from someone who is so willing to pick at some of the nation's most tender scabs. Beck's statement that the president's legislative agenda is driven by Obama's desire for "reparations" and his "desire to settle old racial scores" is hardly a uniting message. While public figures tend to eventually learn (some the hard way) that Nazi, Hitler, and Holocaust comparisons inevitably offend a lot of people, Beck seems not to care. In a forthcoming book about Beck, *Tears of a Clown*, the *Washington Post* columnist Dana Milbank writes that in the first fourteen months of Beck's Fox News show, Beck and his guests mentioned fascism 172 times, Nazis 134 times, Hitler 115 times, the Holocaust 58 times, and Joseph Goebbels 8 times.

In his quest to root out progressives, Beck compared himself to Israeli Nazi-hunters. "To the day I die I am going to be a progressive-hunter," he vowed on his radio show earlier this year. "I'm going to find these people that have done this to our country and expose them. I don't care if they're in nursing homes."

"Raising questions" is Beck's favorite rhetorical method. Last year during the health care debate, Beck compared Obama's economic agenda to Nazi Germany—specifically he paralleled the White House chief of staff Rahm Emanuel's statement that "you never want a serious crisis to go to waste" with how Hitler used the world economic crisis as a pivot point. Photos of Hitler, Stalin, and

Lenin then appeared on screen. "Is this where we're headed?" Beck asked. He allowed that "I am not predicting that we go down that road."

President Obama is not a Muslim, Beck has said, correctly. But Beck can't help wondering this aloud on his show: "He needlessly throws his hat into the ring to defend the Ground Zero mosque. He hosts Ramadan dinners, which a president can do. But then you just add all of this stuff up—his wife goes against the advice of the advisers, jets to Spain for vacation. What does she do there? She hits up the Alhambra palace mosque. Fine, it's a tourist attraction. But is there anything more to this? Are they sending messages? I don't know. I don't know."

Beck and his friends emphasize that he is driven by principles, not politics. He has been critical of Republicans as well as of Democrats, of George W. Bush as well as of Obama. He says that American citizens who are terrorist suspects should be read their Miranda rights, and he opposes a constitutional amendment that would ban flag burning. His friends object to any hint that Beck has merely fashioned his worldview according to a marketplace that rewards shock, chutzpah, and discord. "If you know Glenn at all, you know he believes every word of what he says," Chris Balfe says. "And he believes it down to the core of who he is."

Beck is also a showman at his core and a workaholic. His insomniac mind spins with ideas for segments and revenue streams (which he will e-mail to his staff at three in the morning). He sleeps little: three, maybe five hours a night if he is lucky, Beck told me. His Mormonism forbids coffee, but he consumes a lot of Diet Coke and chocolate.

He begins his day with a seven thirty meeting with about six or seven writers, researchers, and producers split between the television and radio teams. Beck, who runs the meeting, throws out ideas for the show, and the staff will discuss them. "When he walks in, he has about sixty percent of what he wants to talk about mapped out in his brain," says Steve Burguiere, a Beck radio sidekick who goes by the name Stu. That, Burguiere says, will form the basic kernel of what he will talk about on the air. I asked Burguiere if Beck worked from a script, which made him chuckle. "If we could only get him to work from a script," he said.

Beck is a strenuous cross-promoter. He spoke constantly on the air about his Washington rally before and after the event. He invites viewers and listeners to visit his Web site and, better yet, the Glenn Beck Store (Restoring Honor photograph books can be preordered for thirty-five dollars) and become an "insider extreme" member for premium video and audio links. He recently started a new Web site, the Blaze, which he also mentions on his television and radio shows.

The cross-promotion can be a sore spot at Fox News, particularly for its president, Roger Ailes, who has complained about Beck's hawking his non-Fox ventures too much on his Fox show. Ailes has communicated this to Beck himself and through intermediaries. It goes to a larger tension between Fox News and Beck in what has been a mutually beneficial relationship. Ailes, a former Republican media guru, runs his top-rated cable-news network like a sharp-edged campaign, speaking with a single voice and—ideally—for the benefit solely of Fox News' bottom line.

To some degree, all of Fox News' top opinion personalities have side ventures—speeches, books, radio—that can invite static from the network. In April, for instance, Fox News bosses vetoed a planned appearance by Sean Hannity at a fund-raiser for a Tea Party group in Cincinnati. But more than any other person at Fox News,

Beck operates as a stand-alone entity. He is the only major personality at the network whose office is not at Fox News headquarters in the News Corp building (Mercury is a few blocks down Sixth Avenue). He employs his own publicist, Matthew Hiltzik, a communications consultant who is the son of Beck's agent, George Hiltzik. Beck receives a $2.5 million salary from Fox News, which bumps to $2.7 million next year, the last of the contract. It is a small fraction of Beck's revenues, the bulk of which he brings in from his radio and print deals.

"There is always going to be the person within the organization who may take issue with or doesn't like the way the network is programming certain things," says Cheatwood, the Fox News executive who oversees Beck's show. "I allow for that anywhere. But in terms of the relationship between Fox and Glenn, it's extremely solid."

Ailes, who declined to comment for this article, has generally been supportive of Beck. But he has also been vocal around the network about how Beck does not fully appreciate the degree to which Fox News has made him the sensation he has become in recent months. In the days following Beck's Lincoln Memorial rally, which by Beck's estimate drew a half million people, Ailes told associates that if Beck were still at *Headline News*, there would have been thirty people on the Mall. Fox News devoted less news coverage to the rally than CNN and MSNBC did, which Beck has pointed out himself on the air.

Off-the-record sniping shoots in both directions. You can view some of this as positioning for what could be a contentious contract negotiation. But the friction is evident in many areas. When I mentioned Beck's name to several Fox reporters, personalities, and staff members, it reliably elicited either a sigh or an eye roll. Several Fox News journalists have complained that Beck's antics are embarrassing Fox, that his inflammatory rhetoric makes it difficult for the network to present itself as a legitimate news outlet. Fearful that Beck was becoming the perceived face of Fox News, some network insiders leaked their dissatisfaction in March to the *Washington Post*'s media critic, Howard Kurtz, a highly unusual breach at a place where complaints of internal strains rarely go public.

While Beck's personal ventures and exposure have soared this year, his television ratings have declined sharply—perhaps another factor in the network's impatience. His show now averages 2 million viewers, down from a high of 2.8 million in 2009, according to the Nielsen ratings. And as of September 21, 2010, 296 advertisers have asked that their commercials not be shown on Beck's show (up from 26 in August 2009). Fox also has a difficult time selling ads on *The O'Reilly Factor* and *Fox and Friends* when Beck appears on those shows as a guest. Beck's show is known in the TV sales world as "empty calories," meaning he draws great ratings but is toxic for ad sales. If nothing else, I sensed that people around Fox News have grown weary after months of "It's all about Glenn." I was sitting with Bill Shine, the director of programming, on the Wednesday after the Restoring Honor event, which was held on a Saturday and still drawing analysis in the news media four days later. At the end of a half-hour interview in which Shine spoke well of Beck, a look of slight irritation flashed over his face. He shook his head slightly. "The president of the United States ends the war in Iraq," Shine said, which Obama did the night before in a speech from the Oval Office, "and on Wednesday we're still talking about Glenn Beck."

No one seems to quite know what to make of Beck these days. On *Fox News Sunday* the day after the Restoring Honor gathering, Chris Wallace asked him, "What are you?"

Beck appears conflicted over whether he wants to be the face of Honor Restored or the voice of a Great American Freakout or whether some fusion of the two is possible. He told me that he has enjoyed himself more since the event of August 28, which included no references to contemporary politics. It is not clear if this new tenor is a trend or phase or whether Beck is in the midst of a fundamental transformation. "I'm a work in progress, man," he told me. "I don't know how to make this transition." It has become a nagging preoccupation. "I wrote Sarah Palin a letter last night about two in the morning," Beck said on his radio show in September. "And I said: 'Sarah, I don't know if I'm doing more harm or more good. I don't know anymore.'"

Beck has made a determination in recent months, Cheatwood told me. "I think what he's realizing is you have to be careful not to just be part of the noise. You have to transcend the noise." In the weeks after the Restoring Honor rally, Beck's Fox News show took a decidedly spiritual, historic, and even high-minded tone. But near the end of September, Beck returned to a more accustomed noise level. He railed against the "clear and present danger" of progressive ideology and attacked the Obama administration more savagely than he had in some time, singling out Cass Sunstein, the White House's regulatory czar, as "the most dangerous man in America."

On September 11, I traveled to Anchorage to watch Beck and Palin perform together at a downtown civic center. A woman outside carried a sign calling Beck and Palin "the dream team," while another dismissed them as "lipstick and dipstick."

The crowd was loud and even festive, despite the somber anniversary. Palin spoke first and then introduced Beck. The pair stage-chatted for about twenty minutes before Palin turned over the stage to Beck. He spoke—with chalkboards—for more than an hour.

Sitting in the row behind me was a truck driver named Jerry Cole, who was from Fairbanks and wore an "I ♥ Woodrow Wilson" T-shirt with a slash through the heart. "He was the start of the Progressive era," Cole said of the long-dead president. "He believed that college intellectuals should decide how the world should be run."

Beck's Anchorage show started late—around nine p.m.—and Beck was still speaking as eleven o'clock approached. He kept going, and going, and delivered a stem-winding ending about how George Washington became terrified at the end of his life about doing something that would dishonor himself and his country. I looked around the crowd of about four thousand, and it seemed no one had left. The room was perfectly silent after two hours plus—late on a Saturday night—to hear a self-described "recovering dirtbag" with not a single college credit to his name teach them history.

Sitting in his Mercury Radio Arts office three days later, Beck told me that he, too, noticed the silence and was astounded. "If someone had told me, 'Hey, why don't you tell some history stories at the end, and there will be dead silence,' I'd have said, 'No way.'" Beck has great distrust of success, especially his own. Friends say he is terrified of something going wrong, someone in his audience "doing something stupid" (presumably code for violence). There is a certain boyish disbelief in Beck as he engages in his real-time assessment, often on the air. "I told my wife, 'I can't believe I actually have reporters following me to Alaska,'" he said. (Note: Reporter's wife said the same thing.)

Beck told me that he recently threw away all of his old tapes from his morning-zoo years, so his kids could not hear them. He has no idea what his role is in the political firmament. The notion seems to bore him. His most animated attacks on Obama in the days after the Restoring Honor rally were over his take on the president's religious convictions, which Beck called "a perversion of the Gospel of Jesus Christ as most Christians know it."

He is fragile, on the edge. There is no template for him or for where he is headed. "I have not prepared my whole life to be here," Beck told me from his plush couch, his face turning bright pink. "I prepared my whole life to be in a back alley." I expected him to cry, but he did not.

The Reluctant Kennedy

March 17, 2013

I n early December, Washington's political class was in one of its
episodic ventilations over who would fill the latest round of job
openings. The intrigue of the moment involved Hillary Clinton's
replacement as secretary of state. Susan Rice, the US ambassador to
the United Nations and onetime front-runner, was taking a public
battering, and the fallback candidate, Senator John Kerry, was looking more likely to get the job. This would in turn mean that another
Massachusetts Senate seat would be up for grabs—the third election
since the death of Ted Kennedy in 2009.

In the midst of all that, I was eating lunch at a private club near
the White House at the invitation of Ted Kennedy Jr. As the namesake of the late senator, he was of course entitled under Massachusetts law to slide happily into any available political seat without so
much as leaving the compound to drop off a ballot petition. There
was only one slight problem with this: he lived in Connecticut, not
Massachusetts. But Kennedys have a way of surmounting pesky

barriers like these, and conjecture about Kerry's seat, if it were to become open (which it has), was on the table.

Ted Jr., as he is known, has eager blue eyes and windswept Kennedy hair. He is friendly and solicitous, but his efforts at ingratiating himself come off as more self-taught than natural, a bit too eager, as when, weeks earlier, he marveled at how really great it was to see me. At one point he asked if I had ever been to the family home on Cape Cod. When I said no, he insisted, "Oh, you have to come down sometime." We had never met before.

He speaks in the patrician New England accent and nasal-honking intonations that conjure his father. He kept saying things like "I am entering a new phase of my life" and "I come from a family of public servants," and it was perfectly clear what Ted Jr. had called me here to discuss. After a lifetime of entreaties, many from his father, the oldest son of Edward M. Kennedy was now, at fifty-one, prepared to join the family business. In the musty parlance of his heritage, he was being "called to service."

For someone so incubated in the heat of public life, Kennedy betrayed a surprising transparency, or maybe naïveté, in explaining to me how he had been preparing for this next phase. "I've been cultivating all sorts of friendships and relationships with people who can be helpful," he said. And then he made clear how I came in. He also kept mentioning to me that "my father and brother had always spoken highly of you," which carried a whiff of declaring me "reliable" within the family. (Was I, too, being called to service?) What he envisioned, Ted Jr. said, was "a foundational story" being written about him. "What's this guy like?" he asked. "What's he thinking?"

This was somewhat unusual. When someone decides to "come out" as a politician, it is typically in connection with a specific job— as in, "I will be running for such-and-such." They don't generally say, "I'm being called to service, please write a foundational story about me." My immediate question involved exactly what service Ted Jr. was being called to. And where? Would it be in Massachusetts, where he purchased the former home of his Uncle Jack, behind the main family compound in Hyannis Port? Or in Connecticut, where he lives in the New Haven suburb of Branford with his wife, Kiki, a Yale psychiatrist, and teenage son and daughter (their oldest daughter is a freshman at Wesleyan)? There was also the possibility of an executive appointment from a president who regarded his father as a crucial Senate mentor and kingmaker. Ted Jr. wanted me to know that he was open to that.

Whatever the case, there was some urgency that the foundational story be done soon, presumably to help get his name "in play" for the imminent job openings. We were joined at the table by Dick Keil, a former White House reporter for Bloomberg News who now works for a media consulting company called Purple Strategies, which was cofounded by Steve McMahon, a Democratic strategist/TV pundit/friend of Ted Jr.'s from the old days, when he worked on Ted Sr.'s 1980 presidential campaign. Keil, McMahon, and Ben Binswanger, another friend, who attended Wesleyan with Ted Jr. and later worked for Senator Kennedy, were all helping guide the soon-to-be candidate-for-something through the delicate paces of his "rollout." Ted Jr.'s brother, Patrick, a former congressman from Rhode Island who now lives in New Jersey, was also part of the small advisory team, as was Kiki.

In addition to the whats, whens, and wheres, there was also the matter of who—as in: Who did Ted Jr. think he was? As we talked over lunch about the rollout, wherever it may be rolling, I thought of a famous line inflicted on Ted Sr. during his 1962 Senate campaign by his Democratic primary challenger, Edward J. McCormack Jr. McCormack told his thirty-year-old opponent—the brother of the sitting president—that he would have no chance in that race if his name were Edward Moore instead of Edward Moore Kennedy.

When I started to recall that line, Ted Jr. interjected with the exact quote: "If it was Edward Moore," he said, "your candidacy would be a joke."

In fairness, Ted Jr. is more than two decades older and far more experienced than his father was in 1962. He has been a long-time advocate for the disabled—having lost part of his right leg to bone cancer at age twelve—and his Manhattan-based management-consulting firm, the Marwood Group, employs 130 people. But the Edward Moore line resonates within the family. Patrick Kennedy—who was elected to the Rhode Island legislature at twenty-one and the US House of Representatives at twenty-seven, and who himself once dismissed the US Senate campaign of Scott Brown in Massachusetts as "a joke"—told me that he entered politics "as a Kennedy" but was "still looking for my identity." His brother, on the other hand, "knows where his true compass is," Patrick assured me, deploying another pet family term—"true compass"—that happened to be the title of their father's memoir.

Entire touch-football rosters could be filled with Kennedys who could never have been elected at their tender ages without their last names. In November, Ted's thirty-two-year-old cousin, Joseph Kennedy III—the son of a former US representative, Joseph Kennedy II—became the latest pledge when he won the congressional seat left by Barney Frank, who retired. Even Ted Jr.'s son, Edward Kennedy III, has announced his intention to run for US senator from Massachusetts someday. He was, at the time of his announcement, eleven.

"There is this question with every member of my family," Patrick Kennedy said. "How do we fit into this amazing legacy that we have been given by dint of our birth?" That is not a sentence most people utter. But his point was that simply running for an office because it is available is the family default option, and it's not necessarily the best one.

Patrick did not seek reelection in 2010 and now devotes much of his life to promoting treatment and research for his twin causes, mental illness and brain injuries. He married, moved to New Jersey, and has two children. He has sad green eyes, a big pillow of red hair, and the gawky bearing of an overgrown boy. But he also has the weary voice of someone who could be sixty-five.

Patrick told me he has no regrets about his career choices, but his own life proves his original point: that the family reflex to run early is not for everyone. He has battled depression and alcohol and drug addictions for years, and he admits that the United States Congress was not the best place to wrestle these goblins. "When you grow up in my family, being somebody meant having power, having status," Patrick told me back in 2006, when I was reporting an article for the *Times* not long after police found him disoriented, having crashed his car into a barrier near the Capitol at 2:45 a.m. "The compensations you got were all material and superficial," he said. "I've come to realize, in the last few months, that that life made me feel all alone." After the article ran, Patrick told me his father was furious at him for unburdening himself publicly. "Save that stuff for your shrink, not a reporter," Senator Kennedy said to him.

Ted Jr. is less the unburdening type. He has granted few interviews and he seemed nervous when we talked, or perhaps a bit suffocated by Keil, who was always with us. Keil, whom I first met back in his journalism days, is a friendly and earnest operator who, like many in Washington, is always working. (I ran into him once at the supermarket and teased him about the work Purple Strategies was doing to help BP "reposition" its image after the spill in the Gulf of Mexico. Without missing a beat, Keil unleashed his own gusher, calling BP the "the greatest corporate turnaround story in history" before moving on to the deli counter.) He sat in on all three of my meetings with Ted Jr., monitored a subsequent phone call, and also stayed close by during my meeting with Patrick. He made backup recordings of all of our conversations, which is not unusual for public-relations people to do, but typically happens with high-level subjects, not with someone who has never run for office and wasn't really running for anything now. The aggressive "management" of the story conveyed an impression of both loftiness and hand-holding—or, at worst, of a Not Ready for Prime Time Kennedy being propped up by consultants.

All of that said, there's something innately likable about Ted Jr. People who have known him over the years generally describe a solid, down-to-earth guy who is quite normal, given his royal lineage. And his instinct to become a fully formed human being before answering the "call to service" was admirable. His priority, by all accounts, has always been to raise a family and nurture them as unassumingly as possible (again, for a Kennedy). As he put it, "I pretty much spent half my life trying to resist other people's timetables." Later, when I asked him to elaborate on this, he added: "My father was the single most important person in my life. But in some ways, we all live our lives resisting what our parents want us to become."

In early 1985 Ted Jr. was twenty-three and living in Somerville, Massachusetts, outside Boston. Tip O'Neill, the district's longtime representative, had announced he would retire at the end of his term. This seemed an obvious starter gig, but Ted Jr. was not interested. His thirty-four-year-old cousin, Joe—Robert F. Kennedy's son—ran and won instead. "I never seriously considered that race," Ted Jr. told me. "My father was strongly considering me." Ted Sr. commissioned a poll that came back "a slam dunk for Ted," said Steve McMahon, who was one of the people then running Senator Kennedy's political operation. Ted Jr.'s decision not to run, McMahon said, "was against the advice and counsel of pretty much everyone around him." Senator Kennedy was disappointed, Ted Jr. told me. "He couldn't understand why someone with all the built-in advantages would not take advantage of the opportunity."

Instead, Ted Jr. enrolled in Yale's graduate school of forestry. Beyond setting a course away from politics, Ted Jr. told me that he was also trying to escape a one-dimensional identity as an amputee and advocate. "I did not want to be seen as a professional disabled person," he said.

He gained weight, grew a beard, drank heavily, and invited concern that he was priming himself for another, more darkly familiar Kennedy fate. He indulged in what the *Boston Globe* described as "a playboy-style high life" and "careless social habits." At about the same time, his cousin, William Kennedy Smith, was charged with rape and faced a subsequent trial that showcased the family's history of boozy carousing—with the patriarchal senator in a leadership role.

At twenty-nine, Ted Jr. enrolled himself in a drug-and-alcohol-treatment program in Hartford. He was always reticent and closed off, he said, which he attributed to being a Kennedy. "It was never very easy for me to express my feelings," Kennedy told the *Globe* in 1993, on the eve of his marriage to Kiki. "I think it's a consequence of growing up in my family and having people prying and feeling like somebody's always trying to get something from you," he said. "Then I realized this is no real way to live a life." His priority, he said, was to start a family and be present as a father. "I realized if I messed that up, it would be the most serious mistake of my life," he told me. He has not touched alcohol in more than twenty years, he said, because "it just didn't take much imagination to see the impact that alcohol had on many different people in my family." Ted's mother, Joan Kennedy, has also faced many public struggles with alcoholism over the years.

As other Kennedys passed in and out of office (and rehab), the great mentioners and orchestrators consigned Ted Jr. to the terminal-ambivalence compound. His father encouraged him to open a Boston office of Marwood, his consulting firm, to establish more of a presence in Massachusetts, but Ted Jr. resisted.

Then, in August 2009, Senator Kennedy died of brain cancer, and Ted Jr. delivered a powerful and much-discussed eulogy. "My name is Ted Kennedy Jr.," he told the mourners assembled at the Basilica and Shrine of Our Lady of Perpetual Help in Boston. "Although it hasn't been easy at times to live with this name, I've never been more proud of it than I am today."

The speech's emotional climax was a story of his father's taking him sledding at age twelve. He was trying to adapt to his artificial limb, and the hill was slick and hard to climb. He kept slipping and started to cry. "And he lifted me up in his strong, gentle arms and said something I will never forget," Ted Jr. said. "He said: 'I know you can do it. There is nothing that you can't do. We're going to climb that hill together, even if it takes us all day.'" The eulogy drew a standing ovation and, almost immediately, renewed talk of Ted Jr.'s political future. "A lot of people were asking, 'Where have you been?'" he told me.

Over lunch at the University Club in Washington, I asked him if he had spoken to anyone in the Obama administration about a job. "I can't talk about that," he said, wincing a little. Then he laughed.

"Have you talked to the president?" I asked.

"I can't talk about that," he repeated. His face turned red, which I found refreshing, given how comfortable most politicians are with stonewalling.

Ted Jr. then turned to Keil. "I need to think of a way to respond to this question that is respectful," he said.

"No, you just did respond," I interrupted. "It's okay."

"But I don't want the quote to be 'I can't talk about it.'" He was slightly plaintive at this point.

"But that's what you said," I noted.

Kennedy laughed again. Later, when I returned from the men's room, he said he regretted that he didn't answer that question differently. He wished he could change the quote. To what? "What I should have said," he told me, "was, 'I would be honored to serve.'"

Obama's reelection created a few possibilities for Ted Jr. There were potential jobs in the administration or seats in Congress being vacated by members who would become cabinet officials. The most titillating prospect involved Kerry's seat. "I haven't thought seriously about that possibility," he said. Except he and Keil and Binswanger met on November 13 to discuss the matter at a tavern in Georgetown, then held subsequent sessions with McMahon and Patrick and Kiki. Team Ted told him that changing his official residence from Connecticut to Hyannis Port would be no problem. They all said he could win, and the time was now.

"Political consultants want everyone to run for office," Ted Jr. said. A former Connecticut senator, Christopher Dodd, a close friend of the family, seconded that notion, saying, "They're either telling you, 'You can never win, and you need me,' or 'You can't lose, and you need me.'" Dodd cautioned Kennedy against the Massachusetts race. If Kennedy lost, Dodd told me, it could preclude future runs in Connecticut. "It could look like he's on a shopping spree."

Once again, to the disappointment of others, Ted Jr. decided not to run. Ted Kennedy Jr. running for the US Senate in Massachusetts in 2013 was "as close to a slam dunk as you're going to get in politics," McMahon told me. I wasn't buying this. When I mentioned to Ted Jr. that he would have faced charges of carpetbagging if he ran for Kerry's seat, he took issue. "Yes, I've lived in Connecticut for twenty-five years," he said. "But the idea of calling a Ken-

CITIZENS OF THE GREEN ROOM

nedy a carpetbagger in Massachusetts is like . . ." He did not finish the thought.

There were other issues at play, too, among them Vicki Kennedy, Ted Kennedy's widow. Strains between Vicki and her late husband's sons were no secret. According to a *Boston Globe* article last July, Ted Jr. and Patrick Kennedy were convinced that their stepmother was mismanaging their father's legacy, in particular the construction in Boston of the $71 million Edward M. Kennedy Institute for the United States Senate. Vicki Kennedy declined to comment for the *Globe* article (as well as for this one), and when I raised the subject of her with Ted Jr., he looked as if he would rather be cleaning an oven. "I never spoke to her about it," he said of his decision not to run in Massachusetts. On the subject of Vicki generally, he said in a separate e-mail: "Vicki was a great source of love and support for my father, and she is working hard to ensure that my father's memory and legacy are properly honored."

Another argument against the "slam dunk" theory: While Ted Jr. was likable and had a good story to tell, he did not strike me as a candidate who would be ready from Day One, given the scrutiny he would endure. He could be stumbling and tentative. My mind jumped to Caroline Kennedy and her ill-fated effort to take over Hillary Clinton's Senate seat in New York. Other than Ted Sr., no member of the Kennedy family has been on the ballot for statewide office in Massachusetts since John F. Kennedy in 1958. Kennedys are always mentioned as potential eight-hundred-pound gorillas in statewide campaigns, but none ever jump. It's safer that way, not to risk being the one who loses and messes up the mystique of invincibility, such as it is.

"The Kennedy mystique is more of a hologram at this point," said Jon Keller, a longtime political analyst in Massachusetts. "You can see it sometimes, but it's not really there in any meaningful way."

Ted Jr. told me that turning away from the Massachusetts option allowed him to "mentally cross a bridge." "I think for me to go into politics with the name Ted Kennedy Jr. was going to be difficult enough," he said. To do it in the state his father represented for nearly forty-seven years would possibly be too much.

In our last discussion, I asked Ted Jr. if he had ever been in therapy. "I think it's very healthy," he said, and then he added an endearing non-answer that I took to be a yes: "I've done a lot of thinking, okay?"

It was early March, and we were on the phone. He seemed more animated and relaxed than when we last met. "I've had a lot to think about in my life," he said. "I've been through a lot." No doubt it all had to be a handful. From what I could tell, he had managed it admirably, raised a nice family, avoided scandal and embarrassment, and seemed committed now to "making a contribution."

I had been pressing Ted on his timing, trying to get an answer to whether this "coming out" was part of some grand plan. He said he had a "general plan, and I kind of stuck to it." I relayed to him something Steve McMahon told me earlier—that he, McMahon, found it poignant that Ted never responded to his father's wish that he run for office when he was still alive. "But now that Senator Kennedy's gone," McMahon said, "it's almost like Ted's responding to his father's call from above."

I asked Ted if he agreed with this, the overly poetic construction aside. He did, he said, and took it further. "All children want to please their parents," Ted said. "I know it would have pleased my father for me to have had political success when he was still alive. But I think in many ways, now that he is no longer alive, that's really freed me up."

That, as much as anything, would seem like the foundational story.

The Patience of Jeb:
While Others Talk of the
Presidency, Bush Focuses
on Florida and Family

February 23, 2003

J eb Bush is talking, as he often does, about family.

"Although it is an intensely private—and at times painful—
matter, you should know that I am rededicating myself to being a
better father and husband," the governor says. He is giving his second inaugural address under a crystalline sky on the steps of Florida's Old Capitol. The crowd of three thousand includes several
people wearing "Jeb Bush for President in 2008" buttons.

The subtext is lost on no one. His twenty-five-year-old daughter, Noelle, is on the stage, on a one-day leave from her court-ordered
drug treatment program in Orlando. She is accompanied by a drug
counselor. "I realize that any sense of fulfillment I have from this
event is meaningless unless they, too, can find fulfillment in their
lives," Bush continues, his voice quivering.

He is the Bush with the angst gene, who seems to labor through
even his pinnacle moments. His capacity for public tears is impres-
sive even by the weepy standards of the Bush family. He cried four

times at his inaugural events last month—one fewer than he did during *Forrest Gump*.

It is, or should be, such a sweet scene. America's Little Brother, decisively reelected, gets sworn in on the same Bible his brother and father used in Washington. George and Bar sit point-'n'-waving at the front of the stage. Four F-15s scream overhead, and a National Guard unit fires nineteen cannon blasts. George P. Bush, Jeb's twenty-six-year-old son and the program's master of ceremonies, talks like he's already in Congress. The forty-first president introduces Jeb. The forty-third president couldn't make it, but he's a busy man.

But it's never so simple with family dynasties. This is mercilessly true for John Ellis "Jeb" Bush.

Bush, fifty, is best known for the melodramas that bubble around him. He is a shy public man who seems destined to suffer in the open. He is the Bush who has acknowledged marital strife, who cries while discussing his daughter's drug problems on the *Today* show—the same show that repeatedly broadcast her mug shot after her arrest on drug charges—whose wife's ill-fated Paris shopping spree made her a Leno punch line, and whose handsome oldest son is a *People* magazine idol. And this doesn't include the famous family Jeb Bush was born into—or, for that matter, the infamous election he was thrust into.

In the Bush family shorthand, Jeb was the anointed one: the driven big-thinker who started kindergarten a year early and graduated from the University of Texas in two and a half years. He has succeeded by any measure: the first Republican to win reelection as Florida's governor. Some fans call him "Bush 44," kidding, sort of. (George P. is "Bush 45.") He might be the most closely watched US politician outside Washington.

He cherishes these subtexts like gum surgery. Friends say Jeb Bush wants nothing more than to be left alone.

"He probably has as complex a situation to deal with as anyone in public office I've ever seen," says John Thrasher, a Tallahassee lobbyist and former statehouse speaker. He is referring to Jeb's web of public expectations and private circumstances.

To Jeb Bush, the governance of Florida is a precious space of his own authority, blissfully apart from everything else. "Florida, Florida, Florida," he says, declaring his focus. This is how he steers conversations away from national matters, especially those that concern his brother. This is smart politics, assuring everyone that his priority is his current job. But there's also a sense that Bush is protecting a refuge.

A pre-inaugural barbecue in Miami is billed as a chance for Bush to mingle with his hometown admirers. But the governor spends most of his time in a VIP tent. When he comes out to work a quick rope line, his supporters, per custom, urge him to run for president. "Florida, Florida, Florida," he says in response to another question about whether he will.

Talking about his presidential plans, Bush says, "is like talking about whatever that group is from outer space." He is referring to the Raelians, the pro-cloning cult that has ties to Florida, naturally. "It's weird," Bush says of running for president. "I never think about it."

He shakes hands with a man in a yarmulke, one in a wheelchair, and another in an Eminem shirt. Several people wear "Jeb!" and "I ♥ Hooters" stickers, which are being slapped on zealously by volunteers (presumably unaffiliated).

Bush is six-feet-four and slightly heavyset with the beginnings of jowls. He lumbers from group to group, switching from English to Spanish. Bush hugs everyone he gets close to, or as best he can manage from behind a waist-high steel barrier. It's as close as he'll come to being a wade-into-the-crowd pol.

"You can understand the enormous comfort level he has with being governor," says Lanny Griffith, a Republican lobbyist and longtime friend. In Florida, Griffith says, "he doesn't have to have everything analyzed in terms of his brother or his dad."

Jeb Bush can be warm and approachable. But compared with the Georges, he keeps a discernible distance. He almost never grants face-to-face interviews and has particular disdain for the national media. They focus, inevitably, on his daughter, his wife, his brother, his father, 2000, or 2008.

Or worse, what Jeb deplores as "navel-gazing" themes, a powerful allergy in the Bush family.

Never Florida, Florida, or Florida. He declined to be interviewed for this article, though a spokesman suggested questions by e-mail, the governor's preferred medium—Bush gives out his Internet address to crowds (Jeb@Jeb.org) and invites citizens to write.

In dealing with the media, e-mail suits the governor's need for control. He picks what he wants to answer, can edit freely, and cc whom he wishes. E-mail is also easy to ignore.

The *Washington Post*'s trial e-mail to Bush concerns e-mail itself: When did he start using it? How often does he use it? What kinds of business does he use it for? It seems a harmless way to open a conversation. And Bush answers within an hour.

> Thank you for writing. I started using email post 1994 but have been an active user since then. I use it now to keep me connected to friends and constituents. I learn from email from folks. I discount the organized email campaigns but I am respectful of the cause. I don't let the press go around our process (once and a while journalists get around them :)) It is

a huge productivity tool that allows me to be focused on the little things that are important all the while I stayed focused on my larger agenda. Happy New Year.

Jeb Bush

In three follow-up e-mails (which Bush also answers promptly), the governor reveals: He has three e-mail accounts, receives two hundred to three hundred a day on Jeb@Jeb.org, and reads most of them. He guesses that 25 percent of the e-mails come from colleagues, 50 percent from constituents, 10 percent from family and friends, and 15 percent from junk mail and list mail. The risk, he says, is in relying too much on e-mail, at the expense of face-to-face nuance. "There is always [the] threat of invading family time!" he writes.

He likes talking about e-mail. But when questions veer into other areas, the door closes. "I am skipping all of the questions," he writes. "I apologize." National attention, he reiterates, is a distraction. "My interest is Florida, Florida, Florida," he writes, and the e-mail proceeds in one long paragraph that concludes:

> If you want to write an article about career service reform, I can lend a hand so long as it is not about me. If you are interested in how a state can reduce drug use, I am interested. You might be interested in how governments are embarking on major technology projects, in which case you might want to look at what we are doing. Did you know that we are the first state to outsource the hr function of government? No profiles.

Jeb Bush

Jeb Bush can be easy to annoy.

"You don't have to do a lot to get under his skin," says US Representative Kendrick Meek (D-Fla.), a former state legislator who clashed memorably with Bush. Three years ago, Meek and a colleague refused to leave the governor's office until Bush met with them to discuss a plan to eliminate race-based admissions preferences at state colleges. "Kick their asses out!" Bush snapped. It was not clear if Bush was referring to the legislators or the gathering press. Either way, film rolled and great TV ensued.

People close to Bush often feel protective of him. His political friends—often the same ones who say it's futile to get to know him too well—are also quick to profess loyalty. He projects vulnerability, with a mopey posture and fleshy face that seems to cry out for caretaking. He is the Bush with soft eyes—not small and squinty like the Georges' or bugged like Barbara's.

"Jeb is the most gifted and talented person any of us have been around," says one former aide who asked not to be identified. "We would run through walls for him. And yet there's this faraway sadness about Jeb you can't miss."

"Jebby is a deep, sensitive kid with lots of compassion and love in his heart," his father wrote in a diary entry in 1971 that was published in a book of the former president's letters. "But I worry that he may take on some crazy idea."

He is a proud mama's boy who was an infant when his next oldest sibling, Robin, died of leukemia at three. Barbara Bush writes in her memoir that after Robin's death, "I devoted my time to our children, spending every single moment with Jebby, and then with Georgie when he came home from school."

The six-and-a-half-year age difference between the Bush brothers precluded serious intimacy or rivalry. George W. was away at school for much of Jeb's childhood. As adults, they mostly communicated through their parents, or at family events.

When reporters sought comment for their Bush brother stories during their simultaneous campaigns for governor, George and Jeb were always blandly deferential—Jeb saying how "proud" he was of George, and George saying that "Jeb is a good man."

There were some exceptions. At the 1996 Republican convention, Jeb told a reporter for the *St. Petersburg Times* about the time George W. was "caught finger painting with something other than his fingers." (It is not clear how old the president was at the time of the finger-painting episode.)

George W. calls Jeb my "big little brother" during appearances (Jeb is five inches taller), and Jeb dutifully plays the goofy sidekick. He introduces George as "my older, smarter, and wiser brother."

Like George W., Jeb loves to tout his admiration for his mother—which is also smart politics, given her popularity—but in a way that can occasionally be treacly. At his inaugural prayer breakfast, Jeb turns to his mother, shakes his head, and lowers his voice. "When I came into the world and woke up, there I was, lying right next to Barbara Bush."

He was not as mischievous as George W., but could be bold and unpredictable. "Jebby is going to need some help I am sure," his father wrote in 1971. "He is a free and independent spirit and I don't want him to get totally out of touch with the family."

Like his brother and father, Bush attended Phillips Academy in Andover, Massachusetts. Jeb struggled with his course work, missed Texas, and experimented with marijuana. He met his future wife as an exchange student in the central Mexican city of León during his senior year. His devotion to Columba Garnica Gallo was avid and obvious from the start. It was also of great concern to his parents. "How I worry about Jeb and Columba," Barbara Bush wrote in a diary entry. "Does she love him?"

Jeb married Columba on February 23, 1974, in the University of Texas chapel. Columba was twenty. Jeb was twenty-one, the first of the Bush children to wed.

They eventually settled in Miami, where Jeb would begin a lucrative career as a real estate developer and become active in local Republican circles. As a pugnacious candidate for governor in 1994—his first run for elected office—Bush called himself "a head-banging conservative" and expressed fondness for the TV show *American Gladiators*. Women on welfare, he said, "should be able to get their life together and find a husband." He spoke of "blowing up" state agencies. In response to a question about what his administration would do to help African-Americans, Bush's answer included the memorable words "probably nothing."

A firestorm ensued, one of many "distractions" that Bush would complain about during his campaign against Governor Lawton Chiles. Another involved comparisons to his father, with one theory positing that Jeb's brashness was a clumsy attempt to forge his own political identity.

Then there was the unforeseen distraction: George W. Bush decided to run for governor of Texas, even though Jeb was assumed to be the Bush most likely to succeed his father in the family spotlight. In a show of pique, Jeb complained that the Bush brother act would render their campaigns "a cute *People* magazine story."

Except that Jeb lost, George W. won, and Jeb's *People* magazine story was just starting.

During the 1994 campaign, a reporter asked Columba Bush the name of the Spanish-language book she was reading. "It is called *Secrets About Men That Every Woman Should Know*," she said. "We've been together twenty years and you stay that way by keeping the romance going."

In fact, their marriage was falling apart. By Jeb's admission, he had neglected his family. Columba's unease with public life had been clear during the campaign. She once complained within earshot of reporters that she "didn't ask for this."

Following his defeat, Bush underwent what he called a "personal transformation" that included a reevaluation of his political, spiritual, and family life. Raised an Episcopalian, he began taking classes in the Catholic faith, Columba's religion. He converted to Roman Catholicism in 1996.

He started a conservative foundation, worked with minority groups, and began using words like "compassionate" in speeches. He ran for governor again in 1998 and won.

Even with his softer oratory, Bush blowtorched his way into Tallahassee. "A lot of people approach public policy as problem solvers," says US Representative Tom Feeney (R-Fla.), a former statehouse speaker and Bush's running mate in 1994. "And Jeb wants to solve problems. But he truly wants to do it in the most conservative way possible."

He introduced a host of what he called "BHAGs"—Big Hairy Audacious Goals, a notion coined by leadership guru Jim Collins, author of *Built to Last* and *Good to Great*. Bush urged his staff to set BHAGs in areas such as education, where he became the first governor to introduce a statewide school voucher plan.

He hired driven, policy-oriented aides, usually under forty years old, to better endure his round-the-clock demands. Bush can be a headbanging micromanager.

At an open house at the governor's mansion after his inauguration, Bush instructed a young aide on where to stand to ensure that the receiving line moved efficiently.

"He has nineteen hands on both arms and is involved in every phase of what everyone is doing," says Tom Slade, the former chairman of the Florida Republican Party.

"Jeb once made the comment that he loved vacationing in Kennebunkport in the summertime," says Feeney. "You know what his reason was? Because it's the place in the country where the sun comes up first. So when it's five thirty, when he's on his e-mail talking to his staff down in Florida, he can watch the sun come up."

He questions relentlessly and disputes small points. "He seems to know exactly what you don't want him to ask you," says Mac Stipanovich, a Tallahassee lobbyist and longtime associate. He'll bring up an obscure similar proposal that failed three years earlier in another state.

"If you think all you have to do is walk in there and slap him on the back, he'll eat your lunch."

His staff, while loyal, tends to turn over quickly. He can be excruciating to negotiate with. "He absolutely will not compromise until he is backed into a corner," says Tom Rossin, a former Democratic leader in the Florida Senate. "You have a sense that he [Jeb] needs to prove something, that he has a chip on his shoulder."

But Bush has a stubbornness that can seem born of a righteous crusade. In his inaugural address, he fantasizes about the government buildings of Tallahassee becoming "empty of workers." The buildings, he says, would become "silent monuments to a time when government played a larger role than it deserved."

Bush is bored with incremental progress. The Florida constitution mandates that this must be his last term. He is a man in a terrific hurry.

At the inaugural ball, there is a running slide show that plays over the $100-a-ticket "black tie and blue jeans gala." The slides reveal the governor in a series of leaderly settings—looking stern at a meeting, laughing amid a cluster of racially diverse children.

But the slide that draws the most notice is one of Bush collapsed over his laptop. He is asleep, or pretending to be. It suits the recurring message: Governor Bush is chronically logged on.

Columba Bush was on Capitol Hill recently in her role as spokeswoman for the National Center on Addiction and Substance Abuse. She is five-feet-two, has perfect red lipstick, and, battling a cold, is trailed by the faint essence of Hall's cherry lozenges. She is listening to Joseph A. Califano, the former secretary of health, education, and welfare, who is addressing a news conference in the Russell Senate Office Building. Columba Bush, who will speak next, sits perfectly still.

Califano is listing factors that make young women susceptible to drug and alcohol abuse. He mentions high-stress environments, big life transitions. Parents need to be closely involved with their children, he says. They need to be attuned to warning signs.

Columba Bush walks slowly to the lectern when she is introduced. She reads in thickly accented English, appearing uneasy. She never looks up and doesn't mention Noelle.

After she speaks, a reporter asks if her daughter's plight has been exacerbated by being part of a political family. "Absolutely," she says, starting to elaborate, then stopping.

She has rarely spoken to the press since June 1999, when she was fined by US customs agents for not declaring $19,000 in clothes and jewelry she bought in Paris. "I did not ask to join a famous family," she said at the time while apologizing. "I simply wanted to marry the man I loved."

Bush considered not running for a second term last year after Noelle was caught trying to buy Xanax with a fake prescription. It was discussed seriously for a few months within his family, sources close to both Jeb and Columba Bush say. But that was ruled out, largely because Jeb was so attached to his job.

When she is asked last week if her husband came close to not running, Columba Bush gives a firm answer. "No," she says. "He always wanted to run."

They never talk about politics, Columba has said, and while many political couples say this, Columba's detachment from her husband's political self is striking.

No one can understand a marriage from the outside, but the

occasional tidbit escapes about the Bushes. Jeb has volunteered that Columba is the only woman he has ever slept with. They attend church and pray together. They go out for Mexican food.

Their three children are all grown and out of the house—the youngest, Jebbie, nineteen, is a freshman at the University of Texas.

The governor tries to be home by six thirty p.m. and returns to work afterward, often via e-mail or phone. He holds policy meetings on Saturdays and plays golf early Sunday mornings.

They have a black lab named Marvin and a Siamese cat named Sugar. Sugar reportedly sleeps on the governor each night. But Jeb disputes this, and it is a matter of enough import that he breaks his silence.

"Jeez," the governor writes in an e-mail. "Sugar sleeps on a red blanket at Colu and my feet every night.

"This is going to be quite a profile. I am not worth it."

He ignores a follow-up question.

Bush has made "strengthening the family" a signature BHAG of his second term. "It is my ambitious goal to provide the catalyst, in small ways and large, that will bring our families together," he says in his inaugural address. "I, for one, intend to begin with my own family."

"I wasn't saying that I'm a horrible dad," Bush told reporters after the ceremony. But Noelle Bush's drug problems and Columba's discomfort with public life bring questions about Jeb's priorities.

On the day Noelle was arrested last year, people wondered how he could adhere to his existing schedule. Or why he wasn't with his daughter in court last October, when she was sentenced to ten days in jail after crack cocaine was found in her shoe at her drug treatment center. Jeb said he stayed away so it wouldn't appear that he was trying to influence the judge.

"I think he has his arms around his family situation," says Al Cardenas, the chairman of the Florida Republican Party and a longtime Bush ally. "But you can't say he spends as much time as he'd like to. There's no doubt when you live that intensely to serve others, you have to constantly balance things. You have to sacrifice."

Whatever strain his family has placed on Bush, a former aide says, he suffers alone. He prefers realms—such as government— where he can achieve tangible results.

He has convened a panel of advisers to make suggestions about strengthening marriages. "Real-life family situations are messy and gray," the former aide says. "So I think Jeb prefers talking about family challenges in terms of public policy."

Last Saturday at 12:43 p.m., before embarking on a trade mission to Spain, Jeb Bush responds to a final e-mail from the *Post*. The seriousness of his marital problems had been overstated, he writes. "I worked very hard to get elected in 1994 and had to spend too much time away from home. There were no marital difficulties beyond the normal." He says he spends more time with his wife as governor than he did before.

"I still work hard, maybe too hard, but I organize my life better to hang out with Columba. I stay in regular touch with my kids. I wish we could do more things together. When we are all together is when I am the most happy, by far!"

By Jeb Bush's rendering, the picture is clean. He loves his job, he loves his family. The melodramas and the subtexts are a media invention.

"You are very correct about my views on navel-gazing," Bush says, concluding his e-mail, fully engaged, albeit facelessly.

Pressure Cooker:
Andrew Card Has the Recipe
for Chief of Staff Down Pat

January 5, 2005

Andrew Card is talking about his kitchen. "I know my kitchen really well, as evidenced by my rotund being," Card says, patting his belly. "I know where the oven is and I know where the microwave is and I know where the sink is and I know where the refrigerator is and the freezer and the cupboards and the table and the chairs."

Card, fifty-seven, is sprawled on the couch of his West Wing office, describing the kitchen from his mind's eye. It is from here that the White House chief of staff organizes the nation's most potent workplace and man-hours. Like his boss, Card is an aggressively lowfalutin character. He is the longest-serving chief of staff in forty-six years, yet he reminds people that he toiled many years at a McDonald's and spent one summer as a garbage collector. "I'm not a very smart person," Card says. "I have to work really hard at remembering things." Which explains the deceptively prosaic tour of the Cards' Arlington kitchen. Card rarely takes notes. He does not make to-do lists or scrawl reminders to himself on Post-its. Instead, he keeps much of the Bush White House in his head or in his kitchen. This is where it gets eccentric for everyman Andy Card.

Card is a student of memory. He practices a technique pioneered by Matteo Ricci, a sixteenth-century Italian Jesuit. Ricci, who did missionary work in China, introduced the notion of a "memory palace" to Confucian scholars. The "memory palace" is a structure of the mind, to be furnished with mnemonic devices. Ricci might construct an imaginary palace room for each of his students— filled with furniture and shelves to represent aspects of that student (a painting to express his appearance, a shelf on which to array his scholastic record).

Memory is central to a chief of staff's job. He must possess enough instant knowledge to execute the president's minute-to-minute pursuits, be it macro (his agenda) or micro (when he's due for a haircut). Brad Blakeman, a former White House scheduler, says it's not uncommon to have someone ask where the president will be on a certain date three months in the future and have Card answer precisely. "He knew the president's schedule a lot better than me," Blakeman says, "and I was the scheduler."

While Ricci used a palace, castle, or other elaborate edifice, Card's palace is his mental kitchen. Every Monday morning when he arrives at the White House, Card performs the ritual of "cleaning my kitchen."

"I view my job as being responsible for the president to have everything he needs to do his job," Card says. "So when I clean my kitchen, it's really about anticipating what it is the president will have to do, what kind of help he will need to do it, and when it has to be done."

When tackling matters of top priority, Card stands at the stove, working his "front and back burners." Intelligence reform is cooking this morning. He needs to call several people: 9/11 Commission chairmen Tom Kean and Lee Hamilton, Representatives Duncan

Hunter and James Sensenbrenner, and House Speaker Dennis Hastert. They are "on my right front burner," he says.

"Then I shift gears to my left front burner, which is second most important," Card says. He will help the president hire a Cabinet secretary, then move to his right rear burner (hiring White House staff for the second term). "I do that all in my kitchen," Card says. "Now the things I want to put off for a long time, I put in the freezer. But then I can go to my freezer and generally remember things that I put there a long time ago." He will store matters that were resolved or tabled yesterday in a cupboard.

"If you go see Andy at his desk, it looks like he's not doing anything," says Andrew Natsios, a close friend of Card's who is head of the Agency for International Development. "It's almost empty, there's no paper anywhere. But he's created this whole system in his head with this mind discipline of his."

So much institutional history and memory of both Bush administrations are stored in Andy Card's kitchen. He has been as entrenched in Bushworld as the family furniture. He is chronically there—as in there in the room, in the meeting, in the photo, on the Sunday shows. Card was there, next to Bush One when he vomited on the Japanese prime minister; there in the Oval when Bushes One and Two choked up together on Inauguration Day 2001; and there, in Bush Two's ear as he read *My Pet Goat* on 9/11.

He wakes at 4:20 each morning, commonly stays at work until ten p.m., and spends most weekends at his office or at Camp David with the POTUS.

He wears his fatigue proudly, advertises his minimal sleep regimen, mentions what bad shape he's in, how he drinks too much coffee and that he needs to spend more time with family—three grown children, four grandchildren, and wife, Kathleene, a Methodist minister, whom he met when both were in the fifth grade. In

2003, he passed out during a three-mile run with the president in Crawford, Texas.

Does his fatigue make it harder for Card to remember things? He shakes his head: "My kitchen is in order," Card says, "though I may not be."

Card loves to doodle, a rare indulgence of paper for him. "I am almost always doodling," he says. He can look at old doodles and recall where he was when he drew them, what meeting he was in, and what was decided. They are his de facto notes.

Card pulls out a doodle from the top drawer of his desk: It is a pencil sketch of a Canadian flag, which Card drew in a meeting during the president's recent visit to Canada. Beneath the flag is a network of circles, jots, lines, and warped squares. It is the driveway, of his summer house in Poland, Maine: "Here's the house," he says, leading a tour of the doodle. Here's the rock garden, the drainage scheme, and a toolshed that he's thinking about building.

"Doodling helps my thinking," Card says, a corollary to creating pictures in his mind. "It helps me to visualize that which I'm listening to."

As Card describes his "kitchen," he is cagey about his front-burner items. "I'm not gonna show you everything I have in my kitchen," Card says. But when less pressing topics arise, Card offers a window into the size and complexity of his kitchen.

An eager storyteller, Card can take a long time with his explanations and descriptions. He is at times compelled to show you every crumb in his cupboard.

Ask Card, for instance, how he chose the exact words he whispered to President Bush on the morning of September 11, 2001: "A second plane hit the second tower. America is under attack."

"Very carefully," Card says, noting that he wanted to give the president maximum information without giving him a chance to respond, avoiding a public conversation. "I wanted to pass on two facts and one editorial comment and then back away."

The rest of his answer—unloaded from Card's 9/11 cupboard—takes twenty minutes.

Card describes the vivid smell of dead fish at the Sarasota golf resort where the president ate dinner on the night of September 10. Walking back to the hotel, Card saw a car parked in a way that blocked a narrow alley. He asked an advance man to remove it.

The next morning, Card became concerned that there was a misspelled word on the blackboard behind the spot where the president would read. The word—Card doesn't say what it was—"was adroitly covered by a book cover," he says, adding that it was written in red, orange, and blue chalk. Bush learned that the first plane had hit the North Tower as he stood at the door of the classroom, just before he was to begin reading. "We're standing at the door, I'm standing to the president's left," Card says. "The president was holding a doorknob in his right hand."

Card first learned the discipline of Matteo Ricci as a high school junior. He was attending a talk given by "some kind of memory expert" at a Rotary Club near his home in Holbrook, Massachusetts, a middle-class suburb south of Boston. The man quizzed the fifty or sixty people in the audience about personal details—their names, where they lived, and so forth. Then, without notes, he repeated all the information back to them.

Card approached the speaker afterward and asked if he had a photographic memory. "No, no, no," the man said. "I work really hard at this." He explained the Riccian principle of linking facts to visual mnemonics. "He said, take something that you know really well and then associate something with it," Card says. "And I began doing that over the course of time."

Card studied engineering at the University of South Carolina while working at a McDonald's in Columbia (rising as high as night manager). As he manned counters, Card tried to calculate the total price of an order before the clerk could punch it into the cash register. "It really turned into great sport," Card says.

Another McDonald's episode bears mention: Once, when money went missing from the cash register, Card threatened to fire everyone unless it was returned. The cash reappeared and the crew kept their jobs. But Card was serious about his threat, and the episode reflects the resolve behind Card's soft edges, a combination that has served him in politics.

Card's father, a small-town lawyer and unsuccessful candidate for the state legislature, was active in Holbrook politics. Card was elected to the Massachusetts legislature in 1974, a Republican moderate who favored abortion and gay rights. "He was always very supportive of the things that the Bush administration has been hostile to, like gay rights," says Representative Barney Frank (D-Mass.), who served with Card in the legislature.

Through his link to George H. W. Bush, Card joined the intergovernmental affairs office of the Reagan White House in 1983. He remained close to Vice President Bush, eventually taking a senior position on his presidential campaign in 1987. He worked closely with Bush's sharp-edged political guru Lee Atwater. "Lee always thought Andy was his guy," says Ed Rogers, a Republican lobbyist and close Atwater associate. "But everyone thinks that Andy is their guy. That's the beauty of him. He has assumed the role of chief therapist in the Bush camp." Rogers also dubs Card "a human Alka-Seltzer" who offsets the acid of clashing egos, ideologies, and agendas in a political enterprise.

He was deputy chief of staff in the Bush administration under John Sununu and gained a reputation for his forthright and pleasant manner, especially when performing unpleasant tasks. "We always said that if we ever got fired, we wanted Andy to do it," said Bush press secretary Marlin Fitzwater.

C ard's signature firing occurred in 1990, when he had to tell his own boss, Sununu, that it was time to leave. There is a vivid scene in Fitzwater's memoir, *Call the Briefing*, in which Card, White House counsel Boyden Gray, and Bush family friend Dorrance Smith nervously enter Sununu's office after the president concluded that it was time for him to go. Smith and Gray hold back, leaving Card to deliver the news. "This kind of thing always winds up falling to Andy," Fitzwater says.

"Hearing bad news from Andy is like hearing bad news from Dudley Do-Right," says Rogers. "You can't shoot the messenger with Andy. And this is a town where the messenger gets shot all the time."

The story of how Card became George W. Bush's chief of staff is, frankly, long. At least it is in Card's retelling, which takes twenty-five minutes.

"This is one of those cupboards you don't open until somebody says, 'Hey, where are those string beans?'" Card says.

Herein, the string beans:

Card tells of discussions he had "that were not very directioned" with Rove, future commerce secretary Don Evans, and Bush.

And how, just before he began working on the campaign, Card took his wife to Bermuda after she graduated from divinity school.

And a conversation Card had with Bush on the night of his acceptance speech in Philadelphia in which Bush told him to "keep your dance card clear."

And the conversation Bush had with Card in Boston on the night of Bush's first debate with Gore ("when Gore had a little too much orange makeup on"). They were on a boat ferrying them from Logan Airport across Boston Harbor (not as polluted as before, "thanks to the good leadership of the former president Bush").

And how, over breakfast, an annoyed Kathleene Card asked her husband, "Are you married to me or George W. Bush?"

And then the phone rang and it was George W. Bush, who told Card to call his gubernatorial chief of staff, Clay Johnson.

And so Card flew to Austin and met with Johnson, who had a bunch of notebooks marked "transition" on his desk, and Card figured they wanted him to run the transition, which Card calls "a pain-in-the-neck job," but one he'd be willing to do.

And then, on his way out of Texas, Card visited the elder Bush in Houston, where he began to believe they were considering him for "The Big One," as he called the chief-of-staff job. (Card arrived in Houston at nine, and the Bushes were out when he arrived. Barbara Bush arrived home at eleven, the former president at midnight. "I woke up early the next day. I made the bed. I showered. I shaved. I got all dressed.")

And then Card flew to Tampa to meet the younger Bush, who was holding a rally in Jacksonville. But Card's flight was delayed and he missed Bush before the candidate went to sleep. ("Karen Hughes was there, her son Robert. Got a bite to eat late at night in the hotel.")

Next morning he met with Bush, who mentioned "The Big One," and the rest, as they say, is in another cupboard.

"Sorry I talked so much," Card says.

Shortly after Bush took office, Mack McLarty, Bill Clinton's chief of staff, and Ken Duberstein, who held the same post under Reagan, co-hosted a dinner for Card at McLarty's Kalorama home. Several former White House chiefs of staff attended—or, as McLarty puts it, "those of us who have held the office of chief javelin catcher in the White House." Guests included McLarty's neighbor Donald Rumsfeld (chief of staff under Gerald Ford), Donald Regan (Reagan), and Samuel Skinner (Bush One).

In a toast at the dinner, McLarty told of how Reagan chief of staff Howard Baker called him when Clinton took office to say, "Congratulations, you just got the worst job in Washington."

Father First, Senator Second: For Rick Santorum, Politics Could Hardly Get More Personal

April 18, 2005

In his Senate office, on a shelf next to an autographed baseball, Senator Rick Santorum keeps a framed photo of his son Gabriel Michael, the fourth of his seven children. Named for two archangels, Gabriel Michael was born prematurely, at twenty weeks, on October 11, 1996, and lived two hours outside the womb.

Upon their son's death, Rick and Karen Santorum opted not to bring his body to a funeral home. Instead, they bundled him in a blanket and drove him to Karen's parents' home in Pittsburgh. There, they spent several hours kissing and cuddling Gabriel with his three siblings, ages six, four, and one and a half. They took photos, sang lullabies in his ear, and held a private Mass.

"That's my little guy," Santorum says, pointing to the photo of Gabriel, in which his tiny physique is framed by his father's hand. The senator often speaks of his late son in the present tense. It is a rare instance in which he talks softly.

He and Karen brought Gabriel's body home so their children could "absorb and understand that they had a brother," Santorum says. "We wanted them to see that he was real," not an abstraction, he says. Not a "fetus," either, as Rick and Karen were appalled to see him described—"a twenty-week-old fetus"—on a hospital form. They changed the form to read "twenty-week-old baby."

Karen Santorum, a former nurse, wrote letters to her son during and after her pregnancy. She compiled them into a book, *Letters to Gabriel*, a collection of prayers, Bible passages, and a chronicle of the prenatal complications that led to Gabriel's premature delivery. At one point, her doctor raised the prospect of an abortion, an "option" Karen ridicules. *Letters to Gabriel* also derides "pro-abortion activists" and decries the "infanticide" of "partial-birth abortion," the legality of which Rick Santorum was then debating in the Senate. The book reads, in places, like a call to action.

"When the partial-birth abortion vote comes to the floor of the US Senate for the third time," Karen writes to Gabriel, "your daddy needs to proclaim God's message for life with even more strength and devotion to the cause."

The issue came up again the following spring. Santorum, a Pennsylvania Republican, appeared on the Senate floor with oversize illustrations of fetuses in various stages of delivery. He described the process by which a physician "brutally kills" a child "by thrusting a pair of scissors into the back of its skull and suctioning its brains out." He asked that a five-year-old girl be admitted to the visitors' gallery, though Senate rules forbid children under six. "She is very interested in the subject," Santorum said, explaining that the girl's mother had been a candidate for a late-term abortion when doctors advised her during her pregnancy that the child was unlikely to survive.

Senator Barbara Boxer objected, saying it would be "rather exploitive to have a child present in the gallery" during such a debate.

Santorum relented, bemoaning Boxer's objection as proof that "we have coarsened the comity of this place."

The same has been said of Santorum. In so many words, or facial gestures.

Senator Mary Landrieu, the Louisiana Democrat, grimaces. "You couldn't quote what I'd have to say about him," she says.

Boxer (D-Calif.) says he has a knack for "becoming remarkably harsh and personal during debates."

Former Democratic senator Bob Kerrey once wondered whether Santorum is "Latin for asshole." Teresa Heinz Kerry called him "Forrest Gump with an attitude." Howard Dean called him a liar. Then there are the crude Web sites and protesters outside his office, all of which Santorum takes with a measure of pride.

"If you have someone who's really effective on the other side, it's nice to get rid of them if you have the chance," he says. "Particularly if you see them, as a lot of them see me, as a fluke. They say, 'How's a guy like this get elected in Pennsylvania? He's just so lucky.'" ("They" is how Santorum generally refers to Democrats and the media. When channeling the views of "they," Santorum's voice acquires an exaggerated whine.) "They say, 'He's always had a bad opponent or ran in a good year.' They see me as an accidental senator."

Santorum has become, perhaps, the most visible Senate Republican other than Majority Leader Bill Frist. He is ensconced in the most divisive issues in America's culture wars: homosexuality, abortion, the role of religion in public life, and most recently the Terri Schiavo controversy. He has compared homosexuality to incest and called the preservation of traditional marriage "the ultimate homeland security issue." He is a proponent of applying religious values to political institutions, and hosts a course on Catholic doctrine for members of Congress (open to Republicans only) in his hideaway office.

Santorum is running in what could be the most closely watched

Senate campaign in the country next year. He will face, in all likelihood, Democrat Bob Casey, son and namesake of the late Pennsylvania governor. The state, which Al Gore and John Kerry both won, is a plump target for Democrats.

Santorum is clearly working to counter the notion that he is a partisan scourge. He has championed an increase in the minimum wage and more AIDS funding for Africa. He has held press conferences with antagonists such as Senator John Kerry and Senate Minority Whip Richard Durbin. He mentions—in three interviews—that he has a "rapport" with Boxer. (She calls their relationship "civil.") Ted Kennedy was one of the first people to call him after Gabriel died, he says. He is pals with Joe Lieberman.

But Santorum is at his most animated when discussing conflict, particularly when it involves him. "I had one guy, a Republican, walk up to me once on the floor of the House and get in my face," Santorum says of an incident that occurred when he was a freshman congressman in the early 1990s. "He says to me, 'I'm gonna get you. . . . I'm gonna find out something about you and I'll get you, I'll bring you down if you don't back off this stuff.'" The aggrieved congressman was referring to the House banking scandal in which he was implicated, and which Santorum helped expose. Santorum does not name the former colleague, only that "the guy got hurt badly and faded into oblivion."

As a freshman senator, Santorum hoisted a Where's Bill? poster in the Senate chamber—an egregious informality—as a way of demanding that President Clinton submit a balanced budget. He tried to oust veteran GOP senator Mark Hatfield as chairman of the Appropriations Committee for not supporting a balanced-budget amendment. (That inspired Kerrey's foray as a Latin translator.)

Santorum's voice assumes a taunting edge when he discusses how Washington renders people in caricature. The Santorum caricature: A "sort of nasty, mean, ideological kind of guy," he says, shaking his head. "Not liked by his colleagues." But really, he says, if his colleagues—at least his GOP colleagues—disliked him so much, would they have elected him chairman of the Republican Conference, the third-ranking job in the Senate? "It's easier for you guys to put someone in a little box and leave him there," Santorum says. ("You guys" is an occasional stand-in for "they.")

But a mention of Gabriel cools his head of steam. He points to the silver angel pin he wears on his lapel in tribute. Gabriel, Santorum says, "fundamentally affirmed how I see the humanity of the child in a womb." Gabriel reinforced his faith, "an affirmation that what I was doing was right."

He often speaks of the "coincidences" that occurred during Karen's pregnancy with Gabriel. "It struck me that if God is into sending messages, then I was getting some," Santorum says.

He recalls the meeting in which Karen's doctor raised the option of abortion. "We were in one of these little rooms, and it had one of those lights with a timer on it." As soon as the word "abortion" escaped the doctor's mouth, the light in the office went off. "It was eerie," he says, "really eerie."

Sitting in his office, Santorum reads a passage from *Letters to Gabriel* about an episode that occurred during the debate on late-term abortion in 1996. "This is not a blob of tissue," Santorum says, quoting from his own speech. "It's a baby. It's a baby." At which point, the book says, the sound of a baby crying was heard on the Senate floor.

"A coincidence?" Santorum reads, enunciating Karen's words. "Perhaps. A visitor's baby was crying just as the door to the floor of the Senate was opened, or closed. Or maybe it was the cry from the son whose voice we never heard, but whose life has forever changed ours."

. . .

I f Santorum wins reelection next year, he will run for his party's second-ranking Senate job, whip. His name is often raised as a potential GOP presidential candidate, just as it elicits a noticeable wince among Democrats—much worse than a "Frist," "Lott," or "McConnell" ever does.

"Frist, Lott, and McConnell are not as passionate as Rick Santorum," says Senator Arlen Specter, Santorum's fellow Republican from Pennsylvania. "He takes on more issues that have an emotional component."

A lot of people do, but Santorum creates and attracts more heat. It might be the pride he takes in his agitator's role. Or, simply, that he's an up-and-comer who knows he's an up-and-comer.

"Obviously in politics, you don't get to be senator at age thirty-six if patience is one of your greater virtues," Santorum says. He is forty-six now but looks a decade younger, with the careening manner of a hyperactive boy. Santorum has a packed schedule, which he is happy to advertise. And like many fast movers, he likes to tell you how little sleep he gets—rarely more than five hours a night, often less. He gets home around seven thirty or eight and plays with his six kids, ages three to fourteen, all of whom are home-schooled by Karen (who published another book last year, *Everyday Graces: A Children's Book of Good Manners*). He stays up until twelve or one, at work on a computer—with part of the screen showing updated statistics on his fantasy baseball team.

"I got about an hour and a half of sleep last night," Santorum says between Senate votes and full-bodied yawns. He was up until nearly four o'clock that morning with his oldest daughter, who had a sinus infection. "And then I was off to play tennis at five fifteen."

And now he's waiting for a vote. And has a reception later. And then a fund-raiser.

"YAWWWNN!"

The discussion turns to professional wrestling.

Santorum used to lobby for the World Wrestling Federation while working at a Pittsburgh law firm in the 1980s. "Do you remember the Hart brothers?" he says excitedly. This would be Bret "Hit Man" Hart and Jim "the Anvil" Neidhart.

"Well, the Anvil assaulted a stewardess," Santorum recalls. "Or flight attendant, I should say. On a US Airways flight." His firm represented the Anvil, leading to his gig with the WWF, now called World Wrestling Entertainment.

In conversations, Santorum tends to use out-of-favor terms, then correct himself in a way that calls attention to the infraction ("stewardess, or flight attendant, I should say"). "I'm supposed to go to a dinner at the American Indian museum," he says later. "Sorry, the Native American museum. I always mess that up."

Earlier that day, Santorum was en route to a news conference in his Chevy Trailblazer when Robert Traynham, his communications director, mentioned something about Costco.

"Oh, I'll have to shop at Costco to get big jars of mayonnaise," Santorum says, affecting a loud nasal voice. He is mocking a woman he read about recently who was pregnant with triplets but wanted only one child. She underwent a procedure to abort two of the fetuses. (Santorum recalls, wrongly, that the woman was carrying twins and aborted one fetus).

"She decided to kill one of the children," he says, then corrects himself. "To abort one of them. Because she couldn't handle two. So she goes off on these things about how it would change her life. And one of them was"—he falls back into the nasally voice—"Oh, I'd have to shop at Costco and buy big jars of mayonnaise.

"And I'm thinking, 'Hey, I shop at Costco and buy big jars of mayonnaise. It doesn't kill me.'"

Santorum is slouched in an SUV passenger seat after a "town meeting" at Bucknell University in Lewisburg, Pennsylvania, his exhaustion showing plainly. A pelting rain outside could choke frogs. "I feel that, right now, the candle is burned out," he says.

At the town meeting, a Bucknell student asked Santorum about the public "cyber-school" in which his children used to be enrolled. The cyber-school is open to Pennsylvania residents, though Santorum's main residence is in Virginia. The Santorums removed their kids from the program last November when a school board member in Pennsylvania questioned the arrangement.

Santorum explains that he wanted his children to study online with other kids from Pennsylvania while they lived in Virginia. He has heard, and answered, this question before.

But after the meeting, there's an unusual tone of surrender in his voice: "You know, if I could do it all again . . ." Santorum is referring to his children's enrollment in the cyber-school and how difficult it was to quit mid-year. "I look back and I think, maybe I shouldn't have done that." A yawn fills the SUV.

"I'm starving," Santorum announces. "I haven't eaten all day."

After stopping for a chicken salad sub, Santorum is spiritedly discussing his 2006 reelection campaign. He catalogs the races he has won in the past that he wasn't supposed to—against Representative Doug Walgren in 1990, and incumbent Democratic senator Harris Wofford in 1994.

Obscured by Santorum's unfiltered talk are his political skills. He is, by all accounts, as pure a political strategist as there is in the Senate. "He is extremely sharp, extremely bright, and he understands the nuances of politics intimately," says senior White House adviser and Deputy Chief of Staff Karl Rove. This includes an encyclopedic grasp of Pennsylvania politics. Santorum was deeply involved in the Bush-Cheney campaign in Pennsylvania. He participated in conference calls, recruited staff, reviewed volunteer numbers, and talked regularly to Rove.

"One of the reasons they like each other," Rove says of President Bush and Santorum, "is that they're both, at heart, an odd combination of idealist and realist."

But Santorum remains afflicted with the politically dicey tendency of saying what's actually on his mind. He has a gift for getting attention, for better or for worse. The most egregious example of "for worse" occurred two years ago, in remarks to the Associated Press about a challenge to the constitutionality of Texas's sodomy law, a matter before the Supreme Court. According to the AP, Santorum said that if the court allows gay sex at home, "you have the right to bigamy, you have the right to polygamy, you have the right to incest, you have the right to adultery. You have the right to anything."

Santorum disputed the AP's account, calling it "misleading." The AP in turn released a transcript of the entire interview, which yielded this: "In every society, the definition of marriage has not ever to my knowledge included homosexuality," Santorum said. "That's not to pick on homosexuality. It's not, you know, man on child, man on dog, or whatever the case may be."

The interview became instant political legend, known to many on the Hill as Santorum's "man on dog" interview.

"Have you seen some of these hate Web sites, Senator? Are you aware of what people say about you?"

The broadcaster is finishing an interview with Santorum at Newsradio 1070, WKOK in Sunbury, Pennsylvania.

"Yes," Santorum says, adding that he doesn't look at the Web sites, some of which include details about a sex columnist's campaign to make his name a synonym for something that cannot be printed in the newspaper. "When you stick your head out of the foxhole people shoot at you. I've stuck my head out of a foxhole."

Back in the safety of his Dirksen office, Santorum is prone to sentimentality, especially after long days, which (he often reminds you) they all are.

He is reflecting on Pope John Paul II's funeral, which he attended with Karen as part of a congressional delegation. He found himself looking around St. Peter's Basilica at all the princes and presidents and dignitaries surrounding him. He was seated next to Jim Caviezel, who played Jesus in Mel Gibson's film *The Passion of the Christ*. "It was one of those moments where you don't see yourself as the person you are," Santorum says, "but as the kid that you know inside you.

"It's part of the awe of this job that I do," he says. "Every day. You're making these decisions and . . ." He fights for the right words. "It's a great—"

"Is it humbling, Senator?" Robert Traynham, his communications aide, interjects.

"Yes, it's very humbling!"

"And it's uniquely American, isn't it, Senator?" prompts Traynham.

"Oh, absolutely."

And Santorum is launched: About how, at the funeral, he turned around and made eye contact with Democratic senator Barbara Mikulski, his colleague and persistent rival, but who on this day he describes simply as "this scrappy woman from inner-city Baltimore."

"And then there's this kid," he says, "who is me."

"I'm Running for Office, for Pete's Sake"

Feel the Loathing
on the Campaign Trail

September 2, 2012

Sometime early last May, I began to have this goofy notion, which turned into a daydream and eventually a recurring fantasy. It went like this: One morning, I would wake up to the news that the previous evening, with no advance warning to the media, Mitt and Ann Romney stopped by the White House at the invitation of Barack and Michelle Obama. No one was certain what happened while they were there or what they talked about or how it came together, though eventually some details would trickle out. The couples told funny stories from the campaign trail and shared pictures of their families. Mitt drank lemonade, and Michelle led a moonlit tour of her garden. Everyone ate hot dogs loaded with toppings, which inspired a cable christening of the "Sauerkraut Summit."

I knew this would never happen. It was dumb, naive, unsophisticated, and frankly out of character for me, someone with little patience for the Kabuki pleasantries of politics. It wasn't immediately clear what drove the fantasy—a desire for less free-floating hostility in the campaign, I suppose, but that seemed too easy. Whatever the case, I was yearning for something that felt big, or at least different, even if it was just a social visit. Something that messed with what the political know-it-alls refer to as the "narrative." This spring, for the first time since I started writing about politics a decade ago, I found myself completely depressed by a campaign. "How am I ever going to get through it?" is not the question you want to be asking yourself as you enter what are supposed to be the pinnacle few months of your profession.

But that's what I was doing to an alarming degree. Maybe it had to do with how bad off the country felt and how outmatched our politicians were by the severity of our problems and how obvious it was that the proverbial "tone" of Washington wouldn't change no matter who won. Or maybe it was because my daughters were getting older and starting to tune in more. I had also just been through a rough winter in which my eleven-year-old suffered a head injury that brought some terrifying and unexplained side effects that incapacitated her for months. There's something about wondering whether your kid will ever be able to go back to school and live a normal life that makes a steady ingestion of super-PAC poison, talking-point Novocain, and fund-raising spam a little harder to take.

This isn't all a setup for one of those gauzy laments about how "our politics have never been meaner" or how "we've lost our civility as a society" and it would all be so much better if our leaders could just emulate the oft-invoked after-hours salons of Ronald Reagan and Tip O'Neill (a tradition way overstated). Nor am I a member of the "deeply saddened and troubled" club, like John McCain (or whoever tweets for him), who recently called this campaign the "worst I've ever seen." This from someone who in 2000 had to field the race-baiting accusation that he fathered his adopted Bangladeshi daughter, out of wedlock, with a black woman.

I am as cynical as any political reporter. And perhaps my recent craving for uplift was a sublimation of my own anger at being a small cog in a giant inanity machine. But I write and read and talk about politics because beneath that cynicism I understand that the stakes are high. On top of which, oddly, the job also keeps me patriotic, a by-product of seeing—as I did at a Romney event in Ohio in July—things like a Korean War veteran in a wheelchair removing his insignia cap and struggling to his feet to salute the flag during the national anthem. (Immediately after which, I looked down at my BlackBerry to learn that the Democratic National Committee had just released a new ad ridiculing Ann Romney's dressage horse.)

But what's been completely missing this year has been, for lack of a better word, joy. The principals don't seem to be experiencing much joy as they go through their market-tested paces. A kind of faux-ness permeates everything this year in a way that it hasn't been quite so consuming in the past. The effect has been anesthetizing and made it difficult to take any of the day's supposed gaffes, game-changers, and false umbrages seriously. The campaigns appeared locked in a paradigm of terrified superpowers' spending blindly on redundant warfare. How many times do they have to blow up Vladivostok?

Where were the surprises, the pleasures of discovery, and the true emotion of the newly vitalized? The volunteers who decided to get involved because so-and-so inspired them, not because the other guy (the socialist or the plutocrat) scared them? They seemed in such short supply. This might or might not be the most important election of our lifetime—as we are told it is every four years—but it really did feel like the most joyless.

I wanted to find a moment in the muck that proved me wrong. So in mid-July I started circulating through campaign rallies and headquarters on a mission to find something that might make me feel, if not joyful, at least more at peace with the joylessness.

. . .

My first stop was a Romney town-hall gathering at a community center in Bowling Green, Ohio. An orderly, almost entirely white procession filed through metal detectors to Bob Seger's "Ramblin' Gamblin' Man," which of course brings Mitt Romney to mind. The traveling media, which often refer to Romney among themselves as "Mittens," was at the back of the room, ignored by the rest of the crowd, with the one sensational exception of Carl Cameron, the oval-headed reporter for Fox News. As is customary for any recognizable Fox personality at a Republican event, Cameron was a popular fuss-object—waved to and asked for photos and autographs, requests which he obliged with the flair of a seasoned senator. "Thank God for Fox News," one man yelled.

Romney is better on the stump now than he was five or six months ago, and surprisingly better in person than he is on TV—more human-seeming, somehow, when seen head to toe. On screen, his hurried asides ("I'm running for office, for Pete's sake") and staccato laugh seem weirder and more pronounced. In person, there's a slightly awkward charm about him. But he still emits a kind of pre-traumatic gaffe anxiety at all times. This is understandable, given today's hair-trigger media, but you sense that it runs deeper. His father and idol, the former governor of Michigan George Romney, saw his presidential hopes blown apart after he claimed to have been "brainwashed" into supporting the Vietnam War (inspiring a classic insult by Senator Eugene McCarthy, who said that with Romney "a light rinse would have been sufficient"). The episode supposedly had a searing effect on Mitt, and people who know him say it sank a hypervigilance in him that has shaped his public demeanor for decades.

As Romney took questions, a self-described "angry mom" went on a rant about how her son's apparel business has suffered under

Obama—"that monster," as she called the president. Some in the crowd laughed, and Romney closed his eyes and ducked his head, assuming a look of either pained meditation or quiet panic. I imagined the data-processing spasm in his brain as he weighed whether to disavow the remark immediately or risk seeming to have endorsed it. Romney clasped his hands at his waist and, after a few seconds, chose action. "That's not a term I would use," he said, and then, "but, but, but, uh, uh," before Kathye Zaper of suburban Toledo told her party's presidential nominee that, because of her status as a mother who was angry, she could call the president a monster if she wanted to.

In his speech, Romney asked everyone in the room who had started their own businesses to please stand. A few dozen people did, some holding signs that said things like "I Opened My Own Business and I Created a Business. Not the Government." "These are fun; these are fun signs!" Romney gushed. "For those who made those signs, thank you for reminding us who it is in America that creates jobs."

After the event, I met one of these business owners, Wayne Michaelis, standing outside the auditorium. I knew he had opened a business, because his sign said so. He is a retired orthodontist. "I build smiles," he said proudly. But he did not build his own "I Opened My Own Business" sign. That was handed to him, as were many others, by the campaign.

Michaelis admitted this to a reporter traveling with Romney, and word spread fast within the press corps—a morsel of gotcha chum bobbing in the water. Other reporters approached Michaelis, seeking verification. "This is all the media is going to focus on for this event," Dick Motten, a financial planner who was standing next to Michaelis, said. He watched with some disgust as the reporters surrounded his friend. "You can see what's happening here," Motten said. "They don't care what Wayne has to say. They just want to know that he didn't make his own sign. And then they'll make a big deal of it." About that, he was right. The homemade-sign revelation was online within hours.

The political media are engaged in their own silly arms race. The treadmill existence of having to file articles around the clock, tweet non-events as they happen, and listen to the same canned speeches and campaign conference calls day after day, waiting for something, anything, to bust up the script so that you can pretend there's news here; this can be the definition of joylessness. Politics operates in "cycles"—news cycles, election cycles—one of those words that has come into fashion in recent years. There's even a political show on MSNBC called *The Cycle* (which, as the *Washington Post*'s Karen Tumulty pointed out, was obviously not named by a woman).

President Obama talks a lot now about how his hair is going gray. It's a useful tool of self-deprecation (the "my big ears" of 2012) and a functional symbol of what his team calls the "grind it out" election, as opposed to the Hope and Change of 2008. In early August, I went to see him speak at a midday rally in the center of Mansfield, in north-central Ohio, in front of the faded brick exterior of an out-of-business department store. Obama does his best to stir the old magic—droppin' his *g*'s and talkin' straight about how his opponents think we "should be goin' back to what we were doin' that got us into this mess in the first place." But his appearances can give off the slightly musty air of Van Halen in the Sammy Hagar years.

After he spoke, the president quickly worked the crowd near the front of the stage. He does a decent meet-and-greet but clearly lacks Bill Clinton's or Biden's "draw energy from the adoring throng" gene. As with Romney, you can picture him grabbing for the Purell as soon as he escapes the rope line. His retail-politicking chores completed, Obama disappeared behind a thick black curtain next to an empty storefront, into something called the "Good News Center"—a place I was not allowed to go.

I originally planned to see Obama at two events in Florida the previous week, but made it only as far as Atlanta, where I missed a connection and stayed in a Motel 6 and woke early the next morning to the ghastly news of the Colorado movie-theater massacre. The campaigns pressed pause. Sitting in the dark motel room, I got a sentimental yearning again—for something that might break with the predictable regiment that followed a Sobering National Tragedy. I knew there would be statements from the candidates and talk of national unity during this difficult time, and then some member of Congress would say something inflammatory (cue Louie Gohmert, the Texas Republican, who blamed the massacre on a lack of prayer), and then some reporter would wrongly say the shootings were politically motivated (cue ABC's Brian Ross, who initially suggested that the suspect was linked to the Tea Party); a cluster of Democrats would call for tougher arms restrictions, and the president would barely touch the issue, because to do otherwise would be to bang his head against political concrete. As the hiatus proceeded—a "highly choreographed détente," Zeke Miller from BuzzFeed called it— the campaigns were quick to advertise all the campaigning they were not doing. "We have asked affiliates to pull down our contrast advertising for the time being," Jen Psaki, an Obama spokeswoman, said.

By Monday, three days later, they were back to pulling down each other's Garanimals. David Axelrod ended the cease-fire with a pair of early-morning tweets about Romney's being "secretive" regarding his tax returns and business career and etc.

"I guess it's back on," Romney's communications director, Gail Gitcho, said when told of the truce-busting tweet.

I was sitting in a bar later that day in Boston's North End with

Gitcho and Eric Fehrnstrom, Romney's longtime press secretary. "Over the weekend, we were constantly assessing when we could return to campaign activities," said Fehrnstrom, a former *Boston Herald* reporter with chubby cheeks and a jittery bearing. He goes to bed every night at eleven thirty, wakes at three, checks his Black-Berry, and then tries to get another hour or so of "not exactly quality REM sleep" before starting the day. He and Gitcho described how restless they felt during the Aurora armistice, and like a couple sharing the same pheromonic response to the news cycle, they both began quivering their knees under the table at precisely the same time.

Romney's campaign staff is known in political shorthand as "Boston," and Obama's is "Chicago"—like the Russians used to be "Moscow" and the Americans were "Washington." Owing to valid security concerns, Romney's North End headquarters feel like a fortress, with no external signifiers that a presidential campaign is being run there. (Obama's headquarters in Chicago are like this, too.) Receptionists in the lobby greet visitors from behind thick glass similar to what you'd find at a gas station in a rough neighborhood. Inside, big framed pictures of Ronald Reagan and George Romney dominate walls, along with prominent renderings of Mitt and Ann. A lone photo of George W. Bush hangs crooked next to a darkened office in a far corner. (The former president and Laura Bush would stop by the headquarters on a visit to Boston the day after I was there, and I imagined young campaign workers scrambling to put up more Bush pictures.)

Gitcho is a forcible presence who wakes most mornings before five for "boot camp" training at a North End gym. She referred to the Obama staff as "the defending champs" three times in a half hour and kept pointing out that as of that day, the Obama reelection campaign had 778 people on its payroll to Romney's 272 (though the Romney staff grew considerably when Paul Ryan joined the ticket). Stuart Stevens, Romney's chief strategist, said the media's trivial focus on things like Romney's gaffes and his tax returns wouldn't amount to anything next to the ravages of the Obama economy. He wanted me to understand that none of the news-cycle fodder amounted to anything. "If Steinbeck was alive today," Stevens said, "you think he would be writing about tweets?"

Officials in each camp like to praise one another in the classically backhanded language of politics. "Obama is a good salesman trying to push a defective product," Fehrnstrom said, to which Gitcho replied, "Oh, that's a good one." Fehrnstrom looked pleased. "You see where I mixed in something nice with something bad?"

Fehrnstrom accuses Axelrod of having "an entire staff of people who tweet for him" (not true), and he makes sneering references to the foosball table at Obama HQ (it's a Ping-Pong table). The intention is of course to contrast the lean, no-nonsense approach of Boston with the indulged, big-government-like behemoth of Chicago. Fehrnstrom was on a roll, seeming eager to dispense a little wisdom about how the political magic happens. "I used to work for an ad agency," he said, "and I always thought the best place to be was on the creative side, because they could get away with anything." He added, smirking, "It's all part of the creative process, I guess. If someone happened to be taking a nap under their desk in the afternoon, you weren't supposed to disturb them, because it's all part of the process."

As it did four years ago, Team Obama often pats itself on the back for basing its campaign in Chicago, far away from the silliness of Washington. The implication is that they are situated among real Americans with real concerns—in the heartland of Michigan Avenue. (Whereas "Chicago" is used as an epithet by the Romney folks, who like to refer disdainfully to Obama's "Chicago-style politics.") For the Obama staff members, "Chicago" has an almost talismanic connection to the full-swagger days of 2008, time that political followers, especially those with press credentials, have spent a good part of this campaign longing for. The Ghost of the Last Campaign looms heavy over this one like a dearly departed sibling. One of the more anticipated cultural events of the Washington winter was the premiere of *Game Change*, the HBO adaptation of the best seller about the 2008 "campaign of a lifetime," by the journo-pundits Mark Halperin and John Heilemann. The red-carpet opening featured the executive producer, Tom Hanks; the star, Julianne Moore (who played Sarah Palin); Brangelina (i.e., Halperin and Heilemann); Joe Scarborough and Mika Brzezinski; and swarms of White House officials, Congress members, lobbyists, and journalists parading into the Newseum on Pennsylvania Avenue, where they grazed a buffet of salmon and marinated hanger steak with Maui onions. "You don't get to go back in time," said McCain's chief strategist, Steve Schmidt (played by Woody Harrelson), in the film. "You don't get to have do-overs in life." No do-overs, indeed, but you can help shape events retroactively: Schmidt, who presided over the dysfunctional McCain campaign and is credited/blamed with encouraging the candidate to pick Palin, has emerged fine from the fiasco in the proud political tradition of failing upward. He scored a pundit gig on MSNBC and a TV studio outfitted in his home on Lake Tahoe, and he was portrayed as a tortured hero in the film.

The film also sent Palin into a tizzy, complaining about its "false narrative." The complaint brought to mind a line I highlighted years ago—in 1993—from a profile in this magazine of David Gergen by Michael Kelly. "Politics is not about objective reality, but virtual reality," Kelly wrote. "What happens in the political world is divorced from the real world. It exists for only the fleeting historical moment, in a magical movie of sorts, a never-ending and infinitely revisable docudrama."

When I visited the Obama headquarters in late July, I was asked to present two forms of identification before entering the offices, which are in a downtown office building on a floor the campaign asked me not to divulge, for security reasons. The nerve center is a sprawling room filled with hundreds of campaign workers, most of them under twenty-five, many sitting under their college pennants. Like many campaigns—and tech companies—it is also something of a sweatshop (this is even more pronounced in the swing-state field offices), where 100-hour weeks are expected, outputs are closely monitored, and discipline enforced. For every kid organizer whose political fervor is ignited on the Obama campaign, there is another—and probably more—who is not making his phone bank numbers, lagging behind ambitious co-workers bucking for administration jobs and resenting the "revenge of the nerds" arrogance of his bosses. Still, the feel of youthful political energy was palpable as I passed row after row of desks en route to the men's room—an unauthorized foray, it turned out, as all visitors require chaperones at all times. In a far corner was an area dedicated to the memory of Alex Okrent, a twenty-nine-year-old staff member who died earlier this summer after collapsing at his desk. Okrent, a veteran of two previous Obama campaigns—2004 and 2008—was a beloved figure here, and many of the Post-its affixed to the shrine were in the vein of Win It for Alex. Okrent's death hit the campaign hard; Obama called the staff from Washington, and Romney tweeted a message of condolence.

On this day, the Obama team was particularly giddy over Romney's mishaps on his recent tour of Europe and the Middle East. ("Mitt the Twit!" the press secretary Ben LaBolt read aloud from his BlackBerry, quoting a London tabloid headline.) I met with four top officials in the office of the campaign manager, Jim Messina. They included Messina, LaBolt, Axelrod, and the deputy campaign manager Stephanie Cutter. On a few occasions, I looked up to see all four simultaneously typing on their BlackBerries. They are wary of speaking on the record, for fear of compromising their message of discipline. "I don't want to be telling Matt Rhoades everything we're doing," Messina told me, referring to his counterpart on the Romney campaign. When he did speak on the record, it was often with a mouthful of string cheese, around which he spewed a litany of poll data ("Univision says we're up 70–22 with Hispanics"), tech stats ("Facebook was one-ninth the size in 2008 than it is now"), and demographic trends ("The fastest-growing population on Facebook is people over fifty").

I then headed down the hall for a brief separate interview with Cutter, whom I've known for years, going back to when she was John Kerry's spokeswoman. "How are you?" I asked.

"Are we on the record?" she replied.

Nine days after Romney announced his selection of Paul Ryan, his aides were marveling at how much "looser" he had become. It was as if "rapport" was their approved theme of the week, and everyone was on message at all times. When I attended a joint town-hall meeting on the quad of Saint Anselm College in Manchester, New Hampshire, a week before the start of the Republican convention, Romney looked as if he was enjoying himself rather than following some "Look as if you're enjoying yourself" stage direction. He sat in a chair a few feet away and cast an adoring gaze upon his new running mate. "We're going to elect leadership," Ryan said, and then the bells of the campus church tolled to signal it was eleven a.m. "At the eleventh hour," Ryan quipped, a deft ad-lib that had the crowd laughing and cheering for several seconds. A few minutes later, Ryan said what will no doubt be a standard part of his stump repertory: When he and Romney win, he said, they will have "the moral authority and the mandate" to enact their agenda. "Moral authority" is one of the most depressing terms in politics, made more so by the fact that whoever wins will likely do it with barely more than 50 percent of the vote.

When I asked Obama's top aides in Chicago how the president's reelection would make congressional Republicans any more likely to work with them, their response was: "Our winning will teach them a lesson. It will make them look at themselves and realize that their positions are untenable. It will, finally, break the fever."

I thought about this as I walked through the Saint Anselm parking lot after the Romney event, past gridlocked cars, several of which loudly played the affirming sounds of conservative hosts on their radios. On this day, the feedback loop was atwitter over remarks by the Republican Senate candidate in Missouri, Todd Akin, and his bizarre comments about "legitimate rape," plus the report in *Politico* about the drunken, skinny-dipping escapades of a congressman in the Sea of Galilee. A few days later, the evangelist Rick Warren would cancel his "civil forum," after neither campaign would sign on to participate. Two days after that, Romney would trot out the old birther canard in front of a cheering crowd in Michigan. So much for the campaign of "big ideas" we were promised when Ryan was announced as Romney's running mate.

My best moment in New Hampshire came when I met Jim Preisendorfer, a semi-retired salesman from Concord. He had a white Fu Manchu and wore a big crucifix dangling over a "Pro-Life to the Max" T-shirt. I waited for him to get in my face about liberal media bias, something that happens a fair amount at Republican events, but he could not have been nicer or more thoughtful—a Catholic, active in his church, completely despairing about politics. I couldn't help it, and trotted out my ridiculous Sauerkraut Summit idea (which a few minutes earlier I proposed to a longtime Romney spokesman, Kevin Madden, who looked at me as if I had sauerkraut between my ears). Preisendorfer liked the idea. But of course Obama and Romney would never do it, he said. Why? "It's pride in themselves," Preisendorfer said, "and fear in one another."

Voter's Block:
New Hampshire Pol
Lou D'Allesandro Took His Time
Making Up His Mind

November 25, 2003

There are times, when the big dogs start calling one after another, that Lou D'Allesandro must realize how vital he is to the democratic process.

Presidential candidates say how honored they are to call him a friend, a dear friend. Campaign operatives and reporters ask the same question over and over:

Who you with for president, Lou?

He is a New Hampshire primary archetype: the courted local dignitary. "I'm just a little guy from a little state," D'Allesandro says with practiced humility.

But his decision is Very Important. Which explains the importance of being Lou.

He is a heady fluke of geography and political math: D'Allesandro, sixty-five, is one of six Democrats in the state senate. He is the only one, until recently, who had not endorsed a presidential candidate. So he is subject to attention and affection and many,

many Christmas cards. This is his reward for being a state senator from New Hampshire instead of, say, Kentucky. It is also his reward for being indecisive—or at least dragging out his choice.

Some cynics may suggest—okay, many do suggest—that the reason D'Allesandro is taking so long to make up his mind is because he enjoys the courtship. He knows that as soon as he announces his decision, the visits and phone calls from John Kerry will cease, as will the ones from Joe Lieberman and John Edwards and Wes Clark and Howard Dean and old pal Dick Gephardt and the rest.

But, no, this is not about Lou D'Allesandro, Lou D'Allesandro says. It's about the country. "I believe this is going to be one of the most important elections in our lifetime," he says. A lot.

A former high school teacher, college president, and basketball coach, D'Allesandro is picking at ham and eggs in the dining room of the Holiday Inn in downtown Manchester. He is a smiley, often buoyant lug who is always urging people to "Have a great American day."

He was raised in a series of working-class neighborhoods in greater Boston. His father was an oil burner mechanic and his mother bled to death from a tubular pregnancy when Lou was seven.

He attended the University of New Hampshire on a football scholarship and never left the state. He and his wife, Pat, have been married forty-two years. They have three children and seven grandchildren.

But those are just the clinical basics of Lou. They ignore the full and solemn burden of his choice. He can't make a hasty one, he says. That would be irresponsible.

To some degree, D'Allesandro shares his burden with other activists and pols in New Hampshire and Iowa. Candidates also court them. But D'Allesandro's (in)decision is a fixture of the pre-voting months. "Every time I come to New Hampshire with a presidential contender, a closed meeting with D'Allesandro is an inevitable part of the schedule," writes Walter Shapiro in *One-Car Caravan*, a book on the early maneuvers of the 2004 campaign.

Why such attention? In part because D'Allesandro is still holding out. But also because, like many Very Important people here, he expects the handwritten notes, "just thinking of you" calls, and podium tributes.

Because he can. And because it's fun.

So ambitious men keep calling, dutifully. And calling and calling and calling. "We've talked more than a dozen times," Senator Edwards says of D'Allesandro.

The North Carolina Democrat might as well be a telemarketer, except that D'Allesandro loves hearing from him—and Edwards's wife, Elizabeth. ("We've become close," D'Allesandro says.)

On a recent bus tour, the Edwardses were accompanied for a leg by D'Allesandro. As the bus rolled through D'Allesandro's senate district—the central and western wards of Manchester and adjacent Goffstown—Edwards was asked by a reporter if he minds the extensive courtship required of people like D'Allesandro, an exercise that has taken up countless hours over several months.

Edwards simply grinned, rolled his eyes slightly, and—what the heck—indulged in a bit of sarcasm.

"Oh, no, this is funnnn," Edwards said, as D'Allesandro sat smiling behind him.

Campaign officials express exasperation with D'Allesandro (behind his back). "He's milking this thing for all its worth," one high-level campaign operative complains. D'Allesandro's been around. He treats the candidates as well as he can. He takes their flattery and returns it. But only to a point. "My motto is, 'Always leave them wanting more D'Allesandro,'" he says, laughing.

D'Allesandro views the high-level attention he receives every four years as a marker of his success. Sometimes, when things get really exciting, he thinks back to his boyhood days at Saint Joseph

School in Medford, Massachusetts. "Sister Nathaniel, God rest her soul, gave me a fifty-five in deportment," D'Allesandro says. She worried that he wouldn't finish eighth grade. "But if she could only see me now. Wow."

You can see where it's easy to get caught up in this. And really, what's the rush?

"I pinch myself sometimes," says D'Allesandro, who was invited to the Clinton White House four times. "I say, 'Only in America.'"

But especially in New Hampshire.

"They take this responsibility very seriously and very personally," says Bob Kerrey, the former Nebraska senator who sought the Democratic nomination in 1992. He is talking about voters in New Hampshire, where the first binding primary of the 2004 race will be held January 27. He once received a "three-part question" from a ten-year-old at an event.

"These people are used to the attention," he says. "They know they're special."

Kerrey recalls being endorsed by a senior citizen activist who he was told could deliver a thousand votes. They walked the streets of Manchester together one day. They shook some hands, stopped in some stores.

"I got a call from my New Hampshire campaign manager the next morning," Kerrey recalls. Apparently Kerrey had forgotten to offer the activist a cookie when they stopped in at a bakery. She was insulted. And she was prepared to endorse Tom Harkin.

"I had to have breakfast with her the next day," Kerrey says. After an extended grovel, he managed to win her back, but this does not sound fun in the retelling.

Kerrey finished third in New Hampshire, behind Paul Tsongas and Bill Clinton, which doomed his campaign. As he left the state, Kerrey posed for a photo, flipping the bird next to a "Leaving New Hampshire" sign.

But the process can be healthy, imposing a humility on the in-herently un-humble. "Humiliation is a more likely consequence than humility," Kerrey corrects.

Even so, New Hampshire's Most Importants are not without an endearing giddiness. At an Al Gore event four years ago, Manchester mayor Bob Baines recalls thinking, "I'm up here endorsing the vice president of the United States. How awesome is this?" The mayor, fifty-seven and still uncommitted for 2004, is giggling like a kid.

"Twenty-five years ago, senators would call me and I'd get all excited about how great I am," says Jean Hennessey, a prominent environmentalist and longtime Democratic activist from Hanover. "I would say to myself, 'Oh, gosh, gee, my reputation goes all the way to Washington. I must be big stuff.' But then you realize what's going on. This person wants to be president. It's perfectly clear why he's doing these calls."

There are good reasons for New Hampshire pols to withhold their endorsements for a while, says Hennessey, who is supporting John Kerry. "If you're running for office yourself, people can hold the wrong endorsement against you." She invokes a baseball anal-ogy. "The last thing you want is to be a declared Yankees fan while you're seeking support from a Red Sox fan."

But even the most earnest New Hampshire bigwig will admit to loving the high-level fuss. Baines says he won't forget how Gore showed up at his victory party when he won election as mayor in 1999. Or how Hadassah Lieberman called to wish him luck in his reelection bid last month, and Kerry called on election night, and Dean and Clark called with congratulations a few days later. Or that he can easily get an audience with any candidate. Does he have their cell phone numbers?

"No, but Lou's got 'em all," he says. "I can get 'em from him."

D'Allesandro has heard from all the campaigns, repeatedly, ex-cept for the skeletal enterprise of Carol Moseley Braun. Kerry and

Edwards called D'Allesandro on his birthday in August. Lieberman sent a letter. Dean and Gephardt sent emissaries to the party.

Wes Clark started calling after he entered the race in September. He met with D'Allesandro at a Manchester hotel. They talked. "We'd really love to have your support," Clark told him. A few days later, Clark called again and asked for another meeting. D'Allesandro obliged.

D'Allesandro never clicked with Kerry. He admires Kerry's intellect, he says, but finds the Massachusetts senator somewhat distant. Still, he hosted a party for Kerry at his home last month.

D'Allesandro doesn't care for the religious overtones of Lieberman's rhetoric.

He is lukewarm on Dean.

He loves Dick Gephardt. They first met when Gephardt ran for president in 1988 and have kept in touch.

He also came to like John Edwards. "We share similar values," D'Allesandro says. And like him, Elizabeth Edwards is Italian-American.

D'Allesandro says he narrowed his decision to Gephardt and Edwards as long ago as last summer. But he still allowed himself to be courted by other candidates. "I did it as a courtesy," he explains. "I want to be helpful to every Democrat."

As time passed, the campaigns began pressing D'Allesandro for his decision.

Finally, in early October, D'Allesandro said he would take a long weekend at a mountain resort in northern New Hampshire, where his wife had a business meeting. When he returned to Manchester, D'Allesandro had made a decision:

He needed more time.

He was preoccupied with a budget battle in the New Hampshire legislature. His daughter got married. His brother was diagnosed with cancer. He discussed his upcoming decision with friends. He went as far as Nashville to consult with one, Al Gore.

At the end of last month, as D'Allesandro traveled to Tampa for a conference on prescription drugs, his decision was almost set. Really. En route to Florida, D'Allesandro stopped in Washington to attend a dinner and meet with Elizabeth Edwards. A few days earlier, he rode in a car with John Edwards from Cambridge, Massachusetts, to Manchester. They talked about their families, their parents, where they thought the country was going, and what could be done about it. Campaign officials believed this, finally, would be the conversation that closed the deal for Edwards. But they had believed this before. And when the car trip ended, Lou said good night and thanked John again for his time.

D'Allesandro would announce his decision at the headquarters of the winning candidate a week later.

A t noon on October 30, fifteen reporters are linked to D'Allesandro by conference call. Also connected is . . . the winner of the 2003 D'Allesandro Primary, John Edwards.

"Hey, Lou," Edwards says, his voice crackling over a speakerphone. "I'm so excited about this."

D'Allesandro says they're going for all the marbles.

"Yes we are, yes we are," Edwards says. "We're gonna be such a good team."

He says he'll be visiting New Hampshire the next week with Elizabeth. "She loves you, too, Lou," Edwards says.

D'Allesandro is asked what he brings to the Edwards campaign.

"I'll bring the small Italo-American community, which consists of my wife and my children," D'Allesandro says to big laughs.

But seriously: "I bring a belief in the process," he says, among other things.

Why Edwards?

"They're all outstanding candidates," D'Allesandro says, statesmanlike. "But I feel the most comfortable with Edwards. Comfortable with his ideas. He's a fresh face, and you need that." Reminds him a little of JFK.

Why now? What took you so long?

D'Allesandro betrays pique at the question. "I made my decision over the weekend," he says. "This was the right time for me. And I get to pick that time. Because it's my decision."

The call ends. None of the other candidates has called since.

Except one. A few days later, D'Allesandro gets his first call from Carol Moseley Braun, seeking his support.

Cheney and Edwards,
The Me 2 Campaign:
In the Midwest, Aiming
for Second Best

August 15, 2004

Dick Cheney and John Edwards have a few things in common: They are both running for vice president and they are both *Homo sapiens.*

But you would struggle to find two greater stylistic opposites in American politics.

Edwards is a populist outsider; Cheney is a capitalist insider.

Edwards, who is fifty-one but looks younger, is known for his oratorical flair and exuberance. Cheney, who is sixty-three but looks older, is known for his reticence and discretion. He takes as a mantra, "You never get in trouble for something you don't say." (A quote he attributes to former House speaker Sam Rayburn.) Edwards's wife, Elizabeth, calls her sunny husband "the most optimistic person I know." Cheney once took a personality test that found him best suited to a career as a funeral director.

Edwards runs four miles a day. Cheney has had four heart attacks.

Edwards is "very beautiful," according to Teresa Heinz Kerry. Cheney is "not the prettiest face in the race," says President Bush.

"People keep telling me that Senator Edwards got picked for his good looks, charm, and great hair," Cheney said in a speech here Thursday. "And I say to them, 'How do you think I got this job?'" The line—a staple of his stump routine—brings giggles. But it also is revealing. These are very different men touting very different tickets to very different constituencies. To compare their manners, themes, applause lines, and crowds is to glimpse the distinct anthropologies of the two campaigns.

Traditionally, vice-presidential candidates have served a set of prescribed functions. They are cheerleaders for their running mates and attack dogs against their opponents. In this campaign, they are playing to carefully screened audiences, who have usually been issued tickets. The crowds cheer, make noise, wave signs, and do what they're supposed to do—look good and giddy for television news clips, convey a sense of momentum.

Both men campaigned last week in battleground states of the Midwest. It's not clear whether either changed any minds.

Campaign venues in a general election are essentially TV studios. This is what it looked like Wednesday when Cheney, accompanied by his wife, Lynne, held a "town meeting" in the southwestern Missouri city of Joplin. The Cheneys sat side by side on a small stage amid flags, Bush-Cheney signs, and three hundred supporters who filled four risers around them. There were, at first glance, no more than two non-whites in the audience.

With muscled security guards standing everywhere, the setting looked a little like *The Jerry Springer Show*—except that there was absolutely no disagreement here about anything. One member of the audience began a question by saying, "Just let Brother Ashcroft know that his fellow Missourians are praying with you guys."

The iconic town meeting provides a forum for citizens to engage community leaders in a vigorous exchange of concerns. The election town meeting provides true believers the chance to ask softball questions and applaud answers they already know and agree with.

On Friday, Edwards participated in a Kerry-Edwards version in front of a little yellow house in Flint, Michigan. The "front porch" meeting—a staple of the Kerry-Edwards campaign's roving studio—convenes the candidate with a group of "regular people" who are going through some hardship, usually economic. The candidate will then tell the "regular people" how his prospective administration would address their concerns.

This could be any neighborly lawn scene, except for the bright lights and boom mikes and huge speakers and the mob of photographers on a flatbed truck and the entourage of about two hundred staffers, media members, Secret Service agents, police officers, and onlookers swarming 4021 Cuthbertson.

Otherwise, it all looked very intimate, authentic, and unstaged.

Friday's meeting was actually held on a front yard because its host—Philip Phelps, a twenty-five-year-old pizza delivery man—doesn't have a porch. Phelps was one of three "regular people" meeting with Edwards, all of whose hardships jibe neatly with the campaign's "Real Plan for a Strong Economy."

"It's very hard, isn't it?" Edwards asked after Phelps detailed his struggle to put himself through college. Edwards, deeply tanned, was hair-sprayed and in a blue dress shirt with no tie. His hands were folded on his lap and his head bobbed in a slow, understanding nod while dozens of cameras clicked and a loud TV reporter did a live shot twenty-five feet away.

It started to rain.

Shirley Wood was telling Edwards how she had just been laid off from her job at GM. He told her he was the son of a mill worker and had seen, firsthand, the ravages of plant closings. And that he and John Kerry were committed to keeping jobs in the United States and enforcing trade agreements.

It started to rain harder.

"Time to wrap up," an advance man said, and the lights went off and everyone slopped through the mud back to their vans and buses and limousines.

And Edwards thanked his panel of regular people for a "really great discussion," which lasted twelve minutes.

Both Cheney and Edwards are at their best before small groups. Cheney, who had planned to teach political science before he entered politics, speaks into his chin, in the matter-of-fact mumbles of a professor who has been teaching the same class for thirty-five years. Sometimes, when the questions are asked, he looks distracted (he began swabbing his ear with his pinkie in Joplin). But he conveys the authority of one who has clearly been around and knows more than he's telling.

Edwards honed his speaking skills in front of juries. He is a whiz at eye contact and holding his hands far apart to project openness. He looks like a terrific listener, cocking his head, nodding rhythmically, asking empathetic questions. He looks like he feels your pain.

Cheney has been briefed on your pain. But his mind is heavy with the ominous. He is at his most commanding when discussing the prospective horrors of the post-9/11 age—bioterror, beheadings. Speaking in a grave monotone, Cheney leaves the "hope and optimism" for the president.

The enemy is "sophisticated, patient, disciplined, and lethal," Cheney said in a speech in Dayton, quoting from the 9/11 Commission Report. It's inevitable that the United States will be hit again. Nodding.

Edwards leaves them pumped. He is a rollicking speaker, with a booming, drawling voice that gains momentum as he goes. After the front porch meeting, Edwards addressed a rally of one thousand people who waited in the rain for him to arrive at Mott Community College in Flint. "HELLO, FLINT!" Edwards yelled like an arena rocker, making sure to sure to "thank y'all for waitin' out in the rain" and stirring his crowds to responsive chants of "Hope is on the way."

Edwards's surefire applause lines include: The GOP is bent on "tearing us apart, not bringing us together," any reference to nonexistent weapons of mass destruction in Iraq, the president's "go it alone" foreign policy, the shame of having 35 million people living in poverty in the United States, the need for a higher minimum wage, and the acknowledgment that the country has "a long way to go" on civil rights.

Cheney's applause lines include: the need to confirm the Bush administration's judicial nominations, the need to curtail "junk lawsuits," mentions of God, particularly as relating to attempts to strike the phrase "under God" from the Pledge of Allegiance, and any mention of "the sanctity of life," tax relief, the right to bear arms, and George W. Bush.

Edwards is often accompanied by his two young children, ages four and six. Cheney was joined last week by his daughter Liz, who was backstage bottle-feeding her five-week-old son, Philip. Lynne Cheney mentioned Philip while introducing her husband in Battle Creek, Michigan, assuring everyone that they are "training him to be a Republican."

Cheney often begins his speeches by saying something about the place he's visiting. "People call Battle Creek the breakfast capital of the world," he said of the city that is home to the Kellogg corporation. "From the looks of things," he said, looking out at the ticket-holding crowd of four hundred, "Battle Creek is the Bush-Cheney capital of the world."

From the looks of things, the Bush-Cheney capital of the world ends at the walls of Lakeview High School. Outside, 150 protesters were holding Kerry-Edwards and other signs ("Where Are the Jobs?" "Where Are Those WMDs?").

Lynne Cheney is an able attack dog in her own right.

"I'd like to direct this question to Mrs. Cheney," one supporter asked in Joplin. "Senator Kerry has made the statement that he'd like to fight a more sensitive war on terror. What could he possibly mean by that?"

He was referring to a speech by Kerry last week in which he said, "I believe I can fight a more effective, more thoughtful, more strategic, more proactive, more sensitive war on terror that reaches out to other nations and brings them to our side and lives up to American values in history."

Kerry's "more sensitive" quote would become the centerpiece of an attack that Cheney would launch against him in a speech the next day. Bush-Cheney spokeswoman Anne Womack said none of the town meeting questions was scripted and that the timing of the man's question was "purely coincidental."

Either way, Lynne Cheney can wax sarcastic in her own right. "I can't imagine al Qaeda is going to be impressed with our sensitivity," she said, going on to say that Kerry's philosophy is akin to "the kind of left-wing foolishness that suggests that problem is somehow with us, not the terrorists who attacked us."

While Dick Cheney derides Kerry with a kind of grandfatherly disdain, Edwards attacks Bush with polished outrage. His eyes go squinty and his voice low. At the Flint rally on Friday, Edwards defended Kerry from Cheney's attack the previous day.

"The vice president picked out one word and distorted it to

argue that John Kerry will not keep America safe." He reeled off the standard litany of Kerry's Vietnam exploits: how he volunteered for duty after college, how he suffered injuries, how he saved the life of a crewmate. And the home crowd loved it.

Cheney says he likes to campaign, to meet people. But his manner on the stump often betrays all the joy of someone vacuuming. After speaking to a rally at a high school in Battle Creek, the vice president grimaced and worked a rope line, the back of his bald head now covered in red, white, and blue confetti. Edwards lunges into crowds, grabbing for every hand and clutching them for several seconds at a time. Cheney approaches handshakes as if trying to pick mosquitoes out of the air with one hand. He makes quick and minimal contact.

Edwards loves babies and toddlers. In Flint, he leaned four-deep into a crowd so he could grab towheaded Bennett Rauscher, two and a half, of East Lansing. He held him, hugged him, and hoisted him for the cameras.

"Hey, he has a sister, too," Bennett's mom yelled to Edwards, and Edwards gladly performed the same routine with twin sister, Audrey.

When a woman in Battle Creek handed Cheney her baby, he carried the kid for a few seconds and then handed him back, no kiss. In the next three minutes, he would quick-pinch about a hundred more hands.

As he walked out a back door, the vice president vigorously rubbed his hands with sanitizing lotion provided by an aide.

Before the Debate, Putting on a Game Face: In the Green Room, It's Not Politic to Mingle

September 27, 2003

Senator Bob Graham is taking an awfully long time in the men's room.

Howard Dean is waiting outside. Senator John Edwards was in before Graham, looking intently in the mirror and breathing deeply (according to a source in the men's room).

Here comes Senator John Kerry, bounding around a corner. Dean eyes him thoughtfully. Things can get a little Darwinian, especially when a political debate is about to begin and there's a shortage of toilets in the backstage green-room area.

"There's a line here," Dean informs Kerry, his archrival in the race to succeed George Bush in the White House and Bob Graham in the john. Both men laugh.

Kerry, who recently underwent prostate surgery, is in no position to wait. The hallway is congested. The debate will last two hours. He asks an NBC staffer to check out the women's room. All clear, she says.

Kerry walks in. An aide stands guard outside the door.

Debate green-room areas incubate a distinctive, if rarely seen, genre of political anthropology. These are tightly restricted places where debate participants (like stage actors or talk-show guests) wait to go onstage. It is a sanctuary in which to perform last-minute preparation rituals. Ronald Reagan drank a glass of red wine in his green room. Bill Clinton sometimes bounced a basketball and almost always ate bananas. Al Gore got snippy if too many people started hanging around. Joe Lieberman does push-ups.

Candidates, like boxers before a fight, would rather not see each other before a debate. "If a candidate has to deal with the awkwardness of coming face-to-face with his opponent right before a debate, that puts him off his game," says Alan Schroeder, author of *Presidential Debates: Forty Years of High-Risk TV*. Unaware of this custom, political novice H. Ross Perot startled Clinton by walking into his green room before a debate in 1992 to say hello. Perot was turned away at the door of President George H. W. Bush's green room, Schroeder says.

But in a multi-candidate field, encounters are inevitable. This was displayed during the two-hour run-up to Thursday's four p.m. debate among the ten Democratic presidential hopefuls at Pace University in Manhattan. (NBC News, which produced the debate, granted a *Washington Post* reporter access to the debate's shared green-room areas, although entry to individual rooms varied with the campaigns.)

Each candidate was assigned a third-floor classroom, upstairs from the debate theater. At one thirty p.m., a paper sign was taped to General Wesley Clark's green-room door that said "Psychology Club Moved."

Each room is equipped with a phone, thirteen-inch televisions, a gift basket, a laser printer and computers, candy, bottled water, and soda. Edwards always has extra Diet Coke in his green room.

Representative Richard Gephardt has bottled water kept at room temperature. Representative Dennis Kucinich requests vegan food, although a staffer is spotted inside eating mozzarella before the candidate arrives.

Special green-room requests are honored, within reason. "But the last thing you want to do is be accused of being a J.Lo," says Erik Smith, Gephardt's press secretary. Smith was referring to actress Jennifer Lopez, whose two-page list of green-room necessities (for a cameo in a benefit music video) was mockingly circulated on the Internet. The list, among other demands, included white couches, white drapes, white flowers, white sheets, French aromatherapy candles, and apple pie à la mode.

"We will eat all colors of M&M's," declares Dean aide Kate O'Connor, a reference to Van Halen's demand that the brown ones be removed from the band's backstage bowl of M&M's.

The candidates begin arriving after two p.m. Terry McAuliffe, chairman of the Democratic National Committee, stands near a bank of elevators and asks each one if he's excited.

"Light 'em up, Al. Light 'em up," McAuliffe says, calling after Al Sharpton, who is rushing into his greenroom.

"What'd you say?" Sharpton says, looking back.

"I said, 'Light 'em up, Al. Like, light 'em up.' In the debate."

"Oh," Sharpton says. "I thought you said, 'White 'em up.'"

McAuliffe laughs.

Sharpton emerges from his green room at two thirty and encounters Graham's wife, Adele, next to the food table. He asks why her Graham for President button is so small. She doesn't want to be too ostentatious, she says, to which Sharpton replies, "I'll be ostentatious enough for the both of us tonight."

That settled, Clark bursts out of the elevator, surrounded by an entourage of fifteen. This includes his wife, Gert, several former Clinton aides, and a man carrying Clark's suit. They walk in a solemn cluster and settle into room E-324 (the sign on the door now says "Wes Wing").

"Light 'em up, General," McAuliffe yells across the elevator banks. "You gonna light it up today?"

Clark does not respond.

There is a backlog in the makeup room at three fifteen. Five candidates—Kucinich, Graham, Sharpton, Edwards, and Clark—are seated along a table, sharing three makeup artists. Elizabeth Edwards, John's wife, walks in for a last good-bye with her husband. Small talk is made among the combatants. The scent of hair spray blows around the food table whenever the door opens.

"Here you have all these adversaries thrown together in a tense place and everyone tries to act like they're best friends," says O'Connor, Dean's aide and a veteran of many green rooms.

Gary Bauer, a candidate for the Republican nomination in 2000, recalls a telling moment in Ames, Iowa. The GOP hopefuls, all backstage in their respective green rooms, were instructed to come out to take the stage at a designated time. "I walk out and I notice that all seven of us are standing alone together in the hall-way," says Bauer, who now heads two conservative groups. "Every one of us has these distinctive media personalities. But suddenly, here we were, alone in the same semidark hallway. No one really knew what to say."

At today's group appearance, Kerry and Lieberman are way be-hind schedule. "Is your guy even made up yet?" NBC's Beth O'Connell asks a Kerry aide. "Has he been miked yet?" No and no.

And where's Lieberman? He doesn't show up until 3:20. Only one of the three elevators is working. He has to take the stairs and his staff is not happy. He ducks into his green room for a few min-utes and comes out at exactly 3:43, humming the theme from *Rocky*.

Lieberman is the last to leave the green-room area, which is now being transformed into the campaigns' "rapid-response" centers.

The makeup room is empty except for three huge shopping bags on a table that say "Surya Henna—A New Concept in Hair Coloring."

Four Pace University students pick over a depleted plate of oatmeal cookies. They are all wearing shorts and seem oblivious to the debate that's starting downstairs.

"What's that smell?" one of the students says. "I smell hair spray."

The Convict's Campaign Staff:
Jim Traficant May Be in Jail,
but Supporters Still Work
for His Reelection

October 27, 2002

Girard, Ohio

W hen your candidate is in jail, it can be a bit of an obstacle," the campaign manager for Jim Traficant says.

This is a rare moment of exasperation for James Bunosky, a political rookie with a knack for understatement. Every day, after Bunosky finishes his work as a substitute teacher, he soldiers to his "life's calling," at the Traficant campaign headquarters, next to Sami's Quick Stop on Route 224. He takes inspiration from God and from a host of volunteers who file in, proclaiming that "Traficant was railroaded."

On a cloudy day in northeast Ohio, the front page of the Youngstown *Vindicator* sums up Bunosky's challenge. Traficant, the former Democratic congressman, "could not attend last night's debate," the paper said, "because he is in federal prison. His campaign did not send a representative to the event."

The media focuses too much on the negative, Bunosky says.

They harp on how Traficant was convicted in April of ten counts of bribery, tax evasion, and racketeering; expelled from Congress in July; and sentenced to eight years in prison. Why not mention Traficant's good points—his stellar record of constituent service, his great speaking skills—and not dwell on the question of whether he could serve in Congress while confined to a federal prison in White Deer, Pennsylvania?

In all likelihood Bunosky is the only political operative in America who has been asked why his candidate can't wear his toupee in prison. "I get a lot of unusual questions," says Bunosky, who gives his age as "thirties, forties, fifties, somewhere 'round there." He is sitting on a black vinyl chair in the back of the campaign office, rubbing his small brown eyes. No one gives Traficant the proper respect, he says. (This would be the Traficant who, upon entering a congressional hearing room last July, yelled, "If you don't get those cameras out of my face, I'm gonna go 8.6 on the Richter scale with gastric emissions that'll clear this room!") But with Traficant unable to make his case to voters, it falls to Bunosky to be the public face of the campaign—and the target of some residual disrespect.

When he appeared on CNN's *Crossfire* last month, Bunosky felt like "a death row inmate on my way to the execution." He was a nervous wreck—this was his first TV interview—and CNN canceled on him twice. The hosts asked whether Traficant could wear his toupee in prison, and if he had the endorsement of his cell mate. "They also said something to the effect of, 'You have thirty thousand dollars in your campaign war chest, does that include kickbacks?'" With such distractions, he moans, it's hard to run a campaign on the issues.

Bunosky is boyish, excitable, and prone to misspeaking. He says that Traficant should have been "found guilty on most counts," when he meant to say "not guilty on most counts"—at which point

Bunosky slaps his forehead and whispers to himself, "Gotta get those words right, Jim."

Like many Traficant supporters, Bunosky says there is a gap between the abuse Traficant gets in the media and the love he receives in his district. "I wish I could go to Traficant's cell and dig a hole for him," says Arlie Woodford, a retired steelworker who is wearing a Traficant for President button and standing under a "We Will Not Be Silenced" sign taped to the headquarters window.

No one has ever been elected to Congress from jail, and few people outside the campaign give Traficant much of a chance. Polls show him getting between 10 and 15 percent of the vote, which is well behind his opponents, Republican Ann Womer Benjamin and Democrat Timothy Ryan. But local political observers say that polls have traditionally underestimated Traficant's support. "He never polls well because no one admits they're going to vote for him," says Bertram de Souza, a political columnist for the *Vindicator*. There are also voters who would not normally support Traficant, but who plan to vote for him as a rebuke to the government. "A lot of people are angry at what happened to him," says campaign office manager Carol Tigert. "They plan to vote for him to make a statement."

Traficant has surmounted legal problems throughout his political career. As a sheriff in Youngstown in 1983, he was indicted after the FBI taped him accepting a $163,000 bribe from local mobsters. He is not a lawyer but defended himself at the trial and told jurors that he took the bribes as part of an independent sting operation that he had not informed authorities about. He was acquitted, then elected to Congress a year later.

The Congressional Research Service issued a nonbinding report last month saying that Traficant's incarceration would not necessarily disqualify him from serving. His supporters say Traficant could be a great congressman, even from prison. "He could do the job from Afghanistan, prison, or wherever he is" says Chris Martin, a landscaper from Poland, Ohio. Traficant's staff could perform his constituent service tasks. Voting? "The House of Representatives will have to make special accommodations once Traficant gets elected," Bunosky says.

Bunosky, who is single, had a long career in sales before he became a substitute teacher last March. He sold radio ads, cable TV ads, and fireworks displays. "I've always had success selling entertainment," he says, which suited him well for selling Jim Traficant's reelection, a nonpaying job he took last August. In a three-week period after Traficant's conviction, Bunosky and a group of volunteers gathered 3,700 signatures to ensure his place on the ballot as an independent.

No staffers from previous Traficant campaigns are involved in this race. Traficant's ordeal has made them wary, Bunosky says. "They don't want the Justice Department to be sending the black helicopters down on them." Bunosky has not spoken to Traficant except for a thirty-second phone conversation in which the jailed former congressman thanked him for his hard work. He says that Traficant's innocence is a "no-brainer" to him. In an odd way, his incarceration solidifies his underdog credibility—something that has enduring appeal in this distressed region. "There's a calling of the spirit to the Traficant cause," Bunosky says. "I've called him the political Baptist. They beheaded John the Baptist and they railroaded Jim Traficant."

Restoring Traficant to Congress will be just the first step in his rehabilitation, Bunosky says. "We're going to get him elected, then freed, then exonerated." But first things first. He envisions a head-spinning party on election night. Perhaps they'll do a satellite hookup to Traficant's jail cell for a victory speech. "I'm a nondrinker, but I'll probably get loaded that night and take a cab home," Bunosky says.

He is raising his voice, sounding evangelical. "We started out as a marble rolling down the hill," he says, "then a golf ball, a tennis ball, then a volleyball, then a basketball. Now it's a beach ball."

He is spreading his arms to demonstrate the building momentum. "By election day, we expect it will be a full-blown hot air balloon," Bunosky says before catching himself in this unwise political image. Rookie mistake. "That's without the hot air, that is," he adds, slapping his forehead.

"We Will Eat All Colors
of M&M's"

"I Am an Entrepreneur, Baby. Don't Forget That. I'm an Entrepreneur."

July 22, 2012

Terry McAuliffe, the former chairman of the Democratic National Committee, is starting a company that makes little electric cars. On a sweltering Friday in early July, GreenTech Automotive unveiled its signature vehicle—the MyCar—at a plant opening in the north Mississippi town of Horn Lake. McAuliffe was puttering backstage before the event with his pals Bill Clinton and Haley Barbour, the former governor of Mississippi and archetypal Republican lobbyist.

The holding area was crowded and somewhat frenzied. People designated as VIPs kept streaming through, many in from China, where GreenTech is building an 18-million-square-foot facility. They arrived, dozens of them, via a Harrah's shuttle bus with a big "Fun in Store for Those Who Ride" painted on the side. As Clinton prepared to go onstage, I asked him if he would ever consider buying a car from McAuliffe, who he once marveled could "talk an owl out of a tree." "Absolutely, I would buy a new car from Terry," he told me. "But a used car? I am not so sure about a used car." He laughed and wheeled around and repeated the line to Barbour ("Listen to what I just told him . . ."), while slapping his fleshy back.

McAuliffe, fifty-five, is eager to be known, foremost, as a businessman and an entrepreneur, and not so much as a political moneyman. That will take some doing. He is "the greatest fundraiser in the history of the universe," Al Gore once said, in keeping with the hyperbole often heaped on McAuliffe, known widely as the Macker, by the politicians who love/need him. McAuliffe, who is in fact quite hard to dislike and is himself a peerless exaggerator, has collected legions of friends over the years. "There are eighteen thousand names in my Rolodex," he boasted to me earlier that morning over coffee. When I pressed him, he revised the number upward, to 18,632. The acknowledgments section of his memoir *What a Party!* runs six single-spaced pages and includes the names of every member of the Democratic National Committee during his time as the party chairman. In a five-minute span of conversation, McAuliffe distilled for me the extent of his psychological complexity: (1) He pinches himself all the time because he's so lucky. (2) He likes to think out of the box. (3) He swings for the fences every day. (4) At the end of the day, it is what it is.

If McAuliffe's trademark is fund-raising, his principal identity is as a Professional Best Friend to Bill Clinton. The subtitle of *What a Party!* might as well be *Let Me Tell You Another Story About Me and Bill Clinton*. (One involved South Korean intelligence agents thinking McAuliffe and Clinton were more than just friends.) If he is not dropping the name of the forty-second president, the Macker is telling you that he just got off the phone with Bill Clinton, or that, what do you know, President Clinton is actually on the phone right now, and can you please excuse him for just a second ("Hello, Mr. President"). And if Mr. President is not on the phone, there is a good chance he is, as today, close by.

Clinton's voice is softer and throatier than you remember. He has lost considerable weight, evident to anyone who has seen him in photographs (once known as the "Big Dog," he's now more "Vegan Dog"). But it is jarring nonetheless to see the svelte version of the former president up close, especially since his head is as big as it ever was—a fact accentuated by the ruddy brightness of his face and pronounced cheekbones. Encountering Clinton these days is like meeting a skinny older guy who is wearing a Bill Clinton mask.

McAuliffe's MyCar debut is the culmination of years of planning for a firm that is trying to reinvent the automobile. Unsaid was that he also hoped it would reinvent Terry McAuliffe as he approaches his own probable run for governor of Virginia in 2013— something he tried in 2009, losing in the primary to a relative political unknown named Creigh Deeds. GreenTech could be the vehicle, so to speak, for McAuliffe to escape his lane as a political rainmaker, carnival barker, and Clinton appendage and reposition himself as "a Virginia businessman fighting for Democratic causes and creating jobs," as his Web site says. It hardly mattered that a lot of these jobs would be in Mississippi, not Virginia, because of a package of tax and infrastructure incentives McAuliffe was able to secure from Barbour, who himself made the successful transition from operative-businessman to public office when he was elected governor of Mississippi in 2003.

GreenTech's story is in part a monument to the power of a politically connected company. The board of its primary investment group is led by Hillary Clinton's brother and includes a former governor of Louisiana and a former IRS commissioner. GreenTech has raised more than $100 million in capital, much of it no doubt deriving from McAuliffe's wide network of political contacts. And as a general rule, former presidents tend not to show up for the openings of plants in Horn Lake, Miss. This is all nothing but good publicity for the company, for Mississippi, for the Macker. It's hard to look around the excitement of this day's festivities in Horn Lake, staged as it is, like a political event, under a massive American flag, and not appreciate the simple wisdom behind the message: "This idea that if you're in one political party you've got to somehow hate the people on the other side," as McAuliffe put it to me, "it's destructive to our country."

After our brief conversation backstage, Clinton walked over to Barbour, who was standing about twenty feet away and was seemingly in possession of many of the pounds Clinton had shed. Like McAuliffe, Barbour is a former party chairman—he was head of the Republican National Committee during the early Clinton years—who also seems completely unburdened by angst, misgiving, or heavy self-analysis. He thought hard about seeking the 2012 Republican nomination for president. In the end he decided not to run, and after his second term as governor, he rejoined the Washington lobbying firm that still bears his name and made him tens of millions of dollars and where he lobbied for tobacco companies.

The columnist Michael Kinsley noted in *Politico* how so many veteran reporters were longing for Barbour to run for president. Why? Barbour, Kinsley wrote, "plays on this social insecurity among journalists." He "doesn't literally wink as he spins, but he manages to send the message: This is all a big game—a big wonderful game—and you have the privilege of playing it with me."

Barbour speaks in a slow, mud-mouthed Mississippi drawl. Unlike the set of terrified modern politicians admired for their "restraint" and "caution," he will imbibe tumblers of Maker's Mark with reporters after hours and tell salty jokes on the record. Like the one that his former White House boss, Ronald Reagan, told him on *Air Force One* about the two Episcopal preachers: "One says to the other: 'You know, times have really changed. I never slept with my wife before we were married, did you?' And the other one said, 'I don't know, what was your wife's maiden name?'" Shoulder whacks and belly laughs.

The Washington Political Class, as it's called by those in the media who are often a part of it, represents a vast and self-perpetuating network of friendships and expedient associations that transcend even the fiercest ideological differences. Membership in the class is the paramount commonality between the various tribes—the journalists, the Democrats, the Republicans, the super-lawyers, superlobbyists, superstaffers, fund-raisers, David Gergens, Donna Braziles, and Karl Roves. They argue on television and often go into business with their on-air combatants. They can be paid tens of thousands of dollars to do their left-right Kabuki thing in front of big organizations. The Macker did this with Rove a while back—a luncheon speech at the ExxonMobil headquarters in Texas. He has a few joint events planned with Barbour for the fall. He has also done partisan duets at a combined fifty grand a pop with "my great friend Eddie Gillespie," a Barbour protégé and former RNC chairman whom McAuliffe bonded with in the green room between their many on-air donnybrooks over the last decade. "I have a love-hate relationship with Terry," Gillespie joked in one of their public debates. "I love Terry. And I hate myself for it."

One quaint maxim of the Political Class is that there is no such thing as Democrats and Republicans in Washington, only the Green Party. Green as in money, not GreenTech, or anything having to do with clean energy. In his speech at the GreenTech opening, McAuliffe said that during the '90s, "President Clinton created more millionaires and billionaires than any other president in the history of this country." At which point, Barbour, who had been chatting onstage with Clinton through much of McAuliffe's remarks, gave the former president a special nudge.

McAuliffe and Barbour became multimillionaires independent of any celebrity imprint. McAuliffe grew up in Syracuse, where he started his first business, McAuliffe Driveway Maintenance, at age fourteen. After snowblowing work, he ironed and starched out each dollar bill to ensure maximum crispness. He was the chairman of a commercial bank at thirty and made at least an eight-figure fortune as an investor in several companies, including a multimillion-dollar windfall in the late 1990s from a $100,000 investment in the tele-communications firm Global Crossing. (The company later filed for bankruptcy. As the Bush administration was taking heat for the Enron scandal, some Republicans tried to make an issue of McAuliffe's profiting from a doomed company while less well connected investors lost big.)

McAuliffe slightly recoils whenever I suggest that he is a "Washington insider." (He lives in McLean, Virginia, a full twenty minutes outside DC.) "I am an entrepreneur, baby," he has said to me several times in recent years. "Don't forget that. I'm an entrepreneur"—albeit one whose wedding party included the former House Democratic leader turned superlobbyist Richard Gephardt; who has been a regular at Sam Donaldson's annual holiday party; who runs into his neighbor Dick Cheney at his daughter's (and Cheney's granddaughter's) soccer games; and who initially put up the money for Bill and Hillary Clinton's Chappaqua home.

McAuliffe goes on an annual hunting trip on Maryland's Eastern Shore with a gang that includes the famed Democratic lobbyist Tommy Boggs, the former Senate Republican leader Trent Lott, and Lott's Democratic lobbying partner, John Breaux, a former Louisiana senator who as a member of the House famously declared that his vote could not be bought but "could be rented." (After a member of the House leadership once called Breaux a "cheap whore," Breaux protested that he was "not cheap.")

McAuliffe has arguably seen the inside of more green rooms over the last two decades than anyone in Washington. That is where he met Barbour, who in his capacity as RNC chairman used to pulverize Clinton on television while McAuliffe defended him. After a while, through repeated exposures, they became friends. In late

1999, Barbour and Tommy Boggs were planning to open a downtown restaurant called the Caucus Room, which the *Washington Post* described as a "red-meat emporium" that "will serve up power, influence, loopholes, money, and all the other ingredients that make American Democracy great." Seeking investors, Barbour called McAuliffe and asked for $100,000, which he sent over immediately. A while later, Barbour called back, said they were oversubscribed, and sent McAuliffe back a check for $50,000. "So I figure I made fifty in the deal," said McAuliffe, who never saw a penny more.

It was around this time that Bill Clinton asked the Macker what ambassadorship he wanted for all the work he'd done on his behalf. McAuliffe had just put together a fund-raiser at Washington's MCI Center that sucked in more than $26 million for the DNC ("the biggest event in the history of mankind, as you know"). He told Clinton that he wanted to be the ambassador to the Court of St. James's, or Britain. But McAuliffe figured his appointment was no sure thing, given that it required Senate confirmation and that Republicans, who held a majority at the time, had little incentive to help a president they had just impeached. McAuliffe enlisted his friend Barbour and asked him to lobby his friend and fellow Mississippian, Trent Lott, then the Senate majority leader, on his behalf.

The next day, Barbour called back and said the conversation went well. When I asked him about the transaction, he seemed mildly annoyed at the suggestion that Republicans in the late '90s would punish a buddy of Bill Clinton's, or, alternatively, that McAuliffe would receive any special treatment because he was Haley Barbour's friend. McAuliffe, he said, was qualified and effective and would have represented the nation with distinction. "It would be awful if just because he was effective for the other side, we punished him," Barbour said. "We need more of those guys, who understand that this is not personal, just because we disagree. This business should not be vengeful."

But it would be wrong to assume that Barbour and Lott were acting out of pure nonpartisan motives. McAuliffe later learned from Lott, his hunting buddy, that when Barbour called him about the appointment, his first thought was how convenient it would be to get the best political fund-raiser in the Democratic Party out of the country in time for the 2000 elections. "Tell the son of a bitch I'll walk him to the airplane," Lott told Barbour, according to McAuliffe.

As it turned out, the 2000 Democratic convention in Los Angeles was in serious financial trouble, and McAuliffe wound up taking it over at the urging (begging) of the nominee to be, Al Gore. After the election, McAuliffe became chairman of the DNC during George W. Bush's first term. He still saw Barbour a fair amount around town, though Barbour eventually headed back to Mississippi in 2003 to run for governor. He took office in 2004, and a year later saw his governorship consumed by Hurricane Katrina, which killed 238 Mississippians, destroyed 68,000 homes, and turned 28,000 square miles, or 60 percent of the state, into a major disaster area. Barbour became a one-man fuse box of political and corporate connectedness. His old friend Sam Adcock, the head lobbyist for the aerospace firm EADS, sent five helicopters and an ambulance plane to Mississippi. Another lobbyist, David O'Brien, donated 100 satellite phones. The CEO of the timber giant Georgia-Pacific (a former lobbying client) offered his firm's services to help salvage storm-damaged timber.

While fully engaged in the grave matters of Mississippi, Barbour retained strong links to the capital. "Washington has been very nice to me," he said. "I have a lot of Democratic friends. I have a lot of liberal friends. I even have friends in the news media." Indeed, on the night before the 2010 White House Correspondents Dinner, Barbour was scheduled to travel to Washington to speak at a book party for the CNBC host Maria Bartiromo—aka the "Money

Honey." Ed Rogers, a founder of Barbour's old lobbying firm, was the party's host. Prudishly speaking, a journalist's agreeing to be celebrated at a party hosted by a lobbyist and headlined by two news makers might be seen as compromising—especially when one of those news makers (Barbour) was thinking seriously at that point about running for president and when the honoree (the Money Honey) wound up moderating a Republican debate the following year.

In the end, Barbour could not make the Bartiromo bash because he had to stay back in Mississippi to tend to the BP oil spill in the Gulf of Mexico, so the Macker took over his speaking duties. He exalted Bartiromo in his remarks as "the greatest economist, the greatest woman ever to be involved in dictating how world economic policy is done." NBC's Andrea Mitchell, who attended with her husband, the former Federal Reserve chairman Alan Greenspan, went on likewise about her colleague Maria. But first she paid tribute to the fun-loving trilogy of McAuliffe, Barbour, and Rogers, singling Barbour out for special citation for his efforts in the gulf. "Haley Barbour is really a hero to a lot of people," declared Mitchell, who has known Barbour since he worked in the Reagan White House, which she covered for NBC.

Soon after, everyone raised a glass—to the Money Honey, to the Macker, to Barbour, to the whole team.

McAuliffe had thought about starting some kind of clean-energy company as far back as 2006. But he focused instead on writing a book and then, starting in early 2007, on being chairman of Hillary Clinton's 2008 presidential campaign. Then there was the ill-fated run for governor of Virginia in 2009, after which he started GreenTech, purchasing a company from China and moving it back to the United States. He sent a team out to scout for locations in several states, but in the end chose Mississippi because, he said, in addition to the tax incentives and abatements he received, "I knew I could trust Haley's word, and he knew he could trust mine." Barbour emphasized to me that GreenTech received no preferential deal, just a standard off-the-shelf package that the state would offer to an automotive company. "The fact that Haley Barbour and Terry McAuliffe are friends is lagniappe," Barbour said.

Lagniappe?

"It's a French word. It means something extra, like a cherry on top."

McAuliffe says he hates to sleep, musters about four hours a night, and downs about seven or eight cups of coffee a day. He was up at five on the morning of the Horn Lake opening. He checked the assembly line, met with his board, and made certain all the American flags were in place and the ribs and catfish ready to barbecue. He donned a GreenTech polo shirt and determined that the first car off the line should also be green.

But this ran counter to the original plan, which was to have the first car be one that was specially customized for the local Domino's, which is purchasing a fleet to deliver pizzas into areas whose roads are restricted to low speeds, like the University of Mississippi, in Oxford. The speed limit on campus is 18 mph, in homage to the famed alum quarterback Archie Manning's old number. (MyCars, which cost upwards of $15,000, are generally limited to roads with a speed limit of twenty-five miles an hour and need a battery charge every hundred miles or so.) Still, even with the late-breaking car-color change, the program went off with few glitches. Barbour gave a great and generous speech, and so did President Clinton, and McAuliffe proclaimed his hopes for the future of the country and the green movement.

After the remarks, McAuliffe, Barbour, and Clinton descended the stage and squeezed into the maiden MyCars for photos amid a furious blaring of "Born in the U.S.A." After a few minutes, McAuliffe and Clinton walked the assembly line, Bon Jovi's "Livin' on a Prayer" resounding, while Barbour bolted for the air-conditioned area backstage. He seemed less than his usual happy-go-Haley self, but Clinton and McAuliffe rejoined him in a few minutes and Barbour regained his game face. Banter ensued:

"Hey, you notice that Clinton refused to get into the car that Terry was driving?" Barbour kept saying. Big laughs.

Barbour told McAuliffe the joke about the two Episcopal preachers.

(Disclaimer: I prodded him.)

"Reagan supposedly had great jokes," McAuliffe said.

"Oh, God, he's great," Barbour confirmed.

A few minutes later, Barbour made his exit, and McAuliffe and Clinton stayed behind to pose for an impromptu group photo with assorted staff and stragglers. "Hey, get in here," someone called out to a young African-American aide to McAuliffe. "We need some diversity in this photo."

"Yeah, we only got one Jewish guy in this picture," Clinton quipped. "That's not enough."

On his way out, the Vegan Dog stopped in the hallway and offered a quick assessment of why politics has become so nasty. (1) Our national leaders don't stay in Washington enough and don't get to know one another. (2) They travel constantly, don't sleep enough, and are jet-lagged. And (3) for good measure, he's really proud of Terry.

With that, Clinton headed out a back door and into his motorcade while the Macker bounded back down the hallway as if he owned the place.

Seventeen Things I Learned from Reading Every Last Word of the *Economist*'s "The World in 2013" Issue

December 12, 2012

I've been telling people I've read the *Economist* since college. Sometimes I actually even do read it, but not as often as I say I do—and not as often as I quote stuff from "London's influential *Economist*," as they call it on NPR. (Which I also listen to, by the way—I am very well informed!)

Like many people who sometimes travel in high-powered circles, I am a complete fraud. I have no idea how I got here. This is an especially familiar condition in Washington, where I live, and where the impostor syndrome is like our psychological common cold. So a lot of people here lie about reading the *Economist*. We probably have the highest number of lied-about subscribers. Because it's important to come off smart and worldly and cognizant that Lagos will overtake Cairo to become Africa's biggest city in 2013. Also, that 2013 will be the first year since 1987 that will have all digits different from one another. And it could be a really big year for neutrinos.

Reading the *Economist* also makes you feel smart. Recall the

Simpsons episode when Homer is handed a copy of the magazine on an airplane. "Look at me, I'm reading the *Economist*," he boasts to Marge. "Did you know that Indonesia is at a crossroads?"

I especially love the *Economist* at this time of year. Holiday parties abound, which creates a constant need for the kind of fancy-pants knowledge the journal confers. I love the wry, punchy leads and the adorable British spellings ("globalisation") and the concern the magazine engenders in me over whether the president of Colombia can regain his momentum (that would be Juan Manuel Santos, obviously); or whether we will learn of sufficient progress in the development of a "virtual liver" at much-awaited conferences next year in Luxembourg, Denmark, and the Netherlands. Damn, gotta book those plane tickets.

December also marks the arrival of the *Economist*'s annual look-ahead issue: a confident and sophisticated accumulation of factoids and predictions for 2013 that can make you seem not only smart but also visionary. I make a point of reading the *Economist*'s "The World in ____" issue every year (well, not really). Cover to cover. And not because the boss is making me read every word of the "The World in 2013" edition, which came out last week, and which I devoured like a big plate of Swiss chard. Or, better yet, like quinoa, because the UN says 2013 will be "the International Year of Quinoa," as I now know.

Here are seventeen things I learned.

1. Next year could be ugly. "From a showdown with Iran over its nuclear plans to a catastrophic breakup of the euro zone, it is not hard to think of disasters that could strike the world in 2013." That is how Daniel Franklin begins his "from the editor" note. Ouch. "With luck, such dangers will turn out to be like the Olympic-pool-size asteroid that will hurtle close to Earth on February 15, 2013: near misses, which might help to concentrate minds." Speaking for myself, I am now fully concentrating.

2. "Obesity sucks." The urbane publication declares thus on page 32, atop a soda-can graphic showing how much fatter the world is becoming. That is one of the great whimsical touches you find in the *Economist*: a discussion of a spreading global health epidemic summed up so neatly, if crassly. The article itself is svelte, but rich in factoid nutrients:

(a) In 2011 the average Mexican guzzled 728 eight-ounce servings of Coca-Cola, a higher rate than in any other country.

(b) Two-thirds of Americans are overweight or obese.

(c) "Japan has set a specific limit to citizens' waistlines. If workers do not slim down, their employers face fines." The *Economist* calls this "overreach," and who is going to argue with them? The *Economist* also says governments should consider "a hefty fine on soda," because "the syrupy stuff is a main driver of obesity." The syrupy stuff! Tastes like a pander to Michael Bloomberg, in hopes that he might buy the magazine, as has been speculated.

3. Big year coming up for superstitious types. Or, in the *Economist*-like way they put it: "Beware the globalisation of superstition." (Why must they terrorise us like that?) There are apparently many people who think about numbers. Not mathematicians per se, or Nate Silver, but numerologists, which the magazine defines as "crackpots who assign mystical significance to certain numbers." Said crackpots, for instance, would know that 20 and 13 add up to 33, which they "consider a 'highly charged master number,' full of meaning."

4. No doubt, the number 2013 is full of meaning. This largely stems from the "13" in 2013, which is unsettling to people who fear that number, known as "triskaidekaphobiacs." The Romans and Vikings used to freak out over 13s. Theories span the map on the origins of triskaidekaphobia. "It was Judas, the betrayer of Jesus, who brought the numbers up to 13 at the Last Supper." (But, as the magazine points out, couldn't the same be said of the other diners?)

Something else to ponder about 13: "It was the women's thirteen menstrual cycles a year that gave the number a bad name when the solar calendar came to displace the thirteen-cycle lunar calendar. Or so it is said by credulous expositors." Next time my editor asks how I know something, I will credit my newest source, "credulous expositors."

5. The issue includes on page 36 a nifty calendar of events for 2013, or (come February) the Chinese year of the snake, "associated with grace, intelligence, and material gain." I have marked my calendar with the following:

(a) March 20 has been designated by the UN as International Happiness Day.

(b) The iTunes store turns ten in April, and everyone should celebrate by downloading "Happy Birthday to You," the magazine suggests. Cute!

(c) World UFO Day is in July.

(d) Naypyidaw, Myanmar's new capital, will be home to the Twenty-Seventh Southeast Asian Games—the first time in forty-four years that Myanmar has been host. Has it really been forty-four years already?

6. "Barack Obama's first inauguration was festooned with hope and change. His second, alas, will be freighted with inertia and foreboding." That is one concise, packed, and authoritative lead. As one who has spent hours puzzling over how to start stories, I am a sucker for excellent leads. The *Economist* is a hothouse of them. I wish I had written, for instance, this: "Peering into the crystal ball at Italy's future in 2013, what you see is a single stark fact wrapped in mists as thick and shifting as those of the Venetian lagoon." Overdone? Perhaps, but I appreciate the effort, especially compared to so many standard news leads which, as the *Economist* says about the coming upheaval in Japan, "is likely to be as enticing as last week's sushi."

7. Department of "Oh, Yeah, I Guess It Is." This will be a big year in America for momentous anniversaries: the fiftieth for both Martin Luther King's "I Have a Dream" speech and John F. Kennedy's assassination.

8. Breaking: Fidel Castro will die in 2013. Only God knows this for sure. And the *Economist*. That's how smart they are.

9. What would a proper reading of the *Economist* be without at least one exploration of Canada's improved trade relations with China? And what better way to tell that story than with, what else, pandas? Turn to page 56: a story headlined "Pandering to China?," which portrays our endangered friends as a kind of ursine Rorschach test. "When you look at the face of a giant panda bear, what do you see? Zoo visitors, who line up in their millions for the three hundred pandas in captivity worldwide, see a cute and cuddly animal. Environmentalists see a clownlike face as a potent symbol in the fight to preserve endangered species. Chinese officials, who have traded on the panda's cuteness and rarity for centuries, see a useful diplomatic tool. And Stephen Harper, the Canadian prime minister who engineered a ten-year loan of a pair, starting in 2013, sees confirmation that his government's China policy is at last showing positive results." This otherwise sweet story includes this one note of poison. China might not be all that into Canada, after all—panda love notwithstanding. "Canadians' sense of their importance contrasts sharply with one recent assessment by a Canadian Sinologist in Beijing that 'Canada is a distant speckle in the Chinese consciousness.'" Now that is one harsh Canadian Sinologist.

10. The capital of Mongolia is? Ulaanbaatar. Thank you very much.

11. Attention, Homer: Indonesia is no longer at a crossroads. On the contrary, the *Economist* says the emerging behemoth "has a chance to shine" in 2013. It has "almost certainly grown faster than India in 2012 for the first time since the Asian financial crisis of the

late 1990s. And it could well repeat that trick in 2013 (when its population will rise above 250m)."

12. One person who is at a crossroads is Hung Huang, "a publisher of a fashion magazine in Beijing," and "one of the most popular microbloggers in China." In brief, Hung can be a bit subversive and undiplomatic in her posts, and she struggles with how far to push. "She has become fearful . . . of the microblog's power to create a sort of mob justice." This is all interesting, but—being shallow—I really like the headline: "Hung Verdict."

13. Australia is doing quite well these days, at least when viewed from afar (and how else to view Australia?). Prime Minister Julia Gillard enjoys a budget surplus of $1.9 billion, and "the government has also promised big spending on insurance for disabled people and on free dental treatment." It goes without saying that this story is accompanied by photo of a kangaroo.

14. A private company in Hunan, China, says that it will finish construction of the world's tallest building, known as Sky City, in the provincial capital, Changsha. Parenthetically, the writer notes that "given that work on this was not even due to begin until November 2012, some skepticism is in order."

15. "Israel will not strike Iran in 2013." Okay, everyone chill.

16. On page 91, the *Economist* publishes its annual "where-to-be-born index," which purports to rank "which country will provide the best opportunities for a healthy, safe, and prosperous life in the years ahead." The winner: Switzerland, beating out Australia at number two and Norway at number three. The United States ties with Germany at number sixteen, just behind Belgium.

17. Cities will become "smarter" in 2013, following a sluggish period. "One of the more useful concepts in any effort to understand the evolution of technology markets is the 'hype cycle.'" In the first phase, a new idea brings outsize expectations. A "trough of disillusionment" follows, and then, finally, a "slope of enlightenment,"

meaning that the technology finally catches up to its initial hype. "And so it goes with 'smart cities,' the idea that information technology and digital data will make cities far more efficient. After much hype in 2010 and growing disappointment in the following two years, 2013 will be the year in which it becomes apparent that cities can indeed become smarter—albeit in different ways than some visionaries imagined." Just imagine how smart cities could be if they read the *Economist*.

It's Not All About Him,
He Said Often

September 2, 2012

Tampa, Florida

B y the looks of things here, Chris Christie was having so much fun, at least for a while. As the New Jersey governor roller-balled his way through Tampa last week, his tough-guy shtick (his YouTube-immortalized reputation for beat-downs of hecklers, re-porters, and teacher-union types) was as basic to his persona as perma-tan is to Snooki's.

Likewise, as fans of his beloved Bruce Springsteen demand "Born to Run" and "Thunder Road" at concerts, people expect Mr. Christie to play to the combative type. He does not disappoint, de-lighting groups of delegates by threatening to "come looking for them" in the event that Republicans do not perform well in their states. He trashed his seventy-four-year-old Democratic counterpart in California, Jerry Brown, as "an old retread" and stood proudly by as Meg Whitman, the Republican who lost to Mr. Brown, told a meeting of the state's delegates a story about Mr. Christie's con-fronting a rude protester at one of her campaign events.

"You have two choices with a bully," Mr. Christie said,

explaining his actions to the crowd in a default voice that resembles someone trying to shout over a vacuum. "You can either sidle up to them or you can punch them in the face. I like to punch them in the face."

This pretty much distills Mr. Christie's approach to politics as well as the tenor of the current campaign. It made Mr. Christie, other than the two guys on the ticket, "the biggest get of the week for anyone," said the conservative radio host Hugh Hewitt, who was the master of ceremonies at the California breakfast.

But, okay, enough about Chris Christie. He would like to talk now, if that's okay, about Mitt Romney.

Recall that Mr. Romney is the actual nominee of the Republican Party. It can be easy to overlook this when you watch Mr. Christie campaign on behalf of Mr. Romney because Mr. Christie typically first spends several minutes talking about himself, his record, his family, and the general wisdom of "how we do things in New Jersey."

He displayed this trait vividly last week while headlining a procession of heat-lamp breakfasts, activist confabs, and beach parties, as well as in a keynote speech in which Mr. Christie expended 1,800 words and sixteen minutes of me-talk before spitting out the name of the soon-to-be standard-bearer.

So after enduring a few days of criticism about what some had dubbed his "me-note" address, Mr. Christie was careful not to forget Mitt, this despite the heavy burden he himself lives with as such a prime source of interest and desire. This week, after all, is about the current standard-bearer, the former governor of Massachusetts, what's-his-name. Mr. Christie wants to talk about that guy.

Specifically, how Mr. Romney has benefited from Chris Christie.

"I was the first governor to endorse Mitt Romney," Mr. Christie says repeatedly. He has traveled to fifteen states for Mr. Romney, raised money for him all over the place, and spoken on Mr. Romney's behalf at several events in Tampa. "And I was honored to be asked to give the keynote address," Mr. Christie said.

On the morning of the speech, Tuesday, Mr. Christie was comparing himself to one of those agitated racehorses. "You know, the horse that's at the starting gate of the Kentucky Derby," he explained to an assembly of Michigan delegates. "Just banging up against that gate, you know?" Mr. Christie kept rolling his broad shoulders back and forth so the delegates could appreciate the full effect of his impatience and excitement. Caged lion, penned-in racehorse, whatever.

He ended his remarks, as he did many times last week, with a warning to the delegates. "I'm in a good mood now," he said. But if Mr. Romney happens to lose their state? Look out. Mr. Christie will be coming back to them, and in a much worse mood. ("We're going to give you some Jersey-style treatment," he told North Carolina Republicans an hour earlier. "You don't want that now.") Indeed, as David Letterman once said, angering Mr. Christie is like crossing a rhino.

After bolting the Michigan breakfast, Mr. Christie threw off his navy suit coat and barreled his way through the Embassy Suites lobby, trailed by a sizable entourage of security, staff, and reporters shouting questions of the "How do you feel?" and "Are you nervous?" varieties.

"No questions today," Mr. Christie shouted back to the group before plopping himself into the passenger seat of a waiting SUV that would transport him two blocks to the convention floor for his "walk-through." One of the prime status symbols of a convention luminary is the size of his scrum—how many people surround him or her at a given moment—which made Mr. Christie a literal Big Man on Campus.

He and his wife, Mary Pat, did a quick walk of the stage and check of the podium before descending to the floor to greet some Jersey friends. "It's crazy, isn't it?" she kept saying to no one in particular. "It's like a pinch-yourself kind of thing."

After about fifteen minutes, Mr. Christie headed off as loud rock and roll blared over speakers. As he stomped through narrow hallways and tunnels in the concourse, the pulsing music nourished a decidedly WWE aura around him.

An interloping reporter (this one) walked up alongside and fearlessly asked if he had a special pre-speech meal planned. "Something light," he said, "maybe a salad, with chicken or something."

Mr. Christie is known by a few readily identified trademarks. First, he is considerably overweight, which might not be worth mentioning except that it is readily evident and he often jokes about it. "Yes, I am familiar with the restaurant industry," he said Tuesday morning after being introduced by a representative of a restaurant trade group. "I am familiar with it in New Jersey, New York, Pennsylvania, Delaware . . ."

(He is trying to shed pounds, knows it's a problem, and has enlisted a trainer.)

Second, he is a big fan of Bruce Springsteen and not just in one of those ways that Jersey pols try to be cool by saying so. Mr. Christie's devotion to the Boss includes an encyclopedic knowledge of his lyrics, attendance at over one hundred concerts, and a convulsive presence at those shows that "is an exercise in volcano management," wrote Jeffrey Goldberg, who plumbed Mr. Christie's Springsteen obsession in the *Atlantic* earlier this year. (Mr. Goldberg wrote that Chris would happily marry Bruce "if he were gay and if gay people were allowed to marry in the state he governs.")

Last, and perhaps most of all, is the YouTube phenomenon: the collection of short Internet videos that show Mr. Christie chewing out the assorted provocateurs who have, at various times over the last three years, ignited Governor Powder Keg. This has imprinted Mr. Christie with a status of the no-nonsense purveyor of "hard political truths" and has granted him a status as the cathartic id of impatient conservatism to counterbalance the cautious Mr. Romney.

To hear Mr. Christie's admirers tell it, there simply has never been another politician, ever, who has told you what he really thinks.

They wear out the numerous clichés to convey a "straight shooter," someone who "tells it like it is," and whatnot.

"What you see is what you get with him," said Gary Felien, of Oceanside, California, who was wearing a hat adorned with buttons that said things like Ted Kennedy for Lifeguard at the California delegation breakfast.

As much as anything, this smash-mouth sensibility is what made Mr. Christie such an intriguing (and potentially perfect) choice to deliver the keynote speech Tuesday.

But he received some rough reviews: "A prime-time belly flop," *Politico* called it. "The most curious keynote I have ever heard," said Chris Wallace of Fox News. The criticism fed a broader suspicion of Mr. Christie: that he has grown slightly big for his already-big britches.

Several things fed the All About Christie suspicions in Tampa— a notion that gained some currency within Mr. Romney's circle. The week began with an article in the *New York Post* saying that Mr. Christie did not want Mr. Romney to pick him as his running mate because he would have to leave his governor's job, and that Mr. Christie thought Mr. Romney was likely to lose anyway. Mr. Christie denied the article's claims, but at least two Romney advisers took note of it and were not amused.

Meanwhile, Mr. Christie's aides stoked expectations for his Tuesday keynote. They established a Twitter account for him (@christiekeynote) that provided a travelogue of his convention escapades and triumphs. There's a shot of the governor hanging with Tom Brokaw, a nice quote about him from Rudy Giuliani, a clip of Condi Rice saying Mr. Christie "stands for truth-telling."

Mr. Christie is sensitive to the impression that he was more focused here on his own career than Mr. Romney's. This seemed especially acute after the keynote.

Mr. Christie likes to tell audiences about the day Mr. Romney won him over, a vignette that doubles as a charming portrait of the Christie family's chaotic household.

It was October 2011. Mr. Christie, by then a full-scale kingpin of YouTube Nation, had become the epitome of a Jersey brand of headbanging Republicanism. People started asking Mr. Christie to run for president. You might remember this, and in case you did not, Mr. Christie was not shy about providing refresher courses last week, usually in the form of ostentatious exasperation at how no one took his denials of interest in seeking the presidency seriously.

"After the eighty-seventh time I said I wasn't running for president, they finally believed me," Mr. Christie told the delegates of South Carolina—a state that, Mr. Christie points out, had its own effort to draft Mr. Christie into the presidential race last year.

He then began a play-by-play of the day last fall that Mitt and Ann Romney paid a two-and-a-half-hour visit to his and Mary Pat's home in Mendham: How the Christie family hurriedly cleaned their house. How Mom and Dad implored their four kids (ages nine to nineteen) to behave, how Mitt and Ann got lost on the way over, how Patrick Christie (twelve) nearly barreled into Mr. Romney on his Rollerblades, and how Bridget Christie (nine) then became jealous of the attention paid to her brother and started performing cartwheels for Mr. Romney.

In the course of this visit, Mr. Christie became convinced that Mr. Romney (who could not have been nicer to Patrick and Bridget) was his man. In his retelling, Mr. Christie can draw out the story for nearly fifteen minutes, or half his speech. It is a winner with crowds and offers a serviceable testimonial to nice-guy Mitt.

After his speech to South Carolina delegates at a country club, Mr. Christie signed autographs, posed for photos, and promised that he would return soon enough to the state before heading out to his waiting SUV. A scrum of reporters followed. One asked him what Springsteen song would best apply to the events of his week.

He thought a few seconds. "'Out in the Street,'" Mr. Christie said finally. "Because I've been out in the street all week, meeting people, having fun, enjoying myself, and doing important stuff."

Now, two days after his keynote, he is still getting questions about it, specifically the "all about Chris" critique. "I've resigned myself to the fact that my future will always be speculated about," Mr. Christie said as sweat glistened from his forehead. "Even if Mitt Romney wins on November 6, as I expect him to, people will start speculating about 2020 then, okay?"

He shook his head. But that's for down the road: four years, eight years, whatever.

That night, Mr. Romney would deliver his acceptance speech, the convention would end, and Mr. Christie would stand on floor with the rest of the New Jersey delegation. He clapped, pumped his fist, and joined delegates in an enthusiastic response to the new nominee. Shortly after Mr. Romney finished, @christiekeynote tweeted a photo of the action—Chris Christie watching.

If He's So Smart,
What Will He Do Now?

January 10, 2010

I n retrospect, maybe the whole Peter Orszag groupie phenomenon was getting a little out of hand early last year with the (ahem)
birth of Orszagasm.com, the fan blog devoted to the allegedly hunky
White House director of the Office of Management and Budget—
aka the guy who is "putting the OMG back in the OMB."

Or maybe it was last March when the White House chief of
staff, Rahm Emanuel, declared to the *New York Times* that Mr.
Orszag has "made nerdy sexy."

Or when the brainiac proved his boss correct by becoming a
bona fide babe magnet, a fixture at decorated dinners and the object
of breathless fascination in Washington gossip columns ("Orszag
really, really likes Diet Coke!" gushed *Politico*).

He became the epitome of Obama-era nerd cool. The president
himself joked lovingly about his favorite "propeller head" at the
White House Correspondents Dinner last May. His dates were
noted (the *Washington Post* publisher Katharine Weymouth, among
others). Some West Wing wags worried that Mr. Orszag's profile

might be getting a tad inflated and that he was getting a little big for his BlackBerry holsters (yes, that's plural).

Now things have become complicated for the forty-one-year-old Mr. Orszag—and not in the way that pension reform, sustainable-growth rates, and risk-based capital standards are complicated; rather, in the way that it's complicated when a divorced father of two with a very important job gets very publicly engaged to a thirty-one-year-old financial correspondent for ABC News, Bianna Golodryga, just weeks after his ex-girlfriend gave birth to his daughter.

Got all that? Good. So did a lot of people around town: the fact that Mr. Orszag's ex—Claire Milonas, a thirty-nine-year-old venture capitalist—was pregnant with his daughter was well known among Beltway swells. "The worst-kept secret in the history of Washington," declared Mr. Orszag's brother Jon, an economic consultant in Los Angeles.

But this "worst-kept secret" gestated into "news" on Wednesday, when the *New York Post* blared: "White House Budget Director Ditched Pregnant Girlfriend for ABC News Gal."

Suddenly the "Orszag love-child story" became a full-term tabloid distraction in a White House otherwise preoccupied by matters like terrorist plots, health care costs, and unemployment reports. Mr. Orszag alerted "the senior people in the West Wing" of the situation, said Kenneth S. Baer, spokesman for the Office of Management and Budget. As a general rule, executive branch spokesmen are not accustomed to worrying about *Inside Edition*—at least since the Clinton years.

"Trying to explain the sustainable-growth rate in Medicare is challenging," Mr. Baer said. "But this is different." He just wants this story to go away—something both sides seem to agree on.

"I think the whole thing is silly," Ms. Milonas said in a brief telephone interview Friday. "I hope this whole thing blows over quickly." Ms. Milonas, a Harvard- and Yale-educated daughter of a prominent Greek businessman, added that she wishes Mr. Orszag well in his upcoming nuptials (it is unclear whether she has done this directly).

But, of course, this is not a story that will easily go away. Friday brought another wave: another *New York Post* story about the "lover-boy budget director." He made the cover of the tabloid *Washington Examiner*. The *Washington Post*'s Reliable Source column was comparing Mr. Orszag to Tom Brady—not so much as a football player, but as simply "a player."

Big questions kept coursing through the corridors of power, particularly this one: Did the Casanova with a calculator really "ditch" his pregnant girlfriend for a younger television news babe?

Depends on what your definition of "ditch" is—and, of course, whom you ask. People in Mr. Orszag's camp say he and Ms. Milonas had broken up well before he started seeing Ms. Golodryga last spring; people close to Ms. Milonas say they are not so sure of the timing (Ms. Milonas would not speak on this matter, and Mr. Orszag declined to comment altogether).

Likewise, some in the Milonas camp suggest that Mr. Orszag had promised to marry her, but then met Ms. Golodryga; the Orszag people say that Ms. Milonas wanted to get married, but Peter did not, at least to Claire.

"We were in a committed relationship until the spring of 2009," Mr. Orszag and Ms. Milonas said in a joint statement Wednesday (spurred by the *Post* article). "In November, Claire gave birth to a beautiful baby girl. Although we are no longer together, we are both thrilled she is happy and healthy, and we would hope that everyone will respect her privacy."

Friends of Ms. Milonas say that Mr. Orszag wasn't exactly asking for privacy in December, when Ms. Golodryga was showing off her engagement rock on *Good Morning America*. The two met at the

White House Correspondents Dinner, the same event at which the president joked that the TLC network would be starting a new reality show called *Jon & Kate Plus Peter Orszag*.

People close to Ms. Milonas say they were surprised when Mr. Orszag announced he was getting married just a few months after he met Ms. Golodryga. People in the budget director's bivouac blame Ms. Milonas's side for leaking the news to the *Post*, which the White House said is driven by a conservative agenda. "It's no secret what the partisan beliefs of the *New York Post* are," Mr. Baer said, "or what the journalistic standards of a tabloid like that are."

It is not clear what role, if any, Mr. Orszag will have in the future of his new daughter, Tatiana Zoe Milonas. He was not present for her November 17 birth and has spent barely any time with her. Mr. Orszag lives in northwest Washington and shares custody of his two children from his first marriage, to Cameron Hamill. Both Ms. Milonas and Ms. Golodryga live in New York.

As with any story of this nature in Washington, the Very Serious People who traffic in it must emphasize that such silliness is beneath them. Mr. Baer said that nearly every press inquiry he has received was prefaced with the requisite faux sheepishness.

"Everyone feels the need to say, 'I'm really sorry I have to ask you about this' and 'I'm only carrying out orders from my boss,'" Mr. Baer said. (For the record: this reporter was only acting on orders from his boss.) And, of course, the Very Serious Media are not writing the Orszag Love-Child Story, they are merely writing about the media frenzy surrounding it.

Perhaps the most fascinating aspect is not so much the time-worn themes of love, life, and heartbreak. "Human relations are a mess," said Marina Ein, a crisis public relations expert in Washington whose messes have included the travails of former congressman Gary Condit. "We're in the same situation as when Adam was trying to dodge the apple that was thrown at him."

Even so, Adam didn't have to deal with deficit forecasts, consumer price indexes, or, for that matter, cable headlines like "Budget Baby Mama Drama" (thanks, MSNBC). And there's a natural intrigue that goes along with an unlikely celebrity who becomes an even more unlikely piece of tabloid fodder. "There is something that a lot of people in Washington find shocking about this story, which is why we keep talking about it," Ms. Ein said. "This is a person who seems so controlled in his professional life." Indeed, someone who carries neat to-do lists in his breast pocket and a copy on his desk of Epictetus, the Greek philosopher who preached self-discipline. "And yet he's so messy in his private life. This is an aha moment."

This goes to another obvious—and recurring—question: whether someone whose personal life has become so complicated is really fit to tackle one of the most demanding, important, and stressful jobs in the universe. "Frankly, I don't see how Orszag can balance three families and the national budget," wrote Joel Achenbach of the *Washington Post*.

Oh, budget, schmudget. This is about one question above all others, and that is this: Is Peter-mania dead? Is he still a celebrity nerd?

"He is, of course, still a celebrity nerd," said Ana Marie Cox, a national correspondent for Air America and unabashed Orsz-a-phile. "He is still a celebrity and he's still a nerd. What part of that isn't true?"

Taking Power,
Sharing Cereal

January 18, 2007

Some of the most powerful Democrats in America are split over a most incendiary household issue: rodents.

"I once had to pick up a mouse by the tail that Durbin refused to pick up," complained Senator Charles E. Schumer of New York, referring to his roommate Senator Richard J. Durbin of Illinois.

This characterization is not fair to Mr. Durbin, interjected another tenant in the Capitol Hill row house, Representative Bill Delahunt of Massachusetts. For starters, it overlooks Mr. Durbin's gift for killing rats. "He will kill them with his bare hands," Mr. Delahunt marveled.

"Oh, will you stop with the rats," said the annoyed fourth roommate, Representative George Miller of California. He owns the house and is sensitive to any suggestion that he harbors pestilence. It's dicey enough that he harbors politicians.

Think MTV's *Real World* with a slovenly cast of Democratic power brokers. While Washington may have more than its share of crash pads for policy-debating workaholics, few, if any, have sheltered a quorum as powerful as this one. About a quarter mile southeast of the Capitol, the inelegantly decorated two-bedroom house has become an unlikely center of influence in Washington's changing power grid. It is home to the second- and third-ranking senators in the new Democratic majority (Mr. Durbin, the majority whip, and Mr. Schumer, the vice chairman of the Democratic caucus) and the chairman of the House Democratic Policy Committee (Mr. Miller).

Mr. Delahunt, a six-term congressman, is the least prominent of the four but perhaps the funniest. More to the point, he is the only one willing to sleep in the living room with a close-up view of Mr. Schumer slumbering a few feet away in his boxers.

Mr. Miller began taking in weary lawmakers in 1982, but this is the first time in twelve years that four members of a Democratic majority have lived here simultaneously. The four men were once host to a fund-raiser for Senator Barbara Boxer of California at their divey dwelling, raising $80,000. Given the prevailing attire in the place on many nights, guests were given pairs of custom-made "Barbara Boxer shorts."

As a general rule, the abode is hardly fit for entertaining, or even for a health inspector. It is used for convenience: sleeping, ditching stuff, and fast-food consumption—the kinds of functions prized by vagabond politicians whose families are back in their home states and who generally spend only their working weekdays here.

"Everybody in the world says they're going to do a television series based on us," said Mr. Durbin, who was collapsed on the couch on a recent Monday night. Still in a tie, he sipped ice water from a massive Chicago Cubs cup while waiting for the Chinese food to arrive.

"But then they realize that the story of four middle-aged men, with no sex and violence, is not going to last two weeks," he said.

The prevailing topics of their discussions are grandchildren and Metamucil, he added.

"Hey, speak for yourself, Durbin," Mr. Delahunt said, protesting the claim of no sex and violence.

"There is a lot of violence in here," Mr. Schumer said.

In fact, the roommates have never resorted to violence, at least with one another. (Crickets are another story.) Their weapons are verbal, and often aimed at Mr. Schumer, who admits to a serious dereliction of roommate duties, like grocery shopping. He is also prone to a blatant disregard for conserving a most precious household resource, cereal.

"I love cereal," Mr. Schumer said, digging into his second bowl of granola, going a long way toward depleting a box that Mr. Miller had just purchased.

The night of the national championship football game between the University of Florida and Ohio State, January 8, was a rare instance of the four roommates being home and awake at the same time. It had not happened since the election in November, and the neighborhood has changed considerably since then. Several Republicans on the block lost their race or left Congress (the latter category includes the disgraced Representative Mark Foley, who lived down the street).

"This street was just devastated by the election," Mr. Miller said. "Who says Republicans are good for property values?"

He added that no Republican had ever set foot in the place, at least to their knowledge.

"We just have to vote with them, not live with them," he said.

Mr. Miller bought the house in 1977 and started taking in renters a few years later. Early tenants included former representative Marty Russo of Illinois and former representative Leon E. Panetta of California, who was forced to move out when President Clinton appointed him head of the Office of Management and Budget.

(Ethics laws prohibited a White House official from paying rent to a member of Congress.)

Mr. Schumer joined them in 1982, and Mr. Durbin moved in a decade later on condition that he get one of the two bedrooms upstairs. Mr. Miller sleeps in the other, bigger bedroom, asserting his ownership privileges, and Mr. Delahunt began occupying the second living room bed four years ago, after a previous tenant, former representative Sam Gejdenson, was evicted by voters in Connecticut.

Mr. Miller charges rent of $750 a month, which Mr. Durbin pays by direct deposit and Mr. Schumer's wife pays by sending Mr. Miller six checks twice a year. Mr. Schumer says his wardrobe at the apartment consists of boxers and suits, nothing in between.

Women rarely set foot in the place, excluding the Haitian cleaning lady who comes every week and who everyone promises is a legal immigrant. The common bathroom upstairs is stocked with supersize bottles of Listerine, CVS cocoa butter, Suave shampoo (with dandruff control), and a hair dryer.

Little thought is given to entertainment besides the big-screen television that Mr. Durbin recently purchased against the wishes of Mr. Schumer and Mr. Delahunt, who liked the old one. The refrigerator is mostly empty, save for apples, grapes, and about two dozen bottles of beer.

"The ice maker is back on," boasted Mr. Miller, pointing to the inside of what might be the most unseemly freezer in Washington this side of Representative William Jefferson's. (FBI agents found $90,000 in the freezer of Mr. Jefferson, a Louisiana Democrat, who is being investigated on bribery charges.)

Once, Mr. Miller's son shot a deer and presented the house with an abundant supply of venison. It remained in the freezer for twelve years, at which point it was deemed to have reached its term limit and was discarded.

"What ever happened to that venison?" Mr. Schumer wondered.

"I think it just got up and walked away," Mr. Delahunt said.

The roommates then repaired to couches to watch Florida–Ohio State and to stuff their faces with Sichuan beef and kung pao chicken. Mr. Durbin began talking about meetings he had last month with the presidents of Bolivia and Ecuador on a congressional delegation to Latin America. Then he and Mr. Schumer started arguing about Mr. Schumer's refusal to make his bed.

Unanswer Man: Scott McClellan Is the President's Spokesman, Which Doesn't Leave Him Much to Say

December 22, 2005

On the Thursday morning after his reelection in November 2004, President Bush bounded unexpectedly into the Roosevelt Room of the White House, where about fifteen members of his communications team were celebrating. He just wanted to thank everyone for their hard work on the campaign, he said, before singling someone out.

"Is Scotty here? Where's Scotty?" Bush asked, half grinning. Bush scanned the room for Scott McClellan, the White House press secretary.

"I want to especially thank Scotty," the president said, looking at his aide. "I want to thank Scotty for saying"—and he paused for effect. . . .

"Nothing."

At which point everyone laughed and the president left the room.

This is one of those quips that distill a certain essence of the game. In this era of on-message orthodoxy, the republic has evolved to where the leader of the free world can praise his most visible spokesman for saying nothing.

Those were considerably less embattled days for the Bush administration, which has since endured a difficult year. It's been "a perfect storm of bad news," says Mark McKinnon, the president's longtime advertising consultant, listing Hurricane Katrina, Iraq, and the CIA leak investigation. McClellan, per his job description, has borne the daily brunt.

The weary White House front man is an iconic Washington role, epitomized over the years by Nixon's Ron Ziegler during Watergate and Clinton's Mike McCurry during Monica. A ceremonial flak jacket hangs in the closet of McClellan's West Wing office, following in a tradition of previous tenants, beginning with Ford spokesman Ron Nessen. The press secretary delivers an administration's daily boilerplate and also serves as a storm wall, or "human piñata" in the words of Ari Fleischer, whom McClellan succeeded on July 15, 2003, the day after Robert Novak outed CIA analyst Valerie Plame in a column.

"It may not look like it," McClellan, thirty-seven, said from the podium after an especially tough week recently. "But there's a little flesh that's been taken out of me the last few days." This is as close as McClellan will flirt in the briefing room with conveying something beyond the preapproved white noise. Indeed, he has been credited—or blamed—for taking the craft of party-line discipline to new heights, or depths.

Last Friday reporters battered McClellan over a *New York Times* report that the president had authorized the National Security Agency to eavesdrop without warrants on people in the United States. Over several minutes, McClellan emphasized that:

• The president is doing all he can to protect the American people from terrorists (ten times);

• The administration is committed to protecting civil liberties and upholding the Constitution (seven times);

• Congress has an important oversight role, and the administration is committed to working with it on these difficult matters (five times); and

• He would not discuss ongoing intelligence activities (five times).

It was all on live television and in the news conference transcripts, which are posted on the White House Web site and then e-mailed around, deconstructed, blogged about, picked over, and scoured throughout a vast electronic briefing space. The words of White House spokesmen have never been so widely or quickly distributed.

"You can't make a mistake," says Marlin Fitzwater, White House press secretary in the George H. W. Bush administration, whom McClellan sought out for advice before he started the job. "So you just get into a routine of repeating the same thing over and over again."

"I would urge you not to confuse clarity with rigidity," says Nicolle Wallace, the White House communications director. "There is great clarity in the way the president wants us to communicate, and Scott embodies that."

When briefings get tense, McClellan's voice can become robotic, as if he's a hostage reading a statement. His body language betrays unease: He starts blinking rapidly and he clenches his shoulders as an interrogator unfurls a question.

"There's no question the dynamic of the briefing room has changed with live TV," says senior White House aide Dan Bartlett. "When you have live cameras rolling, it makes for an even more stressful working environment. You're talking about difficult issues, and mistakes get compounded."

Colleagues (on message) say McClellan has held up well in

these difficult months. Others (off message) say he's had a tough time, has lost hair, gained jowls, and looks stressed, especially over the Valerie Plame case, which made a return to the briefing room Thursday after an absence of a few weeks.

It started when the president told Fox News' Brit Hume last week that he believed that Representative Tom DeLay was not guilty of money-laundering charges in Texas. This undercut McClellan's vow that he would not comment on the Plame matter because it is an "ongoing investigation," something he has repeated hundreds of times in recent months. We join Thursday's episode in progress:

Reporter: "Why would that not apply to the same type of prosecution involving Congressman DeLay?"

McClellan: "I just told you we had a policy in place regarding this investigation, and you've heard me say before that we're not going to talk about it further while it's ongoing."

In a flurry of follow-ups, McClellan repeated that the White House had a policy on the Plame case (four times) and that the policy was not to comment (three times).

NBC's David Gregory broke in, declaring the administration to be "inconsistent," then "hypocritical."

"You have a policy for some investigations and not others, when it's a political ally who you need to get work done?" Gregory asked.

McClellan: "Call it presidential prerogative; he responded to that question. But the White House established a policy." He mentioned that the DeLay case is a "legal proceeding."

Gregory: "As is the Fitzgerald investigation. . . . As you've told us ad nauseam from the podium."

After more back-and-forth, McClellan said, "You can get all dramatic about it, but you know what our policy is."

Which ended that exchange.

"We've come to understand that no matter how we slice and dice something, Scott's going to stick to the recipe," says Ken Herman, White House correspondent for Cox News Service. "I can't think of any topic where on the sixth or seventh iteration of a question we get something different from the original answer. By somebody's measure, that's the definition of doing the job well. Certainly not ours."

As with most people who do regular televised battle with McClellan, Herman says McClellan is a nice guy, polite and friendly off camera. "He seems to have the right temperament to be a punching bag," Herman says.

"Who knows, maybe he goes home at night and kicks his dog?"

It should surprise no one that McClellan is an unexpansive interview subject. He toggles on and off the record, although the latter offerings are only slightly more revealing than the former.

Over lunch at the Occidental at the Willard Hotel, McClellan says that he is "honored" to serve George W. Bush, that he will "vigorously defend the president and his agenda," that "Washington can be an all-consuming town if you allow it to be," that there are "a lot of bright people working in the White House," that he has "great trust in the American people to make the right judgments," and that he's merely "part of a team."

And that: "It's a good team."

And that: "At the end of the day, this is about the president and his agenda."

The maitre d' addresses McClellan as "Mr. Secretary," which means he is either mistaking him for a Cabinet member or believes this is the appropriate way to address a press secretary.

"Sometimes the nature of this job will put you in a tough spot," McClellan says. He is speaking about the Plame investigation, which has been a source of great strain, according to people he has confided in privately, including several reporters.

He has anguished that his credibility has been harmed by his statements in 2003 that Karl Rove and Scooter Libby "have assured me they were not involved in this," this being the outing of Plame as a covert CIA agent.

Today Libby is under indictment, Rove's involvement has become apparent, and McClellan's public statements haunt him. "His credibility is shot," the *San Francisco Chronicle* said in an editorial calling for McClellan's resignation.

Over lunch, McClellan will refer to the leak investigation as "the thing I can't talk about," "the thing that's put me in a tough spot," "the investigation," and simply "it." You can see McClellan's spine stiffen when the case is raised, his normally fast speaking style slowing to a grind.

He says, repeatedly, that he would like to say more about the investigation, and in time he will, "hopefully sooner rather than later."

Asked if he's spoken to Rove about Rove's assurances that he was not involved, McClellan says: "That's asking me to talk about it and I'm not gonna do it."

Asked if he was wrong in a 2003 briefing to characterize suggestions that Rove and Libby were involved as "ridiculous," McClellan says: "That's not something I can get into."

Asked why he himself has not hired a lawyer, McClellan says: "I'm not going to talk about it."

In the course of researching this story, the following Scotty fun facts were extracted:

• McClellan's wife, the former Jill Martinez, volunteers part time in the White House. They were married in November 2003, live in Arlington, have no kids, no iPods, two cars, two dogs, and three cats—all of them rescued strays and none of which McClellan has ever kicked.

• McClellan, a Methodist, is reading Rick Warren's best seller *The Purpose Driven Life*.

• McClellan, who was a varsity tennis player at the University of Texas, often wakes—at five a.m.—to a BBC radio broadcast, then switches to NPR, then alternates between news radio and country music for the fifteen-minute commute to work in his Chevy Tahoe.

From the podium, McClellan will often bring up his "close relationship" with the reporters who cover the White House. He keeps talking about the "trust" he's established and how they know each other "very well."

"I think this is an example of Scott talking in code," Gregory says.

Saying that Rove and Libby "assured me they were not involved" is different from saying "Rove and Libby were not involved," says Fitzwater. "Assured me" is a classic construction among spokesmen, he says.

"That's a signal that most press members can get. The press secretary vouches for the president every day. He does not vouch for the staff."

Several White House reporters say that as much as McClellan is liked personally, the administration has left him with no meaningful freedom from the podium beyond jackhammering that day's message and providing mundane updates. ("The president had a good discussion with a group of Senate Democrats and Republicans earlier today.") It has diminished the daily briefing to a playacting spectacle in which he recites lines while reporters play the part of exasperated inquisitors.

"The fate of a press secretary is always tied to events," says Mary Matalin, a White House adviser. "They're not good or bad on their own. By definition they are constrained to what the message is. It's such a limited lane, you can't strut your stuff there. But in such a limited lane, Scott is perfect."

McClellan was cautious from an early age. His mother, Carole Keeton Strayhorn, was a three-term mayor of Austin whose youngest son "went from diapers to shaving working on my campaigns," she says. As free-speaking as her son is tight-lipped, Strayhorn instilled in her four boys a sense that their transgressions could easily become public. "I remember my mom saying to me that what your friends do is one thing, but what you do could be on the front page of the paper," McClellan says.

Strayhorn says that her son required stitches many times as a child—tree-climbing accidents, falls onto concrete and whatnot. And not once did she see him cry.

"I think he had eight stitch jobs before two," Strayhorn says. "In this day and age, they'd probably call me an abusive mom."

Strayhorn, now the Texas comptroller and a candidate for governor, describes her son as "one of the most focused people on earth" and tells this story: McClellan once returned home after playing tennis and started telling her about his match when a fuse blew and the house went dark. But he kept talking, on message, as if nothing had happened. "We were like, 'Uh, Scott, haven't you noticed that every light in the house just went off?'"

McClellan's parents divorced when he was ten. His father, Barr McClellan—who now resides in Buffalo and whom McClellan says he speaks to infrequently—published a book in 2003 claiming that Lyndon Johnson was behind the assassination of John F. Kennedy.

"I'm wondering if you agree with your father," McClellan was asked during one briefing in 2003.

"Thank you for the opportunity," McClellan replied. "But I'm not going to have any comment on it. Thanks."

As McClellan is leaving the Occidental, the maître d' urges "Mr. Secretary" to tell "Mr. Bush" that he's doing a great job. Bush is in Minneapolis on this day, and McClellan is heading back to his office, assuring the reporter he just ate with that he said more than he usually does. It's not clear what exactly.

"I think I talked about how badly I wanted to talk about it," McClellan says by phone a few days later, referring to the thing he can't talk about.

After a Grim Diagnosis, Determined to Make a "Good Ending"

August 27, 2009

The once indefatigable Ted Kennedy was in a wheelchair at the end, struggling to speak and sapped of his energy. But from the time his brain cancer was diagnosed fifteen months ago, he spoke of having a "good ending for myself," in whatever time he had left, and by every account, he did.

As recently as a few days ago, Mr. Kennedy was still digging into big bowls of mocha chip and butter crunch ice creams, all smushed together (as he liked it). He and his wife, Vicki, had been watching every James Bond movie and episode of *24* on DVD.

He began each morning with a sacred rite of reading his newspapers, drinking coffee, and scratching the bellies of his beloved Portuguese water dogs, Sunny and Splash, on the front porch of his Cape Cod house overlooking Nantucket Sound.

If he was feeling up to it, he would end his evenings with family dinner parties around the same mahogany table where he used to eat lobster with his brothers.

He took phone calls from President Obama, house calls from

his priest, and—just a few weeks ago—crooned after-dinner duets of "You Are My Sunshine" (with his son Patrick) and "Just a Closer Walk with Thee" (with Vicki).

"There were a lot of joyous moments at the end," said Dr. Lawrence C. Horowitz, Mr. Kennedy's former Senate chief of staff, who oversaw his medical care. "There was a lot of frankness, a lot of hugging, a lot of emotion."

Obviously, Dr. Horowitz added, there were difficult times. By this spring, according to friends, it was clear that the tumor had not been contained; new treatments proved ineffective and Mr. Kennedy's comfort became the priority.

But interviews with close friends and family members yield a portrait of a man who in his final months was at peace with the end of his life and grateful for the chance to savor the salty air and the company of loved ones.

Befitting the life he led, Mr. Kennedy was the protagonist of a storybook finale from the time of his diagnosis in May 2008. It was infused with a beat-the-clock element: his illness coincided with the debate over health care ("the cause of my life") and the election of a young president he championed.

Mr. Kennedy raced to complete his legislative work and his memoirs ("I've got to get this right for history," he kept saying), leaned heavily on his faith, enjoyed (or endured) a procession of tributes and testimonials, and just recently petitioned Governor Deval Patrick of Massachusetts to push for a speedy succession so his Senate seat would not be vacant long.

The knowledge that his death was approaching infused Mr. Kennedy's interactions with special intensity, his friends say.

"He was the only one of the Kennedy boys who had a semi-knowledge that his end was near," said Mike Barnicle, the former *Boston Globe* columnist and an old friend who lives nearby on Cape

Cod and visited the senator this summer. "There was no gunman in the shadows, just an MRI. It was a bad diagnosis, but it allowed for the gift of reflection and some good times."

Even as Mr. Kennedy's physical condition worsened over the summer, he still got out of bed every day until Tuesday, when he died in the evening, said Senator Christopher J. Dodd, Democrat of Connecticut and one of Mr. Kennedy's closest friends in the Senate.

"I'm still here," Mr. Kennedy would call colleagues out of the blue to say, as if to refute suggestions to the contrary. "Every day is a gift," was his mantra to begin conversations, said Peter Meade, a friend who met Mr. Kennedy as a fourteen-year-old volunteer on Mr. Kennedy's first Senate campaign.

Some patients given a fatal diagnosis succumb to bitterness and self-pity; others try to cram in everything they have always wanted to do (skydiving, a trip to China). Mr. Kennedy wanted to project vigor and a determination to keep on going. He chose what he called "prudently aggressive" treatments.

"He always admired people who took risks, like Teddy and Kara did," Mr. Dodd said, referring to two of Mr. Kennedy's children, who both beat cancer with bold treatments. And he vowed to work as hard as he could to lead a legislative overhaul of the nation's health care system.

"He was the irrepressible Ted Kennedy," said Senator John Kerry, the Massachusetts Democrat, who visited with his longtime colleague last week. "He was determined to get things done, but he also understood he had limitations."

Mr. Kennedy deputized Dr. Horowitz, who lives in the San Francisco Bay Area, to research all treatment options before deciding on an intensive regimen of surgery, chemotherapy, and radiation—hardly a clear-cut choice with an almost inevitably lethal disease and a patient of Mr. Kennedy's age. Some physicians assembled at

Massachusetts General Hospital considered his tumor inoperable—
and measured his likely survival time between six weeks and a few
months.

Before he traveled by private plane from Cape Cod to Duke
University Medical Center for his surgery in June 2008, Mr. Kennedy made sure to put his affairs in order—his will, his medical di-
rectives, and even his legislative instructions, family members say.

On the way to the airport, he called two Democratic colleagues:
Mr. Dodd, telling him to take over a mental health bill he had been
working on, and Senator Barbara Mikulski of Maryland, instruct-
ing her to take over a higher education bill he had been shepherding.

"Barbara," he boomed over the phone, "as if he was at a Red
Sox–Orioles baseball game," Ms. Mikulski said in an interview. Just
days after the surgery, Mr. Kennedy began following up with Ms.
Mikulski. "He was Coach Ted," she said.

Mr. Kennedy took no comfort, friends say, in hearing how
missed he was in Washington, or how in his absence he had become
something of a "spiritual leader" on issues with which he is identified, like health care. He kept in close touch with his staff and colleagues, and he was engaged in a running conversation with Senator
Harry Reid of Nevada, the majority leader, on the delicate subject of
whether Mr. Kennedy would be available to vote.

Mr. Reid assured him that he would not ever ask him to come
to Washington unless his vote was essential. (His disease and treatments made Mr. Kennedy vulnerable to infections, so wading into
crowded areas was risky.) When a crucial Medicare provision came
up last summer, Mr. Reid asked Mr. Kennedy if he could make it
down.

Mr. Kennedy's family and staff debated the issue until the senator ended it. "I'll be there," he said, according to a member of his
staff who was involved in the decision. He received a standing ovation when he returned to the Senate floor, and the bill passed easily.

Vicki Kennedy fiercely guarded her husband's privacy, but Mr. Kennedy's illness had an undeniably public component. His setbacks and hospital visits often drew news-media attention. After his emotional speech at last summer's Democratic convention in Denver, it was disclosed that he had been suffering from kidney stones and had barely been able to get out of his hospital bed a few hours earlier.

He had to memorize the text of his speech because he struggled to see the teleprompter (his surgery had left him with impaired vision). The seizure Mr. Kennedy had at an inaugural luncheon at the Capitol led his son Patrick to joke that his father was trying to overshadow Mr. Obama on his big day.

Mr. Kerry remembers Mr. Kennedy telling him on the Senate floor in March that he was having trouble preparing for an event he had been extremely excited for—throwing out the first pitch on opening day at Fenway Park.

While Mr. Kennedy typically told people he felt well and vigorous, by spring it was becoming clear that his disease was advancing to where he could not spend his remaining months as he had hoped, helping push a health care plan through the Senate.

He left Washington in May, after nearly a half century in the capital, and decamped to Cape Cod, where he would contribute what he could to the health care debate via phone and C-SPAN. He would sail as much as possible, with as little pain and discomfort as his caretakers could manage.

He also told friends that he wanted to take stock of his life and enjoy the gift of his remaining days with the people he loved most.

"I've had a wonderful life," he said repeatedly, friends recalled.

Mr. Dodd, in an interview, said: "At no point was he ever maudlin, ever 'woe is me.' I'm confident he had his moments— he wouldn't be Irish if he didn't—but in my presence, he always sounded more worried about me than he was about himself."

Starting in late July, Vicki Kennedy organized near-nightly

dinner parties and sing-alongs at the Kennedy compound in Hyannis Port. The senator was surrounded in the dining room by his crystal sailing trophies and a semi-regular cast of family members that included his three children, two stepchildren, and four grandchildren. Jean Kennedy Smith, Mr. Kennedy's sister, had rented a home down the street this summer and become a regular, too. Instead of singing, she would sometimes recite poetry.

Even as Mr. Kennedy became frustrated about his limitations, friends say his spirit never flagged. "This is someone who had a fierce determination to live, but who was not afraid to die," said Representative Bill Delahunt, a Democrat and a Kennedy friend whose district includes Cape Cod. "And he was not afraid to have a lot of laughs until he got there."

In recent years, friends say, Mr. Kennedy had come to lean heavily on his Roman Catholic faith. In eulogizing his mother, Rose Kennedy, in 1995, he spoke of the comfort of religious beliefs. "She sustained us in the saddest times by her faith in God, which was the greatest gift she gave us," Mr. Kennedy said, his voice stammering.

He attended Mass every day in the year after his mother's death and continued to attend regularly, often a few times a week.

The Reverend Mark Hession, the priest at the Kennedys' parish on the Cape, made regular visits to the Kennedy home this summer and held a private family Mass in the living room every Sunday. Even in his final days, Mr. Kennedy led the family in prayer after the death of his sister Eunice on August 11. He died comfortably and in no apparent pain, friends and staff members said.

His children had expected him to hold on longer—Mr. Kennedy's son Patrick and daughter, Kara, could not get back to Hyannis Port in time from California and Washington.

But the senator's condition took a turn Tuesday night, and a priest—the Reverend Patrick Tarrant of Our Lady of Victory Church in Centerville, Massachusetts—was called to his bedside.

Mr. Kennedy spent his last hours in prayer, Father Tarrant told a Boston television station, WCVB-TV.

Mr. Kennedy had told friends recently that he was looking forward to a "reunion" with his seven departed siblings, particularly his brothers, whose lives had been cut short.

"When he gets there, he can say 'I did it, I carried the torch,'" Mr. Delahunt said. "'I carried it all the way.'"

ACKNOWLEDGMENTS

Continued thanks to Arthur Sulzberger, Mark Thompson, Dean Baquet, Jill Abramson, Bill Keller, and everyone at the *New York Times* for your support professionally, and even more so personally. You run the best newspaper in the world, but, more important, you know what matters.

I feel enduring affection and gratitude for Don Graham and everyone at the *Washington Post*, a great newspaper where I spent nine familial years.

Thanks to my editors, mentors, and betters at the *Times, Times Magazine*, and the *Post* who helped shape and nurture these pages over the years; likewise, to a bipartisan cabinet of wise men and women from various career stations. They would be too numerous to start listing here—and perilous to omit—but oh what the hell: Rebecca Corbett, Dick Stevenson, Hugo Lindgren, Joel Lovell, Jon Kelly, Jake Silverstein, Janet Elder, Rick Berke, Bill Hamilton, Gerry Marzorati, Megan Liberman, Laura Marmor, Steve Reiss, Tom Frail. and Researcher Supreme Kitty Bennett (!). I think about Robin Toner all the time, and will never forget my first editor and boss, the late, great Caroline Knapp, whose wisdom still echoes.

Elyse Cheney is the best agent! Exclamation point! (Special thanks, also, to Alex Jacobs and Sam Frelich at Cheney Literary.)

David Rosenthal at Blue Rider/Penguin is a perfect combination of wicked genius, mensch, and friend. He remains everything a writer would want in an editor and publisher—and I am so lucky to have him at the helm of this ride, as well as the incomparable flack Aileen Boyle and everyone at Blue Rider press: Jason Booher, Linda Cowen, Linda Rosenberg, Phoebe Pickering, Eliza Rosenberry, Wesley Salazar, David Chesanow, Janice Kurzius, and Anna Jardine.

This book is dedicated to a far-flung battalion of blood and non-blood relatives: my oldest pal, Josh King, and the King family of Agawam Road; Paul Farhi and all the Farhim; endless affection for my Michigan and Boston friends, and also the Oyster-Adams *comunidad*. Greatly cherish our kibbutzian life merge with Hanna Rosin, David Plotz, and all the Markey-Daveys, with whom we share the most sacred of occasions and ordinary of minivans.

Big and eternal love to my parents, Joan and Miguel Leibovich, whose grace, survival skills, and unconditional support have sustained and inspired me; and to my amazing sister, Lori Leibovich, whose love and friendship I will hold forever dear. Parents 2.0 Ted Sutton and Betty Grossman are godsends, as are in-laws Jack and Barbara Kolbrener, *hermanos* Bill and Michael Kolbrener, and Larry Kanter (of Resistor!), and kids 2.0 Carlos and Clara Kanter. I am guided every day by the memory of my brother, Phil Leibovich, but mostly I just miss him.

Best for last: To my daughters, Nell, Lizey, and Franny, who make my heart grow a million sizes every day. I could never put this crazy love into words. Likewise, my wife, Meri Kolbrener, who has always been too grounded to care about public shout-outs—"Just don't make me seem long-suffering," she told me. So I'll skip that part and suffice with this: she makes it all possible and joyful, and me the luckiest.

INDEX

ABOUT THE AUTHOR

Mark Leibovich is the *New York Times Magazine*'s chief national correspondent, based in Washington, DC. He is the number one *New York Times* best-selling author of *This Town*. Leibovich lives with his family in Washington, DC.